The *Elvis Presley* SCRAPBOOKS

The
Elvis Presley
SCRAPBOOKS
1955-1965

Edited by
Peter Haining

ROBERT HALE · LONDON

© Peter Haining 1991
First published in Great Britain 1991

ISBN 0 7090 4347 3

Robert Hale Limited
Clerkenwell House
Clerkewnell Green
London EC1R 0HT

PICTURE CREDITS

All illustrations courtesy of the official Elvis Presley Fan
Club of Great Britain.

Photoset in Ehrhardt by
Derek Doyle & Associates, Mold, Clwyd.
Printed in Great Britain by
St Edmundsbury Press, Bury St Edmunds, Suffolk,
and bound by WBC Bookbinders.

'Elvis Presley was unique and irreplaceable; he has become a world-wide symbol of his country's vitality, rebelliousness and good humour. His rise from poverty to international fame was an inspiration to everyone. His death has deprived our country of a part of itself. His music and his personality, fusing the styles of white country and black rhythm and blues, permanently changed the face of American popular culture.'

President Jimmy Carter
18 August 1977

Introduction

ELVIS the KING RETURNS

WIN

A WORL DATE

REVEALING S SHOCK CRET

appearan of Elvis

ELVIS PRESL

STAR OF STAGE, SCREEN, RADIO, RECORDS AND T

ELVIS PRESLEY MAY VISIT LONDON
"Evening News" Reporter

AMERICAN rock 'n' roll king, Elvis Presley, may come to London next year. He has been offered about £250,000 Johannesburg make 25 per nces in

ELVIS ARMY

ELVIS

kissed me

PRESLEY — that's all we had at the ele on ELVIS

ELVIS 50th ELVIS PRESLEY

HART

Some Records from the Past

The telephone call came out of the blue one spring morning while I was working in my study. On the other end of the line from Leicester was the familiar voice of Todd Slaughter, the man who runs the Official Elvis Presley Fan Club of Great Britain, and a friend of the legendary star and his manager, Colonel Tom Parker. After the usual exchange of pleasantries, Todd said to me in his matter-of-fact manner:

'We've been having a clear out in the attics of the old fan club offices in Heanor and we've found a box of old scrapbooks. They cover the first ten years of Elvis' career – I think perhaps you should have a look at them. They might provide the material for a book.'

The face of a young man destined for immortality

Even from such a bald statement I couldn't have agreed more. Although, of course, there had already been hundreds of books about the star, this discovery certainly sounded like something rather different …

A couple of years earlier I had written a book, Elvis in Private, to commemorate the tenth anniversary of the star's death, and the help of Todd and the fan club's archives had been invaluable, not to say vital, in its creation. The club's collection of photographs, documents, taped interviews, books and magazines had proved hugely informative on the man about whom more words have been written than probably any other entertainer of the twentieth century. Now here was Todd telling me of the unearthing of a treasure-trove of material that had lain forgotten in the club's attic in the small Derbyshire town – once known to British fans as 'Elvisville' – for a quarter of a century.

I assured Todd I would travel up to visit him as soon as I could. And, in fact, less than a week later I made the drive from East Anglia to Heanor and was soon sitting in my friend's office with the box of scrapbooks in front of me. There were more than two dozen of them – typical large-size books of grey, heavy duty paper bound in colourful covers on which in most cases portraits of Elvis had been pasted. I brushed off the dust of twenty-five years and began to leaf through them with a mounting sense of excitement. For the cuttings from daily papers and magazines, the advertisements for films and records, and the array of souvenirs such as postcards, streamers, transfers, even chewing-gum cards – not to mention literally dozens of fan photographs of Elvis – offered a unique picture of the star. Indeed, here was history in the making – not the observations of people in hindsight, as so many books about Elvis have been, but made at the very time his legend was developing.

'The King' – rock star, film star and concert star

The scrapbooks had clearly been assembled by a number of fans, both male and female, living in various parts of the United Kingdom. The clue to this was the different newspaper and magazine titles on the cuttings – and these had in turn been augmented by others obtained from America and, on occasions, Europe, too. They began with a mere trickle of reports in 1955 which soon swelled to a tide and by 1965 had become a flood. It was evident that the scrapbooks had been given to the fan club for safe keeping all those years ago, and it somehow seemed appropriate that they should have emerged again at a time when Elvis, though dead for almost fifteen years, was still as famous as ever.

As I went on turning the pages, I couldn't help wondering if those who had so carefully pasted the items into the books year by year could ever have imagined that there would still be such an amazing interest in their hero all these years later …

The cuttings told with graphic and immediate detail of the emergence of the young sharecropper's son who was to change irrevocably modern popular music with a style of singing that at once became the subject of heated debate and in time the admiration of uncounted millions of young people around the world. The cuttings and pictures, initially from Elvis' own Southern homeland, then from the whole of the American continent, and finally across the Atlantic, described the public reaction to this rock 'n' roll phenomenon – as well as what the young man himself was thinking about it all. They ranged from the sceptical to the sarcastic and from the absurd to the amusing.

Where these items had the advantage over much of what was to be written later was in access to the star himself. In time, of course, Elvis retreated behind a reclusive shield, and what the newspapers were unable to find out about him they simply invented. And even what so-called friends and associates told reporters was open to serious question, if not being actually downright untrue.

I also found it intriguing that the scrapbooks covered so precisely the most vital years of Elvis' career from his days as a new recording artist in Memphis to his confirmation as 'The King' of modern music when the only other artists to match his world-wide fame, the Beatles – who by their own admission had been profoundly influenced by him – came to pay their respects in Hollywood, then as now the entertainment capital of the world. It was almost as if those who had kept them had somehow sensed the crucial importance of those ten years. For, in a sentence, the books encapsulated the golden decade of Elvis Presley's career.

Once I had finished going through the dusty volumes with their pages of glued and Sellotaped clippings, I was in complete agreement with Todd's suggestion that their contents should be made public for the benefit of the many Elvis fans who still cherish his memory. People like myself who had been teenagers when he blazed into our consciousness, and those, such as our children, who had more recently become aware of the magic of his music which is still, thankfully, preserved on record and film.

In the pages which follow, then, is my choice of the best of the scrapbooks: a mixture of reports and pictures chosen to illustrate and inform on Elvis Presley's extraordinary rise. There is drama here as well as humour, not to mention talent, determination and the generation of an overwhelming fame which ultimately – and inevitably, I think – changed the man himself. It may well be that, apart from being the most successful ten years of Elvis' life, they were also his ten happiest years. Certainly they were not lacking in incident for him as a person as well as an artist!

I am grateful to the newspapers and magazines who have allowed the reports from their pages to be reproduced here, as well as the photographers, both professional and amateur, whose cameras have captured Elvis' magnetic personality in the various aspects of his life, at work, at play and when he was relaxing. He has undeniably left his mark on his times, and if his life was sadly short-lived it was none the less influential and important to more people than he can ever have imagined. And, whatever his detractors may say, his music has entertained and delighted millions for almost half of this century – and will surely continue to do so in the new era already on the horizon.

PETER HAINING
Boxford, Suffolk
1990

1955

ELVIS
the KING
RETURNS

WIN

A WO
DATE

EVEALING
S SHOCK
CRET

appearan

of Elvis

ELVIS PRESL

STAR OF STAGE, SCREEN, RADIO, RECORDS AND T

**ELVIS PRESLEY
MAY VISIT LONDON**

"Evening News" Reporter

AMERICAN rock 'n' roll
king, Elvis Presley, may
come to London next year. He
has been offered about
£250,000 a Johannesburg
make 25 per
nces in Euro

ELVIS

kissed me

ELVIS 50th ELVIS PRESLEY

HART ENTR

The beginnings of the Elvis Presley legend have, of course, been written about many times by authors all over the world during the past thirty-five years. But the very first reporter to write a feature article on this young man destined for immortality was a television columnist in his home town of Memphis named Robert Johnson. A staff writer on the daily Memphis Press-Scimitar, *Johnson commented on TV and radio programmes of interest and also covered the local music scene. He was in touch with record companies and radio stations and ideally placed to learn about any new artists on the scene. On 5 February 1955 he felt that the emerging talent of teenager Elvis Presley was worth a feature and wrote the following article. A yellowing copy of the clipping pasted on to the first page of the oldest scrapbook reveals with unique, firsthand knowledge just how the Presley phenomenon started …*

SUDDENLY SINGING ELVIS PRESLEY ZOOMS INTO RECORDING STARDOM

By Robert Johnson

One sultry night late last July, Dewey Phillips flicked a turntable switch with one of his cotton-pickin' hands and sent a strange rhythmic chant spinning out from WHBQ.

'Well that's all right Baby … that's all right, Baby … '

The record ended. Radio, like Nature, abhors a void and Mr Phillips hastens to fill the breach.

'That'll flat git it,' he said authoritatively.

That same night, Sleepy Eye John over at WHHM loosed the other side of the record

on his admirers – and the same voice which had been reassuring Baby now sang plaintive praise of 'Blue Moon of Kentucky.'

Someth'ng Happened

Time didn't exactly stand still, but something happened. Bob Neal of WMPS played the record too. The pop jockeys, entranced by something new, began slipping 'That's All Right' and 'Blue Moon' in among the more sophisticated glucose and bedlam of Teresa Brewer, Nat Cole and Tony Bennett.

In less than a week, a momentous change began for a young teen-ager, working on an assembly line, who liked to sing and play the guitar.

His name: Elvis Presley.

Elvis' first record was on the Sun label of Sam Phillips' small but ambitious Memphis Recording Service, 706 Union. It wasn't the first time that Sam's Sun had created a good-sized ripple in the frenzied circles of record business. Sam is largely responsible for a new trend in the field which the trade publications call R&B (for rhythm and blues) and country (for hillbilly) music, and for making Memphis the R&B capital, as Nashville is for rustic rhythm.

Within a Week

Within less than a week, Sam was frantically and happily trying to press enough copies of Elvis' debut platter to catch up with a 6,000 back-order which hit him before the record had even gone on sale, before it had been released in any market outside Memphis.

And overnight, a restricted but indubitable

Elvis with Memphis DJ Dewey Phillips who played his first record on radio

mantle of fame settled about Elvis, as the record went spinning out across the country – 100,000 ... 200,000 ... 300,000 ... still going.

Within a month, Elvis was invited to appear on hillbilly heaven. Nashville's Grand Ole Opry. Veteran entertainers kept him singing backstage, after the show.

On Juke Box Jury

The record was played on *Juke Box Jury*. 'Blue Moon' had been written and first recorded some years earlier by a famous, Grand Ole Opry entertainer, Bill Monroe of Kentucky. Tennessee Ernie Ford, on the *Juke Box Jury* that night, drawled: 'If ole Bill Monroe hears this, he'll just take his li'l ole country band and head back for the hills.' Monroe himself, far from being offended, sent Elvis a note of thanks. After Elvis brought it out, six other companies made it with their stars.

Billboard gave Elvis' first record an 85 score, very high, on both sides. Over a 15-week period, only one other record in the same category had an equal rating, and that was by the established star, Webb Pierce.

Sam Phillips still hasn't figured out which was the big side. 'That's All Right' was in the R&B idiom of negro field jazz, 'Blue Moon' more in the country field, but there was a curious blending of the two different musics in both.

Two More

Sun brought out two more Elvis records – 'I Don't Care' and 'Good Rockin' Tonight'; 'Milk Cow, Blues Boogie' and 'You're a Heartbreaker.' *Billboard*'s annual poll of disk jockeys for 1954 landed Elvis in the list of Ten Most Promising artists on the strength of them.

Ruben Cherry of Home of the Blues said: 'Just three records, and every one has been a hit. People have come in to buy them who never bought records before.'

Country music had been thought to have more appeal for older people, but the teen-agers picked up Elvis.

All at once, he had crowds screaming for him. He got a manager, Bob Neal, and a regular job on CBS Louisiana Hayride from Shreveport every Saturday night.

He had more money than he ever saw before.

'I got my own office,' he said. 'It's listed in the phone book – Elvis Presley Enterprises, 160 Union.'

Terrific Appetite

He also has enough money to buy all the cheeseburgers he wants. When he has music on his mind, he forgets eating, then gets a terrific appetite which may demand eight cheeseburgers and three milk shakes at a sitting.

To that new office of his come between 60 and 75 letters each day, most requesting pictures.

Elvis at first sent the pictures free. Now he charges 25 cents for them; on mass-orders they cost 8 cents each.

In the past three months he has traveled more than 25,000 miles on personal appearances, played to crowds of 3,000. He travels by car with his instrumental teammates – Scotty Moore, hot guitarist, and Bill Black,

bass, both Memphians. Their schedule for one week – New Orleans, Friday; Shreveport, Saturday; Ellis Auditorium in Memphis, Sunday; Ripley Miss, Monday; Alpine, Texas, Thursday; Carlsbad, N.M., next Friday and Saturday.

Elvis will be 20 this month, and things are moving fast.

Came From Tupelo

Elvis is the son of Mr and Mrs Vernon Presley, 462 Alabama. He spent his first 14 years in Tupelo, Miss. The music he heard was mostly negro, with some country influence from his parents' brothers.

When he was 13 Elvis bought a guitar for $12.95. He taught himself to play it, still doesn't read music. At Humes High, he lugged his guitar with him played it with little urging at any time.

The guitar Elvis has now cost $175. He still is peevish about what happened. 'The man gave me $8 on the trade-in,' he said. 'Then he threw it in the waste-basket. Shucks, it still played good.'

Sam Phillips, who had been a WREC engineer seven years, had been scouting for talent on the side. He let it be known that he would listen to anyone who wanted to sing or play.

No Big Names

He still will – and that even includes children whose mothers think they have talent. 'I've never made a record with an established star yet,' he said.

But Sam has established some stars.

He listened to Jackie Brenston's group from Clarksdale, Miss., and recorded his first hit, 'Rocket 88'. This was genuine, untutored negro jazz, not the white man's music adapted by some of the famous negro

In 1955 Elvis Gave Ole Han

By KEN JONES
Press-Scimitar Staff Writer

The first act after intermission was supposed to be a warmup for Hank Snow, the headliner for the country music caravan that played Mobile, Ala., halfway through a southern tour in May of 1955.

As the crowd drifted back from the concession stands and settled into the seats of Ladd Stadium, no one was in the mood for another warmup act.

"Let ole Hank pick and sing so we all can go home," yelled one good ole boy as he cracked open a peanut and wiped the sweat, prompted by a humid Gulf Coast night, from his brow.

As he was yelling, some of the crowd started chuckling. Three guys dressed in blushing pink were taking the stage, led by a slender, but muscular, young man with shaggy sideburns and slicked down ducktails.

They looked out of place. Country music fans had become accustomed to stage dress of rhinestones, sequins and embroidered wagonwheels, but pink was out of character in 1955.

The chuckles were quickly drowned out. Scotty Moore unleashed his electric guitar into a pulsating frenzy. Bill Black's upright bass fell straight into a very uncountry beat, and the young singer, gyrating like a congo dancer, virtually attacked the microphone.

Have you heard the news?
There's good rocking tonight.

Mobilians were having their first encounter with Elvis Presley, and they were immediately in a state of silent shock,

which lasted until the first quitar brea[k] Then a tumultuous roar almost eclipse[d] the frenzied music, a roar that for the nex[t] 22 years was to be a byproduct of Elv[is] Presley concerts.

Each time the roar would nearly fade some Presley innovation would revive i[t] In the middle of a song, he would hold u[p] his hand and stop everything while h[e] hitched his pants before picking up th[e] frenzied pace once more. The crowd yelle[d] its vocal support for his each and ever[y] move.

The emcee had told us the performe[r] was just 19, and it stretched the imagina[-] tion that one so young could have so muc[h] stage presence.

At least one high school junior, attend[-] ing the concert with his first heart throb who was destined to be his first hear[t] break, had a distinct feeling he was seein[g] show business history develop.

The youngster, raised with Hank Wi[l-] liams and Lefty Frizzell in his soul, didn'[t] understand the new music, the new bea[t] and only about half the lyrics. But he felt [a] connecting link with this guy dressed i[n] blushing pink.

Perhaps it was because the singer was o[f] the same generation, and maybe it wa[s] because he dared to be different. And i[t] could have been because the singer led th[e] youth's girl, from whom he had neve[r] been able to coax into a goodnight kiss, t[o] shreik, jump up and down and lose virtual[-] ly all inhibitions.

Elvis Presley in those days was his ow[n] emcee, interrupting the pulsating music t[o] exchange gags with Bill Black or to moc[k] the country music he was supposed to b[e] representing. He would introduce a son[g]

HANK SNOW
In 1955 the country music star didn't know much about the kid with sideburns — but he soon found out.

a Real Snow Job

THE EARLY TRIO
Elvis is shown in this 1955 photograph with, left, Scotty Moore and Bill Black.

with, "We call this song, 'Little Darlin', when you went away you broke my heart, but when you come back I'm gonna break your jaw.'"

Then he would erupt into his own inimitable version of "That's All Right, Mama," or "Blue Moon of Kentucky."

Poor Hank Snow. The headliner never had a chance. When he walked onto the stage after 45 minutes of Elvis Presley, the crowd's energy had been sapped. There was nothing left for applause, requests or even the ordinary foot-patting that goes with country music.

Perhaps few in the audience would forecast what would happen to Elvis Presley in the next 18 months — the national television appearances, the millions of records sold, the movies, the controversy caused by his non-conformist dress and rebellious manner.

The stealing of the show, at every stop on the tour, did not escape the expert eyes of one particular man in attendance, however.

Hank Snow, the man who had to follow the act, was at that time managed by Col. Tom Parker.

musicians. Sam considers Ellington, Lunceford, etc., white man's music.

As word got around, Sam's studio became host to strange visitors. Negroes, with field mud on their boots and patches in their overalls, came shuffling in with battered instruments and unfettered techniques. Most tried to impress him with white man's music. Sam outwaited them, listened for a wisp of original melody, a happy sound or an unconventional riff. Beale Street boys came, in cool drapes, moaning melodies Handy never knew.

One Big Oversight

B.B. King of Memphis made 'My Baby's Gone' and '3 O'Clock Blues' with Sam, his first commercial record. Sam overlooked getting a contract. He didn't forget when Elvis came along. There were Joe Hill Louis of Memphis; the Howling Wolf from across the river; Roscoe Gordon, and others, all introduced by Sam.

Phillips brought out 'Bearcat,' with Rufus Thomas of WDIA, the first Sun record, about two years ago. It sold 200,000, and he was in business. Since then he has brought out 32 records, now has distribution in every state.

Elvis lugged his guitar into the studio one Saturday afternoon, wanted to make a 'personal' record. He sang pop ballads. Sam listened, tucked the name away in his file. Eighteen months later, Sam got a ballad, picked thru the file and pulled out Elvis' name. It didn't go. Sam told Elvis to sing everything he knew, listened for several hours. 'That's All Right, Baby' resulted.

In A Class Alone

Sam deoesn't know how to catalog Elvis exactly. He has a white voice, sings with a negro rhythm which borrows in mood and emphasis from country style.

Marion Keisker, who is WREC's Kitty Kelly and Sam's office staff, calls Elvis 'a hillbilly cat.'

While he appears with so-called hillbilly shows, Elvis' clothes are strictly sharp. His eyes are darkly slumbrous, his hair sleekly long, his sideburns low, and there is a lazy, sexy, tough, good-looking manner which bobby soxers like. Not all record stars go over as well on stage as they do on records. Elvis sells.

If the merry-go-round doesn't start spinning too fast for a 20-year-old, he'll end-up with enough cheeseburgers to last a Blue Moon.

Spin 'em again boys.

Another Memphis Press-Scimitar *reporter, Ken Jones, remembered from firsthand experience the impact the young Elvis had on his audiences – and fellow-singers – in the spring and summer of 1955. Later he recalled these in an evocative article for his newspaper. (See previous pages.)*

Two other early contributors to the Presley scrapbooks were Bill Black, the singer's bass player, and Bob Neal, a local disc jockey and Elvis' first manager. Bill Black talked about the making of the first records for Sun and the trio's life on the road in an interview with a country and western music magazine. Bob Neal's recollections were published in the Memphis Press-Scimitar.

'SEE IF YOU CAN WORK OUT SOMETHIN''

A talk with Elvis's bass player

Memphis musician Bill Black clearly recalls the day when Sun Record boss Sam Phillips asked him and his friend, guitarist Scotty Moore, to 'See if you can work out somethin''. Because the person they were to work it out with was a young man named Elvis Presley, now the nation's most popular young country star.

'Sam Phillips was interested in recording this young guy and asked Scotty to take a listen to him,' says Bill Black. 'So he came over to Scotty's house and we played some numbers together. Later we went over to Sun Records and laid down some tracks – I believe the first was "I Love You Because".

'After that Elvis began fooling around singing "That's Alright Mama" and I took it up, sort of slappin' and clownin' on the bass. That's how we made that first disk.'

The bass player continued, 'In the beginning Elvis had curly hair and looked about 12, even with his sideboards, which he grew to make himself look older. We weren't really a group, just Scotty, me and Elvis. The drummer, D.J. Fontana, didn't join us until later. We formed a kind of syndicate splitting our money three ways with Elvis getting double what Scotty and I got.

'We barnstormed all across the Southern States, travelling about 50,000 miles in six months, I guess. Sometimes we spent more money on petrol than food!

'Elvis himself was playing guitar in those days. We all got on swell. We used to play penny-ante cards, read each other's crime books, visit disc jockeys wherever we stopped, taking copies of our records, and going to the movies or watching TV in our hotel rooms.

'Elvis was the youngest of the four of us, but he was the boss. He was fun to be around. We used to kid him about the first time a female shouted, "Elvis I love you, I love you" at him. No, it wasn't a teenager. It was a woman who told us later she was over 70!

'That was because he was so young looking, I guess. She was feeling very maternal towards him.'

'Later working with Elvis got dangerous. And expensive! I had my bass stamped to splinters in Kansas City and my clothes plucked off like chickens eat corn. But after a bit Scotty and I got cunning when it came to avoiding the fans. We used to go the opposite way Elvis went when leaving a theatre and then make out we were part of the crowd looking for Elvis!

'Mostly the noise of the audience was so loud we couldn't even hear ourselves when we hit a sour note!' adds Bill Black. 'But they were great days those early days on the road!'

Country-Western Jamboree
Winter 1956

I KNEW ELVIS WOULD BE A BIG HIT

Memphis Dee-jay Bob Neal Star's First Manager

'I first met Elvis Presley when I was promoting an outdoor concert in The Overton Park in Memphis', Bob Neal told the *Press-Scimitar* at his record shop on Main Street.

'Sam Phillips of Sun Records called and asked, "Why don't you put Elvis on the show?" I had been a dee-jay for a number of years when Elvis' first record became a hit in Memphis, so I obliged and put him in the show. It was the first big public appearance the boy had made and he stole the show completely.

'I went on playing his records and the hits kept coming. One day I asked Elvis if he had a manager and he said no. So we made a deal and I became his manager.

'He was a sensation every place he went,' says Bob Neal. 'First playing around Memphis, and then as a member of the Louisiana Hayride. We also played a lot of concert tours across Texas. And every place he went, even though he wasn't known nationally, he was a tremendous hit and a great favourite.

A 'beefcake' photograph of Elvis used by his first manager, Bob Neal, to promote the rising young star

*Two other famous rock 'n' roll singers
with whom the young Elvis appeared:
Bill Haley and Johnny Cash*

'Elvis is a very polite and pleasant person and I enjoyed working with him. He was very ambitious and often said his ambition was to be a big star. But he doesn't want people to think he is uptown.

'I remember one day last year we were standing in front of this record shop, Neal recalls. 'Elvis was getting some recognition by then, known as "The Hillbilly Cat", and earning two hundred a week, a large bundle of money for a boy his age. A crowd of boys came by. Maybe they were a little awed by his success, maybe they were afraid of a snub. At any rate, they barely nodded, gave him a quick sideways glance and kept right on going.

'Elvis turned pale as he watched them go on up the street and there were actually tears in his eyes. "Now, what's eatin' them?" he asked. "I went to school with those kids. They were my friends and now they won't even stop to pass the time of day." Elvis is finding that the higher he climbs, the lonelier he gets.

'That's not how the girls treat him, though. We've had to clean our windows ten times as much since Elvis became popular. The girls leave lipsticky kisses on his picture displayed there!'

Neal goes on, 'I was Elvis' manager for about a year, and then late in '55 I got Colonel Tom Parker interested in watching him and using him on some shows. I had a partnership with the Colonel for a while.

'But the trouble was I was already involved in many things in Memphis. I had the radio show, the promotions, the record shop, as well as a big family. I didn't want to be out of town on the road all the time so I dropped out of the picture in 1956.

'I had gotten Colonel Parker involved because he was promoting some shows nationally and could put Elvis into them. I felt Elvis was going to be big. Instead, he's become a sensation!'

Memphis Press-Scimitar
Undated, *c*. 1956

By the autumn of 1955, Elvis was a big enough artist to headline his own show and on 11 October The Elvis Presley Jamboree *played dates in Texas, Arkansas and Louisiana. Among the co-stars in the Jamboree was another singer destined for fame, Johnny Cash. As a result of his increasing success, Elvis had been able to pay for his parents to move into a new home, a bungalow at 1414, Getwell Road, Memphis. And it was there that Gladys Presley gave one of the very few interviews of her ill-fated life to the* Memphis Commercial Appeal *just after Elvis had left on his first starring tour.*

WE CALL HIM BABY OR AGELESS

[Says Mother of New Singing Star]

Mrs Gladys Presley, mother of Memphis' new singing sensation, Elvis Presley, told the *Commercial Appeal*, 'Our boy always comes first with us.

'Even today he don't seem growed up to me. I still see that little tow-head riding the trike we gave him when he was three round and round the kitchen. He called me 'Baby' – and he still does.

'When he's away on tour he phones home every night and says, "How are my babies?" I call him Baby or Ageless. That's because when he was little, his cousin couldn't say Elvis.

'Elvis wanted a brother or sister real bad when he was little,' Mrs Presley recalls. 'He was kind of a lonely child and we were just as anxious to have more children. I'm one of eight children myself. And poor as we were,

Gladys Presley with her son 'Ageless' and a girlfriend

we spent money for doctors – lots of different ones – to try to remedy it, but nothing happened and Elvis is all we have. He is our whole world, he's what we live for.

'I know lots of parents don't let their children know when things are troubling them, but I don't believe in that. Elvis would hear us worrying about our debits, bein' out of work and sickness and he'd say, "Don't you worry none, Baby. When I grow up, I'm going to buy you a fine house and pay everything you owe at the grocery store and get two Cadillacs – one for you and Daddy and one for me."

'And little as he was, the way he'd look up at me, holding on to my skirt, why, you know, I'd believe him.'

Memphis Commercial Appeal
Undated, October 1955

Just over a month before his twenty-first birthday, Elvis took a major step in his career when he left Sun Records and signed for the giant international label, RCA-Victor, on 22 November 1955. There was no acrimony between the young star and Sam Phillips, the man who had given him his start, as the report which appeared in the Memphis Press-Scimitar *reproduced here reveals. Though the money paid for this transfer was not revealed in the story it was, in fact, a then unprecedented sum*

of $35,000. The reporter was once again the newspaper's talent spotter, Robert Johnson.

Elvis signs for RCA-Victor. This historic Memphis Press–Scimitar *photograph, taken on 22 November 1955, shows Elvis shaking hands with his mentor Sam Phillips. Behind the singer stands his manager-to-be Colonel Tom Parker …*

MEMPHIS SINGER PRESLEY SIGNED BY RCA-VICTOR

Elvis Presley, 20, Memphis recording star and entertainer, who zoomed into bigtime and the big money almost overnight, has been released from his contract with Sun Record Co of Memphis and will record exclusively for RCA-Victor, it was announced by Sam C. Phillips, Sun president.

Phillips and RCA officials did not reveal terms, but said the money involved is probably the highest ever paid for a contract release for a country-western recording artist.

'I feel Elvis is one of the most talented youngsters today,' Phillips said, 'and by releasing his contract to RCA-Victor we will give him the opportunity of entering the largest organisation of its kind in the world, so his talents can be given the fullest opportunity.'

Negotiations were handled by Colonel Tom Parker of Hank Snow Jamboree

Attractions, Madison, Tenn.; Bob Neal, Presley's personal manager; and Steve Sholes of RCA-Victor.

Elvis Presley Music, a publishing firm, has been set up to handle much of Presley's music, in conjunction with Hill and Range Music Inc., New York City.

Bob Neal, WMPS personality, continues as Presley's personal manager, and will handle his personal appearances and other activities, but Hank Snow Jamboree Attractions will handle Presley enterprises in radio, TV, movies and theatre.

Also taking part in negotiations were Hank Snow himself, RCA-Victor's longest-term western star.

Memphis Press-Scimitar
22 November

PRESLEYMANIA – 1955

BOB NEAL, personal manager of 20-year-old country singer, Elvis Presley (Sun) who in a few short months has catapulted to a top spot on the Louisiana Hayride, announces that an office is being opened at 160, Union Avenue, Memphis, to handle Presley's affairs. Neal invites deejays to write for samples.

Billboard, 12 February

☆ ☆ ☆

TV NOTES: Among the stars on NBC's half-hour show from the Louisiana Hayride, Sunday, will be Sun's country singer, Elvis Presley, from Memphis, making his television debut. Plus Scotty Moore, hot guitarist, and Bill Black, bass.

Memphis Press-Scimitar, 2 March

☆ ☆ ☆

ARKANSAS: Mike Michael who airs over Station KDMS, El Dorado, Ark. says Elvis Presley's 'You're A Heartbreaker' and 'Milk-Cow Blues' are going strong in his area. Last week Michael staged a Jamboree which drew a full house at the El Dorado High School with Elvis Presley, Scotty and Bill.

Billboard, April

☆ ☆ ☆

HANK SNOW'S All-Star Jamboree, underwritten by Hank Snow and Colonel Tom Parker, kicked off a three-week tour of Louisiana, Alabama, Florida, Georgia, Virginia, North Carolina and Tennessee on May 1. Headlined by Snow, the unit includes Slim Whitman, Faron Young, The Carter Sisters, Jimmie Rodgers Snow and Elvis Presley.

Cashbox, May

☆ ☆ ☆

IN 1954 the sale of fresh dough-nuts went soaring in the Southern States of America. This was due to a sultry voice which sang a commercial for dough-nuts on a show called "Louisiana Hayride." The singer was an up-and-coming young man named Elvis Presley.

ELVIS PRESLEY : My quiet upbringing

MY upbringing was pretty quiet. I was never out of my mother's sight until I was 16. All the kids would go swimming in the creek and my mother wouldn't let me go. And I never really dated until I was 16.

When I was 15 I got crazy about football, but my folks thought it was too dangerous and tried to stop me. After school the white boys would team up against the coloured boys and they'd all come home with their clothes torn.

One thing, though, I was always taught the difference between right and wrong. I remember once when I was five, I took two empty Coke bottles from a neighbour's porch, and got a spanking from my dad.

CAR BLAZE. Elvis Presley, Sun records new country star, saw red early last week when flames devoured his pretty pink Cadillac on the road between dates at Hope and Texarkana, Ark.

Billboard, 25 June

☆ ☆ ☆

POLL WINNER. First Annual Country and Western Popularity Poll run by Bobby Ritter over WTUP, Tupelo, Miss drew letters from 16 States … Elvis Presley was first among the top 10 male vocalers.

Billboard, 6 July

☆ ☆ ☆

AUDIENCE PULLERS. Overton Park Shell was jammed with an overflow audience last night for the wind-up of the eighth annual Bob Neal County Music Jamboree Series. Several hundred who wanted to hear in person Johnny Cash and Elvis Presley and some 22 other country music and comedy performers had to be turned away, while 4,000 more lucky people enjoyed the show.

Memphis Press-Scimitar, 6 August

☆ ☆ ☆

FRENZIED REACTIONS. Elvis Presley created pandemonium among the teen-age country fans at Jacksonville, Florida recently and before he could be rescued from his swooning admirers they had relieved him of his tie, handkerchiefs, belt and the greater part of his coat and shirt. Says Manager Bob Neal, 'We hadn't gone out and arranged for anybody to squeal and scream. Those girls screamed spontaneously. For a long time there's been nobody who'd done that – not since Frank Sinatra fifteen years ago.'

Billboard, 13 August

☆ ☆ ☆

POPS & COUNTRY WESTERN COMBINE. Colonel Tom Parker of Jamboree Attractions instituted a new policy when he presented a combination of popular and country & western music on a recent one-nighter tour. Parker teamed Bill Haley and His Comets with Hank Snow for an extended tour which opened in Omaha October 10. Elvis Presley joined the Snow-Haley tour in Oklahoma City.

Cashbox, October

☆ ☆ ☆

FIRST NUMBER ONE. Elvis Presley's 'Mystery Train' (Sun) hit number one spot in the Country Charts this week as disk jockeys at annual Nashville fest voted the Memphis star 'Most Promising New Singer' …

Billboard, 2 November

1956

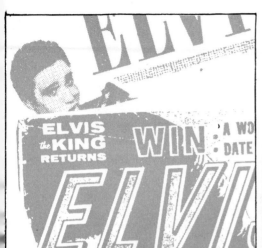

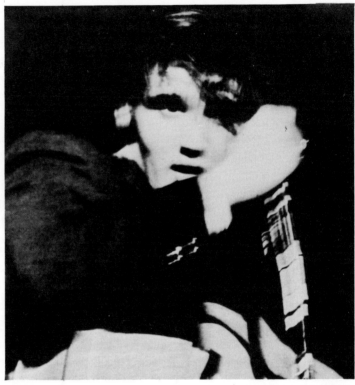

ELVIS the KING RETURNS

WIN A WO DATE

ELVIS

EVEALING S SHOCK CRET

appearan of Elvis

ELVIS PRESL

STAR OF STAGE, SCREEN, RADIO, RECORDS AND T

ELVIS PRESLEY MAY VISIT LONDON

"Evening News" Reporter

AMERICAN rock 'n' roll king, Elvis Presley, may come to London next year. He has been offered about £250,000 a Johannesburg to make 25 per ances in Euro

ELVIS ARMY

ELVIS kissed me

ELVIS 50th

ELVIS PRESLEY

CHART

RESLEY— that's all we had at the ele on ELVIS

Two days after his twenty-first birthday, Elvis made 'Heartbreak Hotel' the record that first turned him into a national star and then an international phenomenon. The session which produced this landmark single was held at RCA's studios at 1525, McGavock Street, Nashville, and was supervised by Steve Sholes who had negotiated Elvis' change of label. Among the musicians who gathered in the company's unprepossessing and rather rudimentary studios were Elvis, Scotty, Bill, drummer D.J. Fontana and piano player, Floyd Cramer.

In the scrapbooks covering this moment of music history are a cutting about Steve Sholes, 'the man who signed Elvis' and an interview with Floyd Cramer. Cramer, born in Shreveport in 1933, had worked as a session man with a number of country artists and had already some personal experience of Elvis' remarkable rise to fame. He talked about this and the recording session in January in the article 'A Lonesome Singer'.

ROCKING TO THE TOP

Steve Sholes the man who signed Elvis
By Georgia Winters

'I will never forget the first time I heard Elvis Presley sing,' said Steve Sholes, top A & R man at RCA-Victor Records. He leaned back comfortably in his big chair and glanced at the picture of Elvis in action over his desk. 'A field man sent me a copy of his first Sun record, "That's All Right". I had been looking for something, I didn't know what – it was a sound or a beat – and I'd been looking for it a long time. When I played this record, I knew I'd found it.'

Steve Sholes was one among many when he flipped over the great singing style of Elvis Presley. But when he called Sun Records he found to his disappointment that Elvis had just signed a seven-year contract.

A month or so later, when Steve was in Nashville to visit the Grand Ole Opry, he was introduced to Elvis.

'When I met Elvis he was 19,' Steve recalls. 'He was wearing a charcoal suit and pink shirt – and on him it looked great. My first impression was that he was an extremely good-looking, warm-hearted, well-mannered, nervous kid. It was his second performance and he was scared, but there was something burning in him.

'I just looked at him and knew this kid had talent. Actually, I should never call Elvis a kid, for as frightened as he was, he went out there and put on a real show. The audience went wild. He really had something.'

After Elvis had been working for Sun for about a year, he met Colonel Tom Parker. Colonel Parker had heard a lot about Elvis and after he saw him perform in Florida he was sold. He became Elvis' co-manager, and eventually his manager.

It was Colonel Parker who arranged the deal that enabled RCA-Victor to buy Elvis from Sun. At that time, his fifth Sun disc, 'Mystery Train' had just gone on the market – but it was his debut performance of Big Boy Cruddup's 'That's All Right, Mama' which had caught Steve Shole's interest.

He had for a long time sensed the significance that Country & Western and negro rhythmn and blues were to have on the pop music field, and in Elvis Presley he saw the makings of an artist who could successfully fuse the two styles.

The deal which brought Elvis to RCA included ten master waxings which had already been issued and six more that were suitable for release. For as with all his signings – million-sellers Jim Reeves and The Browns were others – Sholes was careful to secure a monopoly of masters. This meant that no other label could muscle in on sales by issuing previously recorded material from the can.

Says Sholes, 'Two-thirds of Presley's first RCA-Victor album were those Sun masters. My policy really paid off.'

It was a real triumph for Steve Sholes who had joined RCA-Victor straight from school in 1929 as a messenger boy in the radio department. But his heart lay in music for he played the saxophone and clarinet with local bands and was excited by the prospects of the disc industry.

So, fatefully as it was to turn out, in the year 1935 – the year of Elvis' birth, of course – he took a $25 a week cut in salary to transfer to disc sales. Here he was introduced to a-and-r work by the then Victor boss, Edward Wallerstein, and during the thirties

The historic session in the RCA studios in Nashville in January 1956 which produced 'Heartbreak Hotel'

gained wide experience of not only pop but jazz and classical recording as well.

It was he, for instance, who arranged the first sessions of such leading jazzmen as Jelly Roll Morton and Sidney Bechet, and he was later associated with others of the order of Coleman Hawkins, Earl Hines and Dizzy Gillespie.

Although in the Army during the last war, Steve continued to supervise waxings – Fats Waller's last among them. In 1945–7 he had a string of hit albums with the Al Goodman Orchestra, and when Country and Western really caught fire in the States and big-name stars were selling 300,000–500,000 with every release, he was at the head of RCA-Victor's work in this idiom.

Then in January 1956 he supervised the recording of Elvis for RCA in Nashville. Everyone, the singer, his musicians and the technicians, worked for two days on 'Heartbreak Hotel'. It was somewhat different from the songs he had been doing, but Steve believed in it.

'I crossed my fingers and prayed,' he recalls, 'and thank heavens I was right.'

Summing up, Steve said, 'As time goes by, Elvis Presley will prove himself to more and more people and will gain untold fans. I am thrilled to know that in some fields he still has an untapped audience to match his still untapped talents. The future looks very bright for this wonderful young man.'

Sixteen Magazine
Undated – *c.* December 1956

A LONESOME SINGER

'I knew Elvis Presley in Shreveport before he was at all well known', says C & W pianist Floyd Cramer who has played an important part in the sensational rise of the star from Tennessee now breaking all disk and public appearance records.

'In 1951 I joined the Louisiana Hayride troupe based at radio station KWKH. Every Sunday we did a big broadcast show and I gained my musical experience playing piano for such country stars as Faron Young and Webb Pierce. In 1954, Elvis was given a try-out on the Hayride and the audience liked him so much, he got a weekly booking. I played piano for him with Scotty Moore and Bill Black.

'Occasionally I went to Nashville for recording sessions, but for a time I was glad of all the work I could get and so I sometimes went out on the road with Elvis, Scotty and Bill.

Elvis performing on grass – a rare photograph from
Sixteen Magazine

'Elvis was just the same then as he is now. He hasn't let success go to his head. And he worked just as hard to get his music across when he was playing live in concert halls as he did in the studio.

'I remember on the first session for RCA in Nashville that we were all very anxious to keep the music simple with no technical exhibitionism. Elvis wanted to get the feelings in "Heartbreak Hotel" across as directly as possible. That tremendous feeling of loneliness in the record was all brought about by the way he sang and the way we played. Nothing else. Still, I have to admit none of us knew quite what a big seller we had made.

'Elvis is very conscientious on a record date,' Floyd adds, 'but he's also very relaxed. His main concern is to get the feeling right and he'll take all the time he needs to do it. I hope to go on working with him, and I'm convinced that his popularity will last a long time.'

Cowboy Songs
Undated, autumn 1956

'The King of Western Bop' – the first publicity photograph of Elvis published in Britain in January 1956

On 21 January 1956, British music fans saw the first photograph and details of America's new singing sensation in the weekly pop music paper, Record Mirror. *This landmark story was written by the well-known show business columnist, Dick Tatham, and is also notable for containing the first use of the sobriquet 'The King' as well as the notorious nickname, 'Elvis the Pelvis'.*

THE KING OF WESTERN BOP

By Dick Tatham

Here he is, girls! America's new wonder boy in the world of warble! The very latest prodigy in the platinum-plated palate profession! Fans: meet ELVIS PRESLEY!

Elvis was 20 [sic] on January 8. He hails from Memphis, Tennessee in the dear ole Southland. He plays rhythm guitar, too, and likes to be known as 'The King of Western Bop'. Publicity boys say he weighs 160 lbs., and is six feet in height – and who are we to doubt a tall story?

His rocket to riches was just a few weeks ago. RCA-Victor bought his disc contract from Sun Records. Reported cost: £13,000. Same time, music publishing moguls Hill and Range signed the versatile vocalist as a songwriter. They've created a special firm: Elvis Presley Inc.

The Inc. was scarcely dry on the contract before RCA-Victor had rushed out their first Presley pressing. One side was 'Mystery Train' which is possibly to do with a mystery train of thought, for it was siamesed with 'I Forgot To Remember To Forget'.

Elvis's sudden fame has brought him Cadillacs, sharp country costumes, a backing group, and his own book: *The Elvis Presley Album of Juke Box Favorites*. And that is surely only the beginning for this good ole boy!

Someone has wisely said, 'The 1950s will be remarkable in history for their worship of mediocrity'. Let us hope the much bally-hooed Mr. P flouts this analysis.

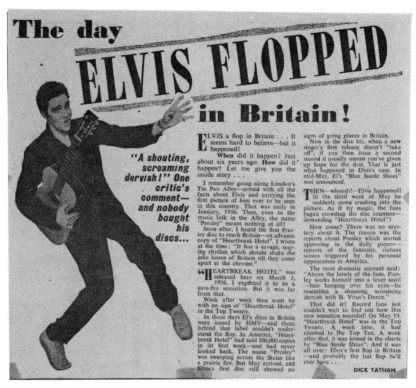

The day ELVIS FLOPPED in Britain!

"A shouting, screaming dervish!" One critic's comment— and nobody bought his discs...

ELVIS a flop in Britain . . . It seems hard to believe—but it happened!

When did it happen? Just about six years ago. How did it happen? Let me give you the inside story . . .

I remember going along London's Tin Pan Alley—armed with all the facts about Elvis and carrying the first picture of him ever to be seen in this country. That was early in January, 1956. Then, even to the music folk in the Alley, the name "Presley" meant nothing at all!

Soon after, I heard the first Presley disc to reach Britain—an advance copy of "Heartbreak Hotel". I wrote at the time: "It has a savage, searing rhythm which should shake the juke boxes of Britain till they come apart at the chrome."

"HEARTBREAK HOTEL" was released here on March 1, 1956. I expected it to be a sure-fire sensation. But it was far from that.

Week after week then went by with no sign of "Heartbreak Hotel" in the Top Twenty.

In those days El's discs in Britain were issued by HMV—and those behind that label couldn't understand the flop. In America, "Heartbreak Hotel" had sold 100,000 copies in its first week—and had never looked back. The name "Presley" was sweeping across the States like a prairie fire. But May arrived, and Elvis's first disc still showed no signs of going places in Britain.

Now in the disc biz, when a new singer's first release doesn't "take off", if you then issue a second record it usually means you've given up hope for the first. That is just what happened in Elvis's case. In mid-May, El's "Blue Suede Shoes" was announced.

THEN—whoosh!—Elvis happened! In the third week of May he suddenly came crashing into the picture. As if by magic, the fans began crowding the disc counters— demanding "Heartbreak Hotel!"

How come? There was no mystery about it. The reason was the reports about Presley which started appearing in the daily papers— reports of the fantastic, riotous scenes triggered by his personal appearances in America.

The most dramatic account said: "Above the howls of the fans, Presley works himself into a fever until —hair hanging over his eyes—he resembles a shouting, screaming dervish with St. Vitus's Dance."

That did it! Record fans just couldn't wait to find out how this new sensation sounded! On May 19, "Heartbreak Hotel" was in the Top Twenty. A week later, it had climbed to the Top Ten. A week after that, it was joined in the charts by "Blue Suede Shoes". And it was all over: Elvis's first flop in Britain —and probably the last flop he'll ever have . . .

DICK TATHAM

Reports from the States suggest, incidentally, he may have to swap his Cadillac for an armoured car, since he's currently enjoying the occupational hazard of having the fans tear off his tie, his shirt, his vest, and stripping him down to the Elvis Pelvis.

Record Mirror
21 January

* FOOTNOTE: *There has been much speculation among Presley fans about* The Elvis Presley Album of Juke Box Favorites *published by Hill and Range Songs, sold for $1, and now of the utmost rarity. The booklet contained the words and music of fifteen songs: 'That's All Right', 'Rag Mop', 'You're A Heartbreaker', 'I Almost Lost My Mind', 'Cryin' Heart Blues', 'Blue Guitar', 'Always Late', 'I Forgot To Remember To Forget', 'Tennessee Saturday Night', 'Gone', 'I Need You So', 'Give Me More, More, More', 'Oakie Boogie', 'That's The Stuff You Gotta Watch For', and 'I'm Left, You're Right, She's Gone'. Of these titles, Elvis only recorded four — and the mystery remains as to*

As soon as Colonel Parker assumed sole responsibility for Elvis' career in March 1956 he began the second stage of his plans to make the young man a nationwide-wide star by booking him on television. In the next three months Elvis appeared six times on the Tommy and Jimmy Dorsey Stage Show *from New York, then followed these with two appearances on the top-rated* Milton Berle Show *in Los Angeles and a strange guest spot on the* Steve Allen Show *(again from New York) where he appeared dressed in a tuxedo of white tie and tails! This had been arranged by Steve Allen following a deluge of criticism in the press about Elvis' 'lewd*

whether the remaining eleven songs were part of his live act at this time which, to the best of anyone's knowledge, he never put on disc. Should he have done so — could this missing cache of treasures still be lying forgotten somewhere in RCA's Nashville vaults?

*In March 1956, Colonel Tom Parker became Elvis' manager – and soon
began to inspire cartoons like this English example by Diz Disley*

movements' during his earlier TV spots. (See the comments in PRESLEYMANIA, p.49.) Aside from the teenagers of America, there were also members of the older generation quite willing to stand up in support of Elvis – including the noted British artist, Feliks Topolski who was working in New York at this time. A cutting from the scrapbooks gives his insider's view of Elvis on television.

ELVIS ALIVE!

Meet the most surprising Elvis Presley fan – Feliks Topolski, world-famous artist. Topolski spent a whole day at the CBS New York television studios watching Presley rehearse, observing him gyrate and bawl his way into his TV show.

And this sketcher of famous people – George Bernard Shaw and Sir Winston Churchill among them – was IMPRESSED. Presley fans take heart. Topolski is on your side against the critics' sneers.

Says Topolski, 'Presley has a natural simplicity and ease about his performance. That is what the teenagers squeal about. I thought there was a terrific tension about his songs, a tense kind of sex appeal.

'At the side of him other male singers seem to be just like little boys trying so hard to please. And I found him a fascinating subject to sketch.'

Topolski's drawings show that he did not have his eyes closed in complete adoration. But *his* criticisms are an artist's criticisms.

He liked the 'good, posed-into-toughness face', but deplored the 'sloppy, half-open mouth and the sloppy half-closed eyes'.

The teenage crush outside the TV studios, said Topolski, was fantastic. 'Mounted police were out, barriers up, but still the youngsters swarmed.'

At the rehearsals, says the artist, it was decided to tone down the sexy jerks with which Presley moves into a number.

Topolski does not, though, class Presley as a great artist. 'He is just a good performer,' he says.

How did Topolski come to illustrate Presley? 'I like to draw life on the move, and Presley is just as much part of life as any of the other famous people I have drawn,' he explains.

Weekend
Undated, c. autumn 1956

By April 1956, Elvis had reached number one in the US pop charts with 'Heartbreak Hotel' and Colonel Parker decided it was time for him to break into films. In between concert engagements, the singer flew to Hollywood and made a screen test for Hal Wallis at Paramount Pictures. The producer concluded that Elvis had 'the same power, virility and sexual drive' on screen as the young Errol Flynn and signed him to a seven-year contract. Back on the road, Elvis' amazing success was featured in a special article, 'A Howling Hillbilly Success' in the nation's biggest selling magazine, Life on 30 April. (See PRESLEY-MANIA, p.48.) However, in Minneapolis two weeks later he was not so favourably reported by the city's leading columnist, Will Jones – though the newspaperman provided some interesting information about Elvis' first experiences in Hollywood, which was soon to dominate his life so completely …

SQUEALS DROWN PRESLEY'S SONGS

By Will Jones

Elvis Presley, young bump and grind artist, turned a rainy Sunday afternoon into an orgy of squealing in St. Paul auditorium.

He vibrated his hips so much, and the 3,000 customers squealed so insistently at the vibrations, it was impossible to hear him sing. None of the smitten seemed to care.

The crowd was much smaller than expected. Presley faced a sea of empty seats. When the noise started, however, even the empty seats seemed to be screaming.

Presley wore a Kelly green jacket, tight blue trousers, and, disappointingly, black leather shoes.

He only sang 'Blue Suede Shoes.' (I couldn't actually hear him sing it, because of the squeals. A girl in tight pink slacks assured me that's what it was.)

Uniform for the Day: Pink Slacks

Tight pink slacks were almost a uniform among the fans. Tight white slacks and tight black slacks were popular.

Presley was wearing tight black jeans and a black silk shirt when he arrived at the auditorium. A dozen policemen marched him into his dressing room. Then he stood around with his hands in his jeans posing for pictures and talking with reporters.

He smiled a faint, half-sneering kind of smile at times. He didn't look nearly so tortured or pouty as he does in most published photographs.

His brown hair doesn't appear so dark, either. He has pimples all over the back of his neck, a few on his chin, and a number of nervous facial mannerisms. The most intriguing is the repeated, rapid puffing of a single cheek. His long eyelashes have a Valentino-like mascaraed look.

'Any advice for all your girl friends?' asked a TV reporter.

'Well, that's a pretty stiff question,' said Presley, 'I have one word for all: Hi!'

People kept handing him pictures and slips of paper to autograph. His right cheek twitched each time he signed an autograph.

His Record Firm is 'the Biggest!'

A radio interviewer asked him about his record successes.

'I switched to Victor because that's the biggest company there is,' drawled Presley.

'You 19 or 21?' asked another. 'I've heard both.'

'Twenty-one,' answered Presley. 'Wish ah was 19.'

Presley came here from Memphis, Tenn., his home. He's been so busy he hasn't had a chance to get home for awhile. He got a few free days by surprise after he flopped at a Las Vegas, Nev., night club. They replaced him with a girl singer. The older customers in Las Vegas just didn't dig him.

I asked Presley about his movie plans. He's been signed for one picture a year for seven years by producer Hal Wallis.

'I was asked to do one of the leading parts in *The Rainmaker* with Burt Lancaster,' he said. 'A young kid, lovesick, real shy. I mean, he wasn't real shy. Real jolly. Real happy, real jolly, real lovesick. It wasn't like me.

'I took this screen test where I came in and was real happy and jolly and I didn't like it. I did this other one where I was mad at this girl, and I liked that better – it was me.'

He's Against Any 'Excess Actin'

As he talked, he gently-stroked the hand of a pretty girl who was standing beside him waiting for an autograph.

'Mr Wallis asked me what kind of a part I'd like, and I told him one more like myself, so I wouldn't have to do any excess actin'. So he's havin' somebody write one for me like that.'

I asked him who was to play the girl in *The Rainmaker*.

Elvis on TV – because of the protests about his pelvic movements, the young singer was only seen from the waist up on the small screen in the summer of 1956, as this example shows

'Hound Dog', recorded by Elvis in July 1956, became one of the biggest of all his hit records

'Katherine Hepburn,' he said, 'if you wanna call her a girl.'

The policemen let a few lucky girls at a time into the dressing room for autographs. One who came in had a haircut just like Presley's. Another one brought him a flattened greasy popcorn box to sign.

He has a way of whipping up the crowd at the start of a song by playing a few introductory notes, stepping to the microphone, and then singing nothing.

Squeals! Another pause, another false start, more squeals, and then finally the song.

The Mob Screams. Closes In

When he wanted silence to announce a number he held up a hand in the traditional platform gesture – but a double-jointed thumb twitched as he held the hand aloft.

In moments of public passion, he clutched the microphone to his forehead. He ended up limp and sweating and loped off the stage half-staggering.

The mob screamed and ran for him. The police marched him to a waiting car. A young, beautiful, well-dressed, highly-made-up blonde tried to get in the car with him. The police barred her.

'I'm a member of his company!' she cried. 'I belong with him! Stupid police!' Presley got away. The blonde walked around in the rain complaining to bystanders while the rain made a soggy mess of her hair.

Minneapolis Globe
13 May

Elvis consolidated his fame during the summer of 1956 with the 'Elvis Presley Show' a tour which took him across America from Florida in the south to New York in the north. These one night stands across the nation were later described as 'the dizzy apogee of Elvis' career as a rock star' and though his young audiences were huge and ecstatic, he ran

into trouble with authority in some states as the cutting from the Jacksonville Tribune *of 11 August graphically reveals.*

ELVIS ORDERED: 'KEEP IT CLEAN'

Elvis Presley, minus his bump and grind dance, continued his two-day show in Jacksonville today after a hectic time yesterday – a warning from a judge and trouble with the Variety Artist Guild.

The teen-age rock 'n roll idol, who was advised before his first show here yesterday to 'keep it clean' or face court charges, met with local Juvenile Court Judge Marion Gooding after the opening performance and was warned sternly to remove the objectionable hip movements from the act.

Judge Gooding, who watched the first performance along with 2,200 screaming youngsters, said today apparently Presley has complied with the order, judging from reports of the later shows last night.

Before talking to Gooding yesterday, Presley appeared bewildered at the request. 'I can't figure out what I'm doing wrong,' he told reporters backstage.

'I know my mother approves of what I'm doing … If I had a teen-age sister, I certainly would not object to her coming to watch a show like this,' he said.

Meanwhile, a representative of the American Guild of Variety Artists told Presley yesterday that unless he joined AGVA and his manager, Tom Parker, posted bond and insurance for other acts in the Presley show, AGVA would prevent other acts from appearing.

The matter was cleared up shortly before show time when Presley accepted membership in the organisation and his manager accepted bond and insurance obligations to AGVA.

Presley, who kept a nonchalant attitude throughout the day, spent his spare time between performances posing for magazine, television and newspaper photographers and answering reporters' questions.

On 26 September 1956 Elvis returned to his birthplace, Tupelo, for what had been named in his honour, 'Elvis Presley Day.' It was here, at the Mississippi-Alabama State Fair in October 1945, that ten-year-old Elvis had made his début in a talent contest and won second prize singing 'Old Shep'. Now in 1956 he was given the 'Key to Tupelo' by the Governor of Mississippi, James P. Coleman, in recognition of his achievements. Among those present in Tupelo to see the star's return was Peter Dacre, chief reporter of the Sunday Express. *The interview he phoned to London was the first to appear in a British newspaper and naturally found a place in the scrapbooks.*

PLEASE, MR. PRESLEY, SIGN MY BACK'

By Peter Dacre

Tupelo, Mississippi, Saturday.
'This,' shouted the State trooper, 'is a heck of a place to interview somebody.'

The place was a crowded, brawling, over-hot tent in a field outside this small farming town.

The 'somebody' was Tupelo's favourite son of the moment, the local boy who has become the biggest phenomenon in show business; Elvis Presley.

Elvis Presley, now 21, has risen in little more than a year from being an unknown lorry driver to the indisputed leader of the riot-rousing cult of rock 'n' roll.

His records have earned more than £2,000,000 so far. (A million copies of his latest have been ordered before it is issued.)

He gets £16,000 for three television appearances. And it is reported he has raked in another £4,000,000 by giving his name to various products.

Elvis Presley and I were trying to talk in what was supposedly his dressing-room.

Around us were four armed State troopers, the governor, the mayor, radio men with thrusting microphones, cameras, and a throng of teenage girls with stars in their eyes and anything autographable in their hands.

Presley, relaxed and gum-chewing, wore a velvet blue shirt (casually open to reveal a bare chest), speckled black trousers, and white shoes.

Gold 'n' diamonds

On the fingers of his left hand were two gold rings, one with black sapphires, the other topped by a diamond horseshoe.

'Mr Presley,' I said, 'do you know the sensation rock 'n' roll music has caused in Britain?'

He surveyed himself in the mirror. 'No, sir, I didn't know. I heard my records were going well over there, though.'

I asked him if he had heard that there had even been riots. A radio man pushed forward. 'I'm from station WELO,' he said. 'Will you give us an interview about that, Mr Dacre?'

I said it was my job to get interviews, not to give them.

'Mr Presley,' I continued, 'can you explain the success of rock 'n' roll and your singing?'

A young girl dashed up, touched Presley's three-inch sideburns and dashed out screaming: 'I touched him.'

Someone else thrust a lipstick into his hand and pleaded: 'Please, Elvis, autograph my back.'

Presley obliged with a practised flourish.

'Mr Presley,' I said, 'about this rock 'n' roll.' 'Oh, yes, sir,' he said. He scratched his mass of hair. 'I wish I knew, sir. I've never been able to explain the reason myself.'

'Why do you sing that way?'

'I like it that way.'

A burly State trooper thrust a pile of photographs between us, 'Sign these, Elvis.'

A young girl took a photograph. Presley kissed her on the forehead, loud and theatrical. 'Oh, Elvis, you are a darling,' she cried, and melted into the background.

'Mr Presley,' I said, 'what do you feel about this adulation?'

Presley moved his gum to the other side, tugged at his trousers, and said: 'This what?'

'All these girls mobbing you like this,' I explained.

'I like it. I wouldn't be human if I didn't.'

From the open-air theatre came an announcer's voice:

'*We've got 500 National Guard and police here, so let's have no trouble. And please keep away from the stage. The last show some of them got burned, some of them were crushed – but none of them got Elvis.*'

Screams 'n' bangs

The warning was justified. From the moment Presley had entered the theatre in his white Lincoln Continental (he also has four Cadillacs, a Messerschmitt runabout, and a motor-bicycle) the tension had mounted.

As he sang, his loose-limbed hip-rolling,

'Elvis Presley Day' in Tupelo, 26 September 1956. Here Elvis stands with his parents as he is interviewed by Peter Dacre of the Sunday Express

his swaying, and his lurching legs started the girls screaming and banging the stage. They tore their hair and held out imploring hands.

Photographers crowded the stage. Police joined them. Presley kept on singing. One blonde climbed hysterically on to the stage and flung her arms around Presley. He kept on singing. She was carried off struggling and weeping.

When it was over, Presley dashed to his car and was away to his crowded dressing tent with his escort.

There I said: 'Mr Presley, do you consider you sway about too much on the stage?'

'Sir, I don't do anything bad. I just move to the music account of the way I feel. I hear it and I gotta move. I can't help it.'

'People tell me, "You've gotta stop squirming like a tadpole," but I'd sooner cut my throat than be vulgar.

'You've seen my folks. They're respectable God-fearing people. They wouldn't let me do anything vulgar.'

Shock 'n' poll

I said I thought he teased the girls something shocking. Presley gave me a shocked look.

'Hiya,' he called to a young man who had just come up. He slapped him heartily. 'When we were kids we used to slip in here under the fence 'cause we had no money. But it's different now.'

'Say, Elvis,' said someone, 'will you have your picture taken with the governor?'

Presley agreed. He put his arm round the governor and said: 'If I ever leave this business I'll go into politics.'

'What'll you run for?' someone asked.

'The city limits,' replied Presley.

I led Presley back to the corner and said: 'Mr Presley, what do you think of your success now?'

'I don't ever think about it except sometimes when I wake up in the morning and say to myself "Has this really happened to you?" '

'Mr Presley … ' I said.

A man pushed a young girl forward. 'Say, Elvis, you remember Leonard's daughter.'

'Sure,' said Presley. 'Hiya.' He hugged the near-fainting girl.

I left and went out into the comparative quiet of 5,000 screaming teenagers.

Among the many newspaper attacks on Elvis during 1956, the occasional sympathetic interview appeared such as the following item from the New York Star *of 29 October in which the writer decided after meeting the singer he was 'a fine lad' – and one teenagers could safely set up as a hero.*

ELVIS THE PELVIS HITS TOWN

By Gordon Sinclair

New York, 29 Oct. – Elvis Presley grabbed New York by the throat today and made the big town cry uncle while declaring that he 'hated' the phrase 'Elvis the Pelvis.'

He is a six-footer of 21, a millionaire with a peaches and cream complexion, and a lad who consistently calls oldsters like me 'sir'.

He neither drinks nor smokes, says he has no time for love life … but would like to have time … and feels that he has 40 years of top earnings ahead of him. Elvis would like to be an actor but is taking no lessons.

Modestly he told me that if he was tops for the next 40 years he might reach the stature of Mickey Mouse 'and that would really be something to yowl about.'

As we talked in a theatre basement, police barricades were stretched for an area of 300 square yards to keep screaming people … mostly teen-aged girls … at bay and 57 constables manned those baricades. Elvis said he was Irish-American and proud of it.

As a first question I said: 'Elvis, the teen-aged crowd have had plenty to say about you; now let's hear what you think about them.'

'Teenagers are my life and my triumph. I'd be nowhere without them. But I think it's terribly wrong for them to think it's smart to get loaded and go out driving a car to force other people off the road or maybe even kill people. Hot rodders are my fans but they go too far … a lot of them go too far. Some of them think it's smart to sass people and get uppity and high and inconsiderate of others.'

Not Short of Cars

'They ripped your car apart … yes?'

'That means nothing, sir. That's a car and I've got other cars but the idea of doing to others what you'd like them to do to you is what's in my craw. It's in the Bible.'

'Many parents seem to feel, Elvis, that you are a menace, evil and wicked and the personification of easy money. How do you feel about that?'

'Sir, I know they feel that way. Lots of them do. And I wish they didn't. I wish I could have a chance to set down and talk to those parents because I think I could change their minds and their viewpoint. Ever since I got to be a sort of name I've examined my conscience and asked myself if I led anybody astray even indirectly, and I'm at peace with my conscience.

'I don't drink and I don't smoke and I don't swear.

'I read my Bible, sir, and this is no story just made up for now. My Bible tells me that what a man sows he will also reap and if I'm sowing evil and wickedness it will catch up with me. I'm right sure of that, sir, and I don't think I'm bad for people. If I did think I was

bad for people I would go back to driving a truck and I really mean this.'

Money Snowballing

'Then how do you suppose these stories got started?'

'Talk about big money got them started and I do make big money. Up to now, this year, I think I've brought in $1,100,000 and the money is snowballing into more money. I can't help it and I can't stop it but I live pretty simple. I don't even have a regular home. A man can't but wear one suit at a time … me, I only have one suit. He can't eat but three meals in a day. I pay back about 85 per cent in income tax and I'm right proud to pay it.'

'Do you ever think of Joe Louis who made the same kind of money and got so far back in his taxes that he can't ever get out of hock so long as he lives?'

'Yes, sir, I thought about Joe Louis in two ways. There was the way he was complaining while he was champ, that he didn't have any privacy. Not even a bit. Well, sir, I do have privacy. I got me a good manager in Col. Tom Parker (he was manager for Edward Arnold until Arnold dropped dead in March) and I insist upon some privacy and I get that some.

'On money, I'm paying more in taxes than I need to pay because I've seen people like Dick Haymes and all and I don't want that to be ol' Elvis because those tax people don't ever forgive a man and I don't see why these should, either. So with me I get, say, a million up to now. That's for 10 months.

Clears $1,200 Daily

'Well, I get allowed a lot for expenses and I have at the end, after all of these taxes are met, about $1,200 extra every day and a fellow can't even spend that kind of money.'

Elvis, the teenager's hero. Presley loved riding motor-cycles and was photographed with his friend Nick Adams, the movie star, in Memphis in September 1956

'Another point that I keep reading about is how, when I get into the army, they're going to give me a special time off to make records and personal appearances and other things at a lot of money. I don't want that, sir.

'First, I think I could enjoy the army life just doing what I'm told to do, and another thing is that all the boys would hate me if I could get things they didn't get.'

Many Ask Questions

This interview was not a strictly Sinclair-Presley interview but one in which many people asked many questions.

There were a good deal of banter back and forth between Elvis and Ed Sullivan, who kept the conversational ball abouncing. The kidding was about cars because Elvis just won't drive the sort of cars for which Ed is a pitchman.

There was also chatter about girls. For example, somebody says, 'You've had more girls than Robbie Burns. Is it true?'

'How would I know? How would anybody know how many girls Robbie Burns had? But Burns knew about love and his verses prove it. Me, maybe I know, too, but I don't have time. Girls are wonderful. Girls are the greatest and mostest and loveliest! Anybody that says he doesn't like girls is missing his life. There wouldn't be anything without girls.'

Has No Special Girl

'How do you feel about Jayne Mansfield on account of somebody says you and Jayne are that-a-way?'

'She's a right nice girl, but a married girl. Not for me.'

'Who is for you, Elvis? Don't you have any one girl; I mean, with all you have to choose from, you a millionaire at 21 with your life

and your fortune ahead of you. Don't you have any one special girl?'

'Sir, I'm honest with you. I do not have such a girl. Not even a hint of a special girl. Think, like you say, I could have one, but with me it's a fight with the clock. I don't have the time.'

Has 40-Year Hope

'And how long can you go on at this hectic pace?'

'I'm not just sure what you mean by hectic, but I sort of got it blocked out at 40 years. Let's say 39. I won't be able to sing that long but I might be able to act if'n I ever get to act. Now this picture coming out soon, it's a civil war picture and the people who write about pictures might tear me all apart. So if they do, I'll have to start all over again. But I'm not going to quit and I'm not going to take lessons because I want to be me.'

'How come you've never been up to Canada?'

'Mostly because I'm pretty young yet and, up to two years ago, I was a nobody driving a truck in the South. Truck drivers from the South don't get much chance to go to Canada. Now I'd like to go to Maple Leaf Gardens. That's in Toronto, and I've been hearing about it. But nobody has invited me to come up, or go up. In letters I get lots and lots from Canada.'

Keeps Fan-Mail Record

'Ever read 'em?' 'Well, I guess, sir, that to be honest you'd say no. I look at some and we keep records of how many.'

'And how do you react to the screaming hysteria of your fans?'

'Honestly, sir ... this will seem like I read it some place, but I keep wondering if it's really me they are screaming at. I keep wondering who is behind me that is causing all the excitement. I say to myself: "Elvis, this is you that is doing it." And then I think it can't be me.

'I don't like them pulling my clothes and writing on my cheeks in lipstick and wanting me to kiss them. I don't see any sense for them to dance a rock 'n' roll on the hood of my car or drive a knife into the upholstery. But some do it and look at me with the queerest look in their eyes while they are doing it. That part kind of frightens me. Mind you, sir, like I say, I can get other cars. People are even wanting to give me cars for free. But I don't like to see kids put knives into them. I wonder why they do it.

Opposed To Drinking

'Now, mind you, these kids have bought these cars. I'd be nobody without them. But some things I wish they wouldn't do, and what they do with cars is one of them. With cars and drinking. Drinking is no good, sir. It is really no good.'

In all of this talk Elvis Presley was poised, composed and cheerful. He flashed a pleasant smile from his dark eyes; eyes that reminded me of the eyes of a Hindu maiden. Not bags or marks of dissipation but a sort of healthy animal glow.

Young Presley used no pretence and no slang. He did not pose or upstage those around him.

As a final question I asked what was his biggest moment up to now. 'Dying,' he said. 'In the picture *Love Me Tender* I die. All the actors I met in Hollywood told me that dying was a big moment, a big scene for anybody in the game. They told me it was a hard thing to do. So I did it. I think it came off pretty good but I'll be waiting to see how the experts feel about that.'

Part of the reason for Elvis being in New York had been to begin the promotion of his first film, Love Me Tender, *which he had made in Hollywood in August for 20th-Century-Fox. Originally entitled,* The Reno Brothers, *the picture had been retitled after one of the four songs performed by Elvis, and was naturally awaited by fans with mounting excitement. American newspaper stories prior to the release that Elvis 'died' in the picture produced a fevered reaction from fans as the story by John Sampson on 29 October reveals. And as to the reviews of* Love Me Tender – *the critics seemed to dislike the picture as much as the fans loved it.*

GIRLS CRY 'ELVIS MUST NOT DIE!'

By John Sampson

New York, Sunday.
'Elvis must not die!' screamed the teenagers.

So all right, Elvis the Pelvis Presley, the rock 'n' roll riot, won't die. That is if his film company likes the alternative ending of his latest film, *Love Me Tender.*

In the original he dies. And when he arrived here today bobbysoxers clamoured outside his hotel screaming their disapproval of the unhappy ending.

So Presley's manager, Col. Thomas Parker, came down and told them about the alternative happy ending.

'We are shooting this ending in New York in the next few days,' he said. 'It is then up to the film people to decide which version to use.'

The bobbysoxers seemed appeased. Then they demanded to see Presley. The colonel agreed to produce him on condition that the fans did not touch him.

They promised. And Elvis the Pelvis appeared.

The new film star learning his lines for his first picture.
A publicity shot of Elvis and his co-star Debra Paget
on the set of Love Me Tender

'He's Divine'

But the girls did touch him. They nearly tore him apart, and those who couldn't get near him cried: 'Oh, what a doll!' 'Isn't he divine?' 'May I touch your sideburns, Elvis?'

Presley dived into a passing taxi and thus remained all in one piece. It drove him away from the girls who again began shouting that he must not die.

What a life!

PRESLEY'S BUMPING OFF IS 90 MINUTES LATE

By Edward Goring

Mr Elvis Presley, known to the initiated as 'The Pelvis,' has made his screen début by courtesy of 20th Century-Fox in a film called *Love Me Tender*, which opens in London this week.

For the 21-year-old American phenomenon of Rock 'n' Roll, who starts a riot every time he opens his mouth, it is a good beginning. He gets bumped off.

This distressed me when I had a preview of the picture yesterday only because it comes 90 minutes too late.

But will it distress British teenagers abreast of US affairs through selective reading, who are dutifully waiting to swoon at the sight of him?

Ghostly

Just in case the fans can't face their soft drinks at the thought of it, Hollywood have made an alternative version with a 'happy' ending in which he does not die.

Even in the version I saw they have softened the blow. After his funeral a ghostly vision of Mr Presley looms across the screen to sing farewell.

Before this he enlivens a drab, slow, mechanical film about a Southern family at the end of the Civil War with a few songs.

Cashing in on the Rock 'n' Roll craze and a reputation which has earned Mr Presley $1,000,000, the producers cast him at the last minute, and he wanders into CinemaScope trundling a plough.

Abandoning this for the guitar, he sings to Mom in her rocking ('n rolling) chair, and 'sends' 'em in crinolines at the country fair.

Watch Him

It's not what he sings, but the way he sings it. His numbers are hilly-billy, but his manner can only be described, without lapsing into bad taste, as Rock 'n' Roll.

For it describes, in its writhing, squirming aggression, one thing, sex. See him at work and you know why youngsters squeal and elders protest. And why he is called 'The Pelvis.'

When it is not wriggling, ploughboy Presley's heavy, sensual features are furrowed with concern.

He took advantage of big brother Richard Egan's preoccupation with the Yankees to marry Debra Paget; and big brother returns with the Yankees on his heel in pursuit of $12,000 spoils of war.

Seeking a simple solution, Mr Presley, beefy and pugilistic, beats up Miss Paget and tries to shoot Mr Egan.

One movie mogul judges him the successor to James Dean.

True, he glowers as sulkily as Marlon Brando, but judging by his first film, all Mr Presley shares with the new school of screen acting is inaudibility.

Elvis made headlines in two very different ways at the end of 1956 – firstly for being involved in a brawl in Toledo, Ohio, and secondly for becoming a millionaire in a year according to the show business magazine, Variety. *The two stories neatly encapsulate the enormity of his impact on the popular culture of the late fifties.*

ELVIS ROCKS JEALOUS MAN

Girls Yell: Save Him
By Gerry McKnight

Rock 'n' Roll singer Elvis Presley is in trouble again – with a jealous husband who says his wife's 'insane love' for the singer caused their separation.

He is 19-year-old Louis John Balint who burst into a hotel at Toledo, Ohio, near midnight last night when Presley, three musicians and a press agent were listening to the cabaret.

Balint, in blue jeans, walked over to the table and yelled, 'Are you, Elvis Presley?'

Presley nodded.

Balint screamed, 'You S.O.B., my wife carries your picture in her handbag and doesn't carry one of me!'

At this Presley tried to get up. Balint lashed out with both fists, connected with the jaw and rock 'n' rolled Elvis' head back.

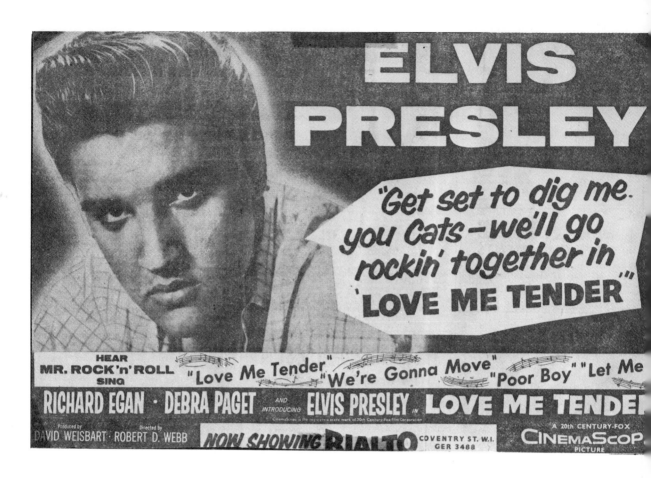

British advertisement for Elvis' first movie; and
(left) a chewing gum card used in the promotion of
Love Me Tender

ONE DAY, EL WAS IN A TOLEDO HOTEL WHEN SOME GUY WALKS STRAIGHT UP TO HIM ...

HEY YOU... MY WIFE CARRIES A PHOTO OF YOU IN HER WALLET... BUT SHE DOESN'T CARRY ONE OF ME! STEP OUTSIDE!

Comic strip version of the incident when a jealous husband attacked Elvis in Toledo. Valentine, *October 1961*

Girl fans in the doorway then screamed out, 'Police! Save Elvis. Save Elvis.'

Patrolman Walter Zalaznski standing outside the hotel heard the cries. He said later he could hear dozens of hysterical woman screaming and thought it sounded like big trouble.

Inside, Zalaznski and fellow patrolman Bill King fought their way through a mob of sobbing teenage girls.

'Hold on Elvis,' they shouted, 'We'll get you out.'

Then they found the singer ... pounding another man with his fists. And it was the other man the police had to rescue!

Said Zalaznski, 'Elvis handled himself well and threw several good punches before we broke it up. He could cuss as well as the other guy, too.'

And Patrolman King added, 'Presley's no slouch – he was really working over that guy. He put up a good fight.'

Sequel: Elvis said he did not want to press charges, but Balint was taken to court and fined $10 for assault.

Outside the Toledo Courthouse, Balint said: 'I thought Elvis was a sissy singer, but he ain't such a bad guy after all.'

Daily Sketch,
24 November

ELVIS A MILLIONAIRE IN ONE YEAR

By Mike Kaplan

Hollywood, 23 October.

Controversy has always meant cash in show business and the latest proof is Elvis Presley, whose jet-propelled career will reach stratospheric heights in his first full year in the bigtime with an indicated gross income of at least $1,000,000. Tally is an underestimation, based on what he has done in the first nine months of 1956.

Despite the carping critics who contend he can't last, reasonable projections of future income indicate he'll do at least as well in 1957, with the tally possibly bouncing even higher as result of his share of an unprecedented $40,000,000 retail sales volume of Elvis Presley merchandising during the next 15 months.

Presley's entry into the bigtime is usually dated from his appearance on the *Milton Berle Show* last midsummer. Actually, he had been a rising performer for some months prior to that as witness hefty disk sales and personal appearances that drew door-busting crowds. Since the Berle show, however, Presley has been a true atomic-age phenomenon.,

Estimate of $1,000,000 for his 1956 earnings is based solely on the known factors, which include unprecedented heights in

Looking every inch a millionaire – a postcard of Elvis published in the winter of 1956

some departments. The near-1,000,000 advance sale of his 'Love Me Tender' disking for RCA-Victor is an indication of the pace of his platters. For the 1956 calendar year, Presley figures to wind up with a total of at least 10,000,000 records sold. Figure represents a royalty return to him of about $450,000. Add to that an estimated $250,0000 in picture deals, including the reported $100,000 for *Love Me Tender* (20th-Fox) as well as advances on his deal with Hal Wallis, and probably another $100,000 in television guest stints. Then, there are the personal appearances, about 40 in all by the end of the year, on which Presley's percentages vary but which are figured to total at least $200,000. There's

$1,100,000 right there, plus returns from his music publishing firm.

Few of the actual Presley figures are available since his manager, Col. Tom Parker, is an astute and close-mouthed guide. Nor is there any concrete indication of the 1956 take on the merchandise tieups, which are figured to be considerable.

PRESLEYMANIA – 1956

THE HILLBILLY JOHNNIE RAY. How do British fans feel about America's newest singing sensation, Elvis Presley? Johnnie Ray fans claim he could never replace their hero, and, while some agree that 'Heartbreak Hotel' is a good disc, they nevertheless intend to remain faithful to Johnnie.

New Musical Express, 6 May

☆ ☆ ☆

PRESLEY RECORD. According to rating figures, 40 million viewers watched the *Milton Berle Show*, in which Elvis Presley starred, April 3. Spokesman for Berle claimed, 'That's one out of every four folks in the US tuned in to us.'

Billboard, 11 April

☆ ☆ ☆

A HOWLING SUCCESS. A lover's lament called 'Heartbreak Hotel' sung by Elvis Presley is the bestselling record in the country this week, and the 21-year-old hillbilly who howls, mumbles, coos and cries his way through it has overnight become the biggest singing attraction for teenagers in the US. On a tour of Texas last week girls kicked through a plate glass door in Amarillo to get him to autograph their arms and underclothes. In San Diego, the Shore Patrol was called out to save him from an overenthusiastic audience. This week, Elvis headed into Las Vegas to pick up about $12,500 for a week's wailing. Asked what it is about him that makes all the ladies go limp, Elvis answers, 'I don't know, but I sure hope it doesn't stop.'

Life, 10 April

☆ ☆ ☆

THE HOOTCHY-KOOTCHY MAN. Jack Gould writes, 'Mr Presley has no discernible singing ability. His speciality is rhythm songs which he renders in an undistinguishable whine; his phrasing, if it can be called that, consists of the stereotyped variations that go with a beginner's aria in a bathtub. He is a rock-and-roll variation of one of the most standard acts in show business: the virtuoso of the hootchy-kootchy. His one speciality is an accented movement of the body that heretofore has been primarily identified with the repertoire of the blonde bombshells of the burlesque runway. The gyration never had anything to do with the world of popular music and still doesn't.'

The New York Times, 6 June

☆ ☆ ☆

GUT BUCKET MUSIC. Popular music has been sinking in this country for some years. Now it has reached its lowest depths in the 'grunt-and-groin' antics of Elvis Presley.

Ben Gross, New York columnist, 8 May

☆ ☆ ☆

ELVIS SPEAKS. 'I don't like being called Elvis the Pelvis. I mean, it's one of the most childish expressions I ever heard. But if they want to call me that, there ain't nothing I can do about it, so I have to accept it. The Colonel made me controversial to get me going, but we haven't done anything bad. I trust him, he is really like a Daddy to me when I'm away from home.'

TV Guide, 1 July

SINGER'S FATHER RETIRES AT 39. Mr Elvis Presley, the 21-year-old American popular singer, has got his wish and is to have a part in the film, *Love Me Tender*. Since becoming a success he has induced his father, who is only 39, to retire, and has refurnished a home for his parents and designed some of the furniture himself. He now owns a publishing company, two Cadillacs (one coloured yellow, the other pink), a station wagon and a motor cycle.

The Times, 9 September

☆ ☆ ☆

MERCHANDISING PRESLEY. Thus far, H.G. Saperstein & Associates on behalf of Colonel Tom Parker have set 51 different licenses for Elvis Presley products and they're still rolling in. Of the items bearing the Presley name, ranging from bookends and bracelets to wallets, 80% are aimed at the female market and 20% at the male market. Campaign is unprecedented in that it is the first all-out merchandising drive aimed at teenagers who have their own money to spend.

Variety, 23 October

☆ ☆ ☆

PETITION AGAINST PRESLEY. Memphis can be a cold and exclusive city, though it prides itself on Southern hospitality. Recently, certain neighbours of the Presley family appointed a spokesman to see if the Presleys wouldn't sell their property to the group. A resident said, 'We've had to call the police time after time to get those screeching female adolescents to go away. I don't like to be thought a snob but, frankly, the Presleys don't belong here.' Mr Presley was said to be upset by the suggestion, pointing out that he couldn't help the youngsters and sightseers, but he wasn't interested in selling.

Dallas Morning News, 22 October

WORK OF THE DEVIL. 'The effect of rock and roll on young people is to turn them into devil worshippers,' says Reverend Albert Carter, a minister of the Pentecostal Church, 'and to stimulate self-expression through sex. To provoke lawlessness, impair nervous stability and destroy the sanctity of marriage. It is an evil influence on the youth of our country.'

Los Angeles Times, 31 October

☆　☆　☆

GOD-LOVING KID. Elvis Presley is a 'God-loving, jelly-kneed kid' who has taken rock 'n' roll out of the category of race or rhythm-and-blues music and made it into pops, according to his personal manager, Colonel Tom Parker. 'Elvis is still a country boy at heart and he's not fixin' to change,' the Colonel says. 'You can't get Elvis into fancy restaurants or night clubs. He doesn't feel right in 'em and I don't know as he ever will.'

San Francisco News, 15 November

☆　☆　☆

GERMAN PITCH FOR ELVIS. 'He walks like Marilyn Monroe but at home he's a model son!' That's the pitch which RCA-Victor is giving Elvis Presley in the promotional pieces attendent to the diskery's expansion into the German record market and its pitch to sell r 'n 'r locally.

Variety, 3 December

1957

ELVIS the KING RETURNS

WIN · A WOR... · DATE

EVEALING S SHOCK' CRET

appearan... of Elvis

ELVIS PRESL...

STAR OF STAGE, SCREEN, RADIO, RECORDS AND T...

ELVIS PRESLEY MAY VISIT LONDON

"*Evening News*" Reporter

AMERICAN rock 'n' roll king, Elvis Presley, may come to London next year. He has been offered about £250,000... a Johannesburg... make 25 per... ces in Euro...

ELVIS kissed me

...ESLEY– that's all we had h...
...s at the ele... on. ELVIS

ELVIS ARMY

ELVIS 50th

ELVIS PRESLEY

...HART ENTR...

When Elvis turned 22 on 8 January, he became eligible for military service and was required to report to the Kennedy Veterans Hospital in Memphis for a medical. Naturally, there was enormous press and public interest in the event, and Elvis passed the examination 1A – 'the highest you can get,' according to Captain E.P. Rowan, chairman of the draft board. In Britain, the news that Elvis was to become a soldier began press speculation that it might bring him to the country – at least in uniform, if not with a guitar under his arm.

In the US, Elvis set out on a series of concerts across the country before returning to Hollywood to make his second movie, Loving You. *He also recorded a new disc, 'All Shook Up', which proved his greatest single release success topping the charts for eight weeks. The items in the scrapbooks from this period include an eyewitness account from his backing group, the Jordanaires; and an insider's view on Elvis and the making of* Loving You *by the movie's dance director, Charles O'Curran.*

TEARING IT UP WITH ELVIS!

The Jordanaires from Nashville are not only one of the most successful, prolific and flexible vocal-instrumental units on the American music scene, but thanks to their association with Elvis Presley are becoming known throughout the world.

The regular group consists of only four – Gordon Stoker, Hoyt Hawkins, Neal Matthews and Ray Walker. But they are augmented from time to time by various other Nashville session men and name artists like Floyd Cramer and D.J. Fontana.

Because of their association with Elvis, both on records and in live performance, The Jordanaires can each dine out for weeks with untold stories of Presley. This is one gem told recently by Gordon Stoker:

'We were on stage with Elvis at a concert in Detroit one evening, when the 10,000-strong audience suddenly seemed to go wild. As the show was finishing, Elvis looked out into the crowd and said:

' "Let's get out of here fast ... they're coming after us!"

'And come they did. It looked as if someone had set loose millions of bees, and they were swarming along the aisles, over seats and on to the stage.

'With Elvis in front, we rushed down the stairs and into a waiting car surrounded by policemen.

'It had been a near thing. Our buttons had been torn off, coats ripped, pockets left hanging.

'As we were pushed, exhausted, into the car with Elvis, and the doors automatically locked as the car set off, we began to congratulate ourselves on saving Elvis from certain disaster.

'With a grin, Elvis, who hadn't been touched, told us, "Man, were we lucky that time. In a crowd like that I usually lose a coat and a shirt!" '

Cashbox
29 April

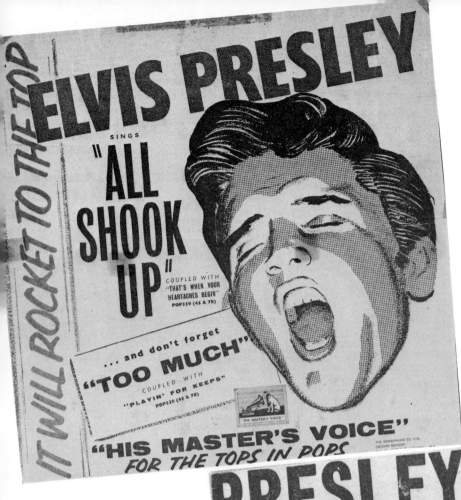

ELVIS PRESLEY

SINGS

"ALL SHOOK UP"

COUPLED WITH
"THAT'S WHEN YOUR
HEARTACHES BEGIN"
POP359 (45 & 78)

... and don't forget

"TOO MUCH"

COUPLED WITH
"PLAYIN' FOR KEEPS"
POP330 (45 & 78)

IT WILL ROCKET TO THE TOP

"HIS MASTER'S VOICE"
FOR THE TOPS IN POPS

THE GRAMOPHONE CO. LTD.
(RECORD DIVISION)

PRESLEY MAY BE HERE AS A DRAFTED GI

NEW YORK, Wednesday.—If Elvis Presley visits Britain this year it will be as a member of the U.S. Armed Forces! Film commitments prevent him from making an overseas tour as a civilian entertainer.

But if Elvis is drafted he may reach Britain as an entertainer with Special Services.

The singer has already been classified 1A in the draft—and he may be called up at any time. Only 30 days' notice is given.

On vacation

Meanwhile, Elvis is currently on vacation following completion of his third film. He still has three more to make.

The next—his fourth—is likely to be started soon, which precludes any possibility of overseas travel this year.

Will Britain's Presley addicts see their favourite next year?

Colonel Tom Parker, Presley's manager, told the MM that he did not rule out the possibility of Presley's visiting Britain "some time in the future if all conditions were right."

ELVIS IS A PERFECTIONIST

Says Charles O'Curran Hollywood Dance Director

People have tried to write Elvis Presley off – and there are many more who would if they could. To many, he's an unpleasing sign of the times, something they dislike without really understanding.

Last week, the *Melody Maker* met a man who believes he *does* understand.

Charles O'Curran – Patti Page's husband – is a dance director who has been working with Elvis on the Paramount film, *Loving You*.

'Actually, I selected his songs,' says O'Curran. 'Hal Wallis is a great producer, but he doesn't know much about pop songs. One of the numbers I picked was "Teddy Bear," which is doing very well.

'How is Elvis? You're going to love him. I hear he is coming over here. Let's put it this way: you're going to like him a lot more than some of the people around him.

'When I say that he's a simple lad, don't get me wrong. He's sharp enough mentally. But, in a way, he's still unspoiled and unaffected. Childlike, perhaps.

'And he's so willing to learn. If you told him to go over in the corner and stand on his head, I think he'd do it.

Unhappy

'He's a perfectionist, too. We saw his first film, *Love Me Tender*, and thought it was awful. Elvis can't bear to think about it. He was most unhappy about that title ballad. Thought he sang it flat. He didn't feel that a straight ballad was his material anyway.

'When we did the recording session for his latest film, I was quite satisfied with one take. "That's perfect, Elvis," I told him. "We couldn't improve on it if we tried all day."

'But he didn't think so. We did it again.

'With his acting, too, he strives for improvement.

'*This isn't the boy from the backwoods who has let fame go to his head*. He's quite humble and conscious of all his defects.

Patient

'Don't take my word for it. Everyone who has worked with him says the same. Naturally, he's made some enemies. In his position, that's unavoidable. He has to be smuggled in and out of hotels and theatres, and in general keep to a plan of campaign mapped out by others. That's bound to offend some.

'But I've seen him signing autographs and he's much more patient than most of us would be. If two hundred people are there, he'll just go on writing his signature until he's satisfied everybody.

'Presley has become an industry. He's so big that ordinary standards don't apply. For example: one magazine wanted him for a special photographic session. That kind of co-operation is normally given free in the name of publicity. But Presley's handlers demanded a fee – a huge one. And I believe they got it.

'How can his teenaged appeal be explained? I think it's simple.

'How free is a teenager?

'They're told not to do this, not to do that all day in school. And it's No, No, No, all the rest of the time at home – a constant process of repression.

'So then they go to an Elvis Presley concert and watch the uninhibited performance of someone who seems just about in their own age group. They get his smouldering, rebellious appearance. And they catch on that this is one time when they *can* let themselves go, let their hair down, squeal and scream and clap. *It's actually allowed.*

'Once they've enjoyed that sort of freedom, no adult can ever tell them to stay away from Elvis. Oh, they've tried it.

'Religious organisations put the ban on him, sent the word out to parents to forbid their daughters and all that. Did it make a scrap of difference? What do you think? You've heard about forbidden fruit …

'And so what happens? He's banned and people write about him. The kids refuse to stay away – and they write some more. If it seems at any time that he's unco-operative, newspapers put in a beef. Does it touch Elvis? Of course not. It's all publicity.

'And, incidentally, although I've heard that Presley has come in for some criticism over here, I notice that you claim to have your own Elvis Presley, Tommy Steele.

'I caught his act on television the other night.

'*Cute.*

'How does it compare with a real Presley performance?

'I'm afraid it doesn't.'

Melody Maker
26 March

Because of the problems caused by teenagers clamouring to see Elvis when he was at home in Audubon Drive and the complaints from neighbours, he returned to Memphis in March and bought a new home in the exclusive suburb of Whitehaven. Built in 1910 as a mansion house with a white-columned portico entrance, it stands in extensive walled gardens, and the new owner decided to call it Graceland for his mother. Elvis paid over $100,000 for the 18-room property and a great deal more to have it customized for himself and his parents. Graceland was Elvis' home for the rest of his life – and has since become the mecca for his world-wide band of fans.

In May, Elvis returned to Hollywood to film his third movie, Jailhouse Rock, *in which he played an accidental killer reclaimed for the world of popular music by the love of a good woman.*

The picture made headlines even before it was released – Elvis' co-star, the vivacious Judy Tyler, being killed in a road crash in strange circumstances; and in Britain there was a battle with the film censor about scenes in which Elvis was flogged. These stories plus one review of the picture and the outcry it brought from the fans appeared in the scrapbooks …

GEM RIDDLE OF ELVIS'S STAR

A private detective was yesterday investigating the riddle of two diamond rings and £5,350 in money belonging to the lovely co-star of the American rock 'n' roll king Elvis Presley.

The actress, Judy Tyler, 24, had just finished filming *Jailhouse Rock*, opposite Elvis in Hollywood, when she was killed in a car crash near Laramie, Wyoming, last week, with her husband, Gregory Laffayette.

The private detective, Mr Charles Littnan, said yesterday that Miss Tyler had only personal papers on her, while only tenpence was found in her husband's pockets.

Miss Tyler, he added, was known to have had two diamond rings on her, and it was also believed that she might have had £5,350 which she was paid for her film work before leaving Hollywood.

THE CENSOR AND THE FLOGGING OF PRESLEY

By Henry Fielding

I understand that the British censors have passed without cuts a vicious scene in the new Elvis Presley film, *Jailhouse Rock*. It shows the rock 'n' roll idol being flogged by a warder and it has stirred excited controversy in America where some states have cut it.

Pelvis-waggling Presley is shown as a prisoner who has killed a man. In the flogging

Publicity still for Loving You *with Lizabeth Scott and Dolores Hart*

Elvis' home in Audubon Drive, and the young rocker photographed outside the house with some fans

Graceland – the new home Elvis bought in 1957 and in which he was able to find seclusion and relaxation

scene you see him 'registering real pain on his face'.

Well, I've registered pain on my face listening to this yelling, side-boarded star. Yet the film has been given an 'A' Certificate for general release.

Frankly, I'm a little worried.

Remember the teenage riots in cinemas all over the country during the showing of the Bill Halley rock 'n' roll films last year? Seats torn out. Police called in. Fights and hysterics.

Presley is bigger than Haley.

Apart from his whipping by a bloody-faced warder, you see Presley getting sloshed on the chin. Presley in a bar room brawl.

And – good heavens! – Presley singing and dancing a mad rock 'n' roll number with a convict chorus!

How much lower can teenage exploitation sink?

Daily Herald
10 December

ELVIS, YOU'RE A BORE!

By Donald Zec

I am suffering from 97 minutes, 8,687 feet of Elvis 'The Pelvis' Presley in a film called *Jailhouse Rock*. A dreadful film. An unsavoury, nauseating, queasy-making film to turn even the best-insulated stomachs.

Why is the film so bad?

I'll break it to you gently. The story is a muddy brew of delinquency, cheap sentiment, bad taste and violence. It is a crude, ugly musical with four beats to every bar – in the State Penitentiary.

And the star performer? Elvis the Pelvis himself – the sombre, sullen, joyless Mr Presley.

Now wait a minute. Do I feel the ominous tremors of a fan-fanned earthquake? Is that a dagger which I see before me with 'I Love Presley' on the tear-encrusted hilt?

With Judy Tyler

1719-135

Well, hold on. The simple point I wish to make is: Elvis Presley should be heard and not seen.

Torment

I like many of his records. I can get in the groove, 'rock' and 'skiffle' with the next man. Tommy Steele, Frankie Vaughan and Frankie Laine are among my closest chums. These stars are all gay, free and breezy.

But not Mr Presley. This droopy, pallid performer sings in torment, mopes in gloom. His tortured incoherence doesn't bother me.

The violence in Jailhouse Rock *was attacked by several film critics, including Donald Zec of the* Daily Mirror *–attracting a predictable outburst from fans!*

(Though I could catch only one word in six.) It's just the side-burned misery of him all that palls – plus those crazy pelvic manoeuvres.

In *Jailhouse Rock* he is sent to gaol for accidentally killing a man in a bar room fight. By mere coincidence he finds his cell-mate has a guitar. And very soon he's singing, 'You're So Young and Beautiful'.

Everything goes quiet in the State Penitentiary. No more angry clamour; no secret sawing through steel bars. Just sighs as 'The Pelvis' sings.

After which in a sudden extraordinary riot, Presley socks a warder and is hauled up for whipping.

Flogging

This flogging scene, with the half-naked Presley dangling from his wrists is clearly designed to shock his fans. They can take it from me, 'The Pelvis' doesn't feel a thing. But he does get £90,000 and 50 per cent of the profits.

Elvis falls in love with The Girl Who Helps Him Become A Star. When she resists his bear-hugging, Elvis leers, 'That's the beast in me, honey!'

Mr Presley should stay off celluloid ... and get back to the groove where he belongs.

FOOTNOTE: On his ATV disc show last Saturday, Jack Jackson offered Presley's picture to the writers of the first 200 postcards to arrive at Television House before yesterday. There were more than 50,000 replies ...

Daily Mirror
16 January 1958

In August 1957 Elvis set out on his first tour of the Pacific Northwest – a jamboree of sell-out concerts which were to be his last tour until the 1970s. Now the unchallenged King of rock 'n' roll, he had a suit to match – a $10,000 gold lamé tuxedo which proved dazzling on stage but hot and cumbersome to wear! The concerts were the most successful ever seen in the US and climaxed in Los Angeles on 28 October where near-hysterical, capacity crowds earned Elvis $56,000.

The triumph of Los Angeles also had a sad side. It marked the end of the partnership of Elvis with Scotty and Bill who had decided to give up the frenetic life on the road for a more sedate existence in Memphis. Though the two musicians recorded again with Elvis, the parting marked the end of an era in which they had become the most famous rock 'n' roll trio in history ... in less than

three years. Once again the Los Angeles concert was attacked by some critics as 'obscene', though Elvis retorted sharply, 'I'm sorry about this, but it won't stop us putting on the best show we can – if they think it's obscene, then that's their problem not mine.' The matter, though, certainly weighed heavily on Elvis's mind as an interview he gave to Photoplay in December revealed.

WHY DO THEY CRITICISE ME?

Says Elvis Presley

Elvis Presley walked over to the large mirror in his hotel room and looked at himself. He ran his hand through his long chestnut brown hair, then slowly tugged one end of the silk string tie he was wearing, sighed and dropped his head. His usually squared shoulders slumped.

The room reflected Elvis's dejection. A sagging bed in one corner was piled high with suitcases, clothing and his guitars.

Gene Smith, Elvis's cousin, sat in the corner mopping his face with a damp handkerchief.

'Tired, El?' asked Gene.

Presley nodded his head. 'But it ain't the work. Never did mind it.' He glanced around the room. His eyes fell on two slightly crumpled newspapers lying beside the armchair in which he had been sitting.

'Stuff like that gets me weary,' Presley said pointing to the headlines.

On page one in large bold type was a story head-lined 'Pastor Flays Elvis. Elvis Presley is morally insane.' The story, quoting the clergyman, said in part, 'The belief of unholy pleasure has sent the morals of the nation down to rock bottom and the crowning addition to this day's corruption is Elvis Presleyism.'

Next to that story, still on the same page was another: A prominent Los Angeles judge, commenting on a serious case of

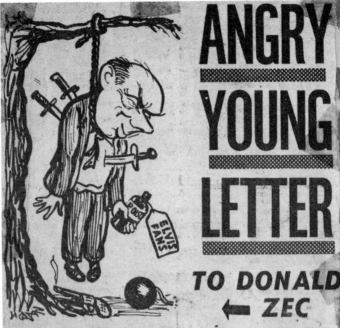

ANGRY YOUNG LETTER

TO DONALD ← ZEC

⭐ Hundreds of "indignant, outraged, disgusted, and murderous" Elvis Presley fans have torn into Donald Zec (by letter, phone and telegram) over his highly critical review of Elvis in the film "Jailhouse Rock."

He wrote: "It is a crude, ugly musical . . . this droopy, pallid performer (Presley) sings in torment, mopes in gloom."

A high-explosive bomb in a youth club couldn't have caused more teenage tumult.

Here, in the form of one big Angry Young Letter, is what the youngsters had to say to . . .

DEAR Square, Fathead, Bighead, Pighead, Stinker, Creep, Donald . . .

People like you ought not to be allowed to live. You are just a drag on the nation. . . .

We hope you're flogged, drawn and quartered for that horrible injustice. You're just a mean, no good, jealous man . . .

You are a vulgar square, and a pompous, self-opinionated humbug with one foot in the grave.

⭐ STINKER

Why don't you either dry up or just drop dead . . . you are a stinker.

Donald Zec ought to be shot at dawn JUST LEAVE ELVIS ALONE OR ELSE . . .

Expect poison pen letters and murder threats to come pouring in by the next post . . .

You have a face like a WET COD FISH. So-long, slob . . .

Because of that article of yours, some of us have been banned from seeing the film. . . .

How long do you intend to live. . ?

You old sour-faced bag of a jellyfish. Please do us a favour. DROP DEAD . . .

You are the biggest, beastliest beast we have ever heard of, you great big hulk of a "square." You are jealous of him because he has something you have not got—sex appeal, a nice wiggle figure, smashing eyes,

'I love Elvis . . .'

smouldering lips, AND ALSO A LOT MORE HAIR . . .

Mr. Z, get lost! Hoping there are no hard feelings . . .

Elvis is much better looking than you, old haybag! You ought to be thrown to the lions . . .

⭐ SHOOK UP

You have a rotten nerve—you narrow - minded, hypercritical old fuddy-duddy . . .

UP WITH ELVIS, DOWN WITH ZEC . . .

DO NOT DO IT AGAIN . . .

We love Elvis — he's all shook up . . .

It's a good job you come from London and not Chester because a whole gang of Presley fans met this morning and all of them are in a hell of a temper.

OF course, not EVERY-BODY disagreed. "Congratulations," "Agree with you one hundred per cent.," "I don't dig Elvis!" wrote some.

⭐ MOSTLY MAD

But mostly the writers were hopping mad. They signed off with . . .

"Take poison, get hung, take a long walk off a short pier, drop dead (seventeen suggested this), get lost, gas yourself, shoot yourself, cut your throat, disappear."

Yours

Faithfully, Sincerely, Truly, Disgustedly, Rebelliously, Murderously, Despisingly, Unsincerely, Most sincerely, Indignantly, Contemptuously, Never, Hopefully,

ELVIS PRESLEY FANS

AND DONALD REPLIES —

DEAR Jean, Carol, Lorraine, Miriam, Thelma, Pat, Yvonne, Pearl, Janet, Christine, Mary, Maxine, Jane, Julia, Anne, Denise, and the others.

Thank you for your letters.

It is so nice to hear from my readers.

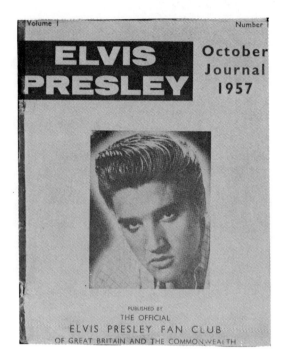

Volume 1   Number 1

ELVIS PRESLEY

October Journal 1957

PUBLISHED BY
THE OFFICIAL
ELVIS PRESLEY FAN CLUB
OF GREAT BRITAIN AND THE COMMONWEALTH

juvenile delinquency, said, 'It is strange that in all these cases involving boys under age, everyone has been wearing an Elvis Presley haircut. I wish,' concluded the judge, 'that Elvis Presley had never been born.'

Gene eyed Elvis critically. He had travelled a lot with his cousin and knew him as few people did. At the moment, he knew that Elvis was depressed.

Suddenly Elvis turned to me and said:

'If I thought for one minute that I contributed to juvenile delinquency I'd go back to driving a truck.

'I wish that those who criticise me could understand what happens to my heart when I see those words in print. Those people know that a 22-year-old fellow from Tupelo, Mississippi, doesn't really contribute to juvenile delinquency.

'For instance, I've cut my hair in a way that I like and feels comfortable with me. A lot of youths my age now have their hair cut in the same way. Some of them get into trouble.

And because their hair is cut like mine, it's Elvis Presley's fault that some confused young guy has done something wrong.

'I wish the people who criticise me, would try to remember how they felt when they were young. Maybe a lot of them didn't think Sinatra was the greatest or that Rudy Vallee was the Vagabond Lover. But at least they could understand why their friends felt that Sinatra was the best or why the girl of yesteryear experienced a funny kind of feeling over a Rudy Vallee record. Why can't they understand that some people like to hear me sing?

'Those who like my records buy them. Those who don't like the way I perform on stage go to see someone else. That's the way it should be.

' 'COURSE SOME OF THE THINGS THEY SAY ABOUT ME ARE TRUE.

'I like cars. All kinds. I have my Cads and my Lincolns and my Messerschmitt and now I have another. A little red racer. Seats one.

'And when they say I like to live it up and have a big time on a date with a girl, why that's true, too. I have as much fun as I can.

'IF THERE ARE PEOPLE WHO FEEL THERE IS SOME SECRET MEANING, SOME EVIL IMPLICATION IN WHAT I DO I CAN ONLY TELL THEM THAT THEY MUST REMEMBER DOING SIMILAR THINGS WHEN THEY WERE YOUNG.'

Photoplay
December

PRESLEYMANIA – 1957

THE RUNAWAYS. Hardly a week passes without at least one 15-year-old girl running away from home and coming to Memphis in an effort to see Elvis Presley. One by one they have been picked up by police, sent to the Juvenile Court, and held until their parents come for them. But they do not get to see Elvis – and in an effort to stem the tide, the singer's mother has addressed a letter to all runaways stating that without their parents' permission to visit Memphis she will ensure that they do *not* see her famous son.

Memphis Press-Scimitar, 15 February

☆　☆　☆

GOLD SUIT. Elvis Presley, shimmering in sequins and a metallic gold cloth suit, writhed and sang last night before a capacity crowd of 11,000 spectators in St Louis' Kiel Auditorium. Promoter Lee Gordon said the gold suit had cost $2,500. 'It's real gold, with impregnated unborn calf skin, or something of the sort,' he said.

St Louis Post-Dispatch, 30 March

☆　☆　☆

MISTAKEN IDENTITY. Gordon Stratton of the Cleveland Ice Hockey Team found out what it is like to be Elvis Presley when the hip-swinging singer played the city. For Stratton looks exactly like Presley, sideburns and all, and during the intermission he was put in one of the star's shirts and left to fight off the crowd. After it was over, Stratton said, 'Gee, I'm glad I'm not a celebrity!'

Cleveland News-Dispatch, 31 March

☆　☆　☆

I HATE ELVIS. A teenaged girl, sporting an 'I Hate Elvis' button was forced to remove it by a group of fans before they would allow her to reach her seat at the singer's concert at the Olympia, Detroit.

Detroit Free Press, 1 April

☆　☆　☆

CANADIAN DEBUT. Hugh Thomson writes: 'I've heard it said that the lurchin' urchin, Elvis the Pelvis, hasn't any kind of singing voice and I was anxious to hear if there was anything in the rumour by attending at the Maple Leaf Gardens. Frankly, after 16 of his rock 'n' roll ballads delivered with a ferocious intensity and manoeuvres known to the burlesque business as 'all-out grinds and bumps' I still have no way of knowing. I just didn't hear one note or one word he sang above the protracted roar of the 15,000 youngsters.'

Toronto Daily Star, 3 April

☆　☆　☆

STAY AWAY FROM ELVIS! Students at Notre Dame Convent have been asked to stay away from the visiting US singer and sign the following declaration: 'I promise that I shall not take part in the reception accorded Elvis Presley and I shall not be present at the programme presented by him at the Auditorium, Wednesday, April 3, 1957. Signed … ' (Eight girls defied this ruling and were later expelled from the convent.)

Ottawa Evening Journal, 8 April

☆　☆　☆

STEALING THE GROUND HE WALKS ON. Report from the Memorial Stadium where Elvis Presley played to 12,000 people last evening, said the only thing organisers had to complain of was a few youngsters who stole soil from the stadium infield where Presley's feet had touched it.

Spokane Review, 31 August

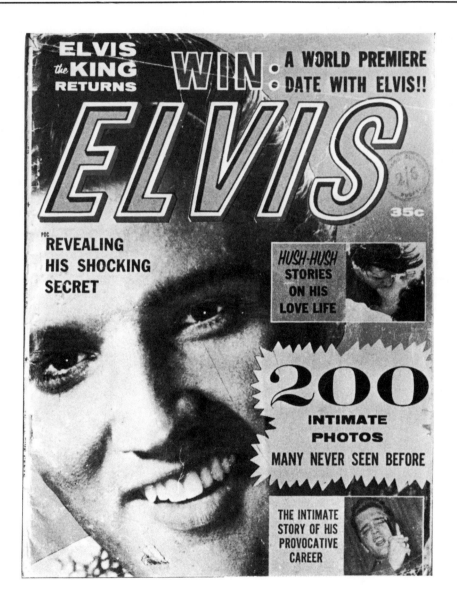

ELVIS PRESLEY ANTHEM. Elvis climaxed the show with what he called, 'The Elvis Presley National Anthem' a frenetic, whirling dervish rendition of 'Hound Dog'. Afterwards he said, 'I lose myself in my singing. Maybe it's my early training singing gospel hymns. I'm limp as a rag, worn out when a show's over. Why, I had a couple of nervous breakdowns a while back when I was making too many of these one night stands.'

Tacoma News-Tribune, 2 September

☆　☆　☆

TRUE OBSCENITY? Dr Ida Halpern, music critic, said Saturday night's concert by Elvis Presley 'had not even the quality of a true obscenity – merely an artificial and unhealthy exploitation of the enthusiasm of youth's body and mind. One could call the whole thing subsidised sex. It was planned artificiality at its best and the gullible and truly worshipful Elvis Presley fans bit,' she added.

Oregon Journal, 3 September

☆　☆　☆

ELVIS TO MARRY? When asked about the many rumours of marriage, Elvis explained, 'Often when I'm supposed to be marrying one girl a certain night, I'm out with another girl on a date. This is confusing to me, and I may be surprised and wake up and hear I'm married sometime!' he laughed.

Portland Journal, 3 September

A DETERRENT TO DELINQUENCY. Elvis Presley and rock 'n' roll music have been hailed as a 'valuable deterrent to juvenile delinquency' by Reverend James H. Elder, the Memphis minister spearheading the campaign for a local youth commission. 'Time will prove that rock 'n' roll music has helped to combat delinquency,' he said, 'rather than contributing to it. It may seem a bit violent to those of us who are already developing rigor mortis, but it can be a valuable outlet of energy for youth caught up in the frantic rush and bewildering problems of our day. Youth will always idolise someone, so I think our city should be proud that so many youngsters of our generation have chosen a young man of clean habits whose witnesses against the danger of drink are proving a powerful inspiration to all American youth.'

Memphis Press-Scimitar, 20 November

1958

ELVIS
the KING
RETURNS

WIN : A WO
DATE

ELVIS

EVEALING
S SHOCKI
CRET

appearan

of Elvis

ELVIS PRESL

TAR OF STAGE, SCREEN, RADIO, RECORDS AND T

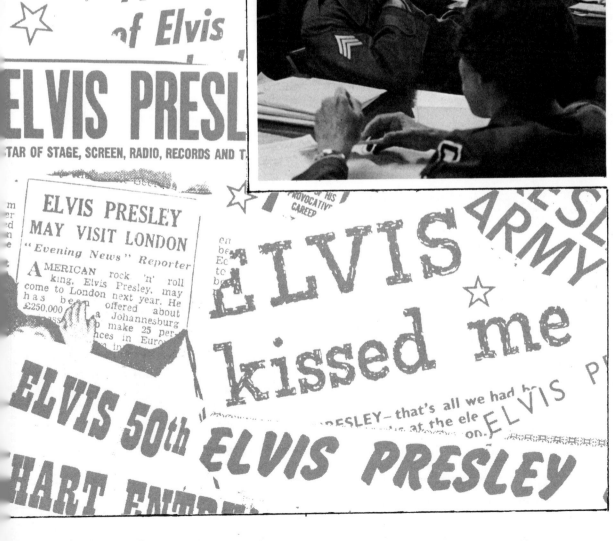

ELVIS PRESLEY MAY VISIT LONDON

"Evening News" Reporter

AMERICAN rock 'n' roll king, Elvis Presley, may come to London next year. He has been offered about £250,000 a Johannesburg to make 25 per nces in Euro

ELVIS ARMY

ELVIS

kissed me

PRESLEY—that's all we had h at the ele on ELVIS

ELVIS 50th ELVIS PRESLEY

HART ENT

Although Elvis was due to begin his Army service in January, he was in fact allowed a sixty-day deferment in order to complete his fourth movie, King Creole, *in Hollywood and New Orleans. This picture represented a determined effort on Hal Wallis' part to give Elvis a more substantial role in a story based on Harold Robbins' tough and violent novel,* A Stone For Danny Fisher. *Pre-publicity for the picture described the star as 'exchanging ballads for a beating', and English pop music writer Ker Robertson wondered in his* Daily Sketch *column if Elvis was about to become 'the new James Dean or the singing Marlon Brando?' Philip Oakes the film critic of the* Sunday Dispatch *was just one of the several writers impressed by Elvis' performance and also drew comparisons with both Dean and Brando …*

THE WILD ONES ARE BACK!

By Philip Oakes

The city streets are slick with rain. Flick knives glint in the shadows. With two shootings, a back-alley stabbing, and sundry beatings-up, *King Creole* (Odeon, Marble Arch), brings the Wild Ones back to town.

But are they still welcome? Brando has traded his leather jacket for a lounge suit. James Dean – the original Rebel without a Cause – is dead and gone. The snarling film cycle which dug deep at the roots of teenage trouble has come to a full stop.

Real job

And *King Creole* marks the end and rockbottom of the line.

Briskly directed by Michael Curtiz and excellently acted by Elvis Presley, Vic Morrow, and Carolyn Jones, it is the classic case of the bad film well made.

Its ethics dip low into the gutter. Violence is met with more violence. The villain is a sadist. The hero is a slob. Justice is never mentioned. And through all the shabby heroics, played out against the moss-hung background of New Orleans, there is not one glimmer of a police badge. *King Creole* makes up its own laws as it goes along.

Apart from a passing interest in the moral sludge raked over by *King Creole* the film's fascination lies in Presley's performance.

This is a real acting job by an already potent performer. None of the songs is memorable; hardly any of them are necessary. Presley shows enough talent here to stand alone.

8 August

Elvis' entry into Army life on the morning of Monday 24 March made headline news around the world with dozens of photographers and hundreds of tearful fans gathering around the Memphis Draft Board headquarters where the star sacrificed his famous sideburns and million dollar life-style. For his initial training, Elvis was stationed at Fort Chafee in Arkansas, but shortly afterwards he was sent to Fort Hood, Texas and assigned to A company of the famous 'Hell on Wheels' Second Medium Tank Battalion. An initial news black-out on the new recruit's activities caused many columnists to fall back on arguments about Elvis' music and the chance of him still being a star when his two-year Army stint was over. Jack Good, later to be famous as a TV producer, wrote the following piece in the British magazine, Disc, *of 5 April.*

Elvis – the new James Dean? A still from King Creole

THE ARMY MAY MAKE A MAN OUT OF ELVIS!

By Jack Good

Well paralyse my pelvis! This is it. All my life I've wanted to be the centre of a high-powered intellectual controversy. But I never imagined that the fuse to this explosion of whip-lash argument would be in my first 'DISC' column.

All I did was to make one remark – just one – about Private Presley. Here it is: 'Elvis Presley is a giant because he has taken the sex in rock 'n' roll as far as it can go. They don't come more sexy than Elvis!'.

That's all. But the Presley fans stiffen with rage and say, like duelling musketeers, 'It is enough. We demand satisfaction.' Or, more precisely (I quote):

'We have read your article in which you made some stinking comments about the sex that Elvis has brought into rock 'n' roll. Just because he puts everything he's got into his songs (unlike Sinatra) you start voicing your stupid opinions. I suppose you are a Tchaikovsky fan, you daft old square. He's much better looking than any of you jealous mob so pack it up or you'll find yourself very unpopular. – Two Elvis Presley Fans.'

All right. I give in. These two fans are right. Let me confess it all. Sitting in the one-and-nines at *Jailhouse Rock* I was eaten away with acid jealousy. I couldn't bear hearing all those screams for handsome Presley, whilst, ugly and deformed, I was ignored by the girls.

Now I see the error of my ways. I apologise deeply to the two Presley Fans and will put it all to rights.

I not only withdraw my statement about Elvis, but, if you please, I will say the opposite, viz: 'Elvis Presley is a dwarf because his rock 'n' roll lacks virility. There can be no one more sexless than Elvis.' – Satisfied?

Now that Presley has gone into the Army it is possible that the most exciting phase of his career has come to a halt. At any rate there can be no more of the 'meteoric rise to the top' angle, since if he shoots any higher he'll disappear into outer space.

So perhaps this is a good time to take note of the criticisms that have been continually levelled at Elvis, during the hey-day of his stardom.

Criticism: 'He is a bad singer.'
Critic: Sinatra fan.
Answer: If you had asked Caruso what he thought of a Sinatra disc (assuming this had been possible) you would probably have got the same comment. In other words, it depends on what you are used to. Presley doesn't try to sing like Como any more than Como tries to sing like Gigli. Their styles of singing attempt to achieve different effects. The question is not 'is it good?'? (which is something that everyone has his own opinion about) but, 'Does it succeed?' As far as Presley is concerned it certainly succeeds – record sales prove this.

Criticism: 'I can't hear the words.'
Critic: Old-school disc jockey.
Answer: When you hear Italian opera you probably get the same impression. You don't complain. You say it doesn't matter, even though words in opera must be of some importance since they tell the story. Again, how many words do you understand in Scots songs if you are a Cockney, or Cockney songs if you are a Scot? Presley's dialect is just as legitimate as either of these. Sometimes, admittedly, he slurs words for deliberate effect. We must then assume that the effect is more important than the words. If the words are of 'My Special Angel' quality, there can't be much argument here. But on the whole, if you don't just 'hear', but listen to Presley's discs, the words aren't too hard to follow.

Two fan photographs of Elvis joining the Army

THERE WAS A SOLDIER

— a yankee soldier..

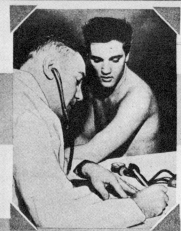

Does that tube really go in that guy's right ear and out the left? Anything can happen in the Army.

What's there to be happy about, man? Dirty jobs and denims. Nothing much to sing about. But there's a good time just around the corner . . . .

Now here's a thing! A real live steel helmet. And all mine. A guy told us they're knitted with steel wool. The Army's full of jokers . . . .

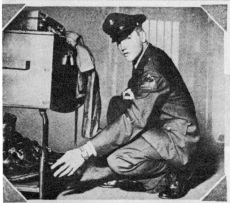

Boots, boots, marching up and down again. This makes a guy long for his blue suede shoes again. Still, they do come in handy for kicking the odd tin can.

That smile means one thing—food. A G.I.'s lot is a hungry one. Say, what's keeping that steak, anyway?

All good things must come to an end. What with reporters and mikes everywhere, a guy can't even snatch a sigh of relief. Still, it's all in the game . . . .

SAD-EYED SEND-OFF is given Presley by (from left) local fan Janet Hall. Starlets Judy Spreckels and Anita Wood, cousin Patsy Presley and aunt Mrs. Vester Presley, and (right) his mother and father.

GI BOOTS, size 12, begin Elvis' metamorphosis. He still wears his own jacket and black pegged pants.

Star is shorn, a new GI born

TOTALLY TRANSFORMED, SINGER PRESLEY SWINGS TO A SMART HEP-2-3-4 UNDER 75 POUNDS OF DUFFEL

Stripped to his shorts in an Army hospital in Memphis, Tennessee, Private Elvis Presley was measured and weighed and—at 185 pounds, 6′1½″—was not found wanting by the Army. The 23-year-old rock 'n' roll king was drafted over moans by his manager who said that his time would cost the U.S. $500,000 a year in lost income taxes. Unmoved, the Army made quick use of Presley's expensive services, putting him in charge of 21 other recruits for the bus trip to Arkansas' Fort Chaffee reception center.

In the next three days the new Private Presley was inoculated, outfitted, barbered and advanced $7 on his month's pay of $78 (he also gets $4,000 a month in record royalties). Then Fort Chaffee's commandant, Brigadier General Ralph Mace, who had announced that Elvis stood the strain of induction "marvelously," sent him on to Fort Hood, Texas for combat training. "It's up to the Army to do what they want with me," said Elvis. "Heaven knows I want to live up to what people expect of me."

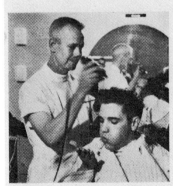

FAREWELL TO HAIR is blown by Presley as Army barber James Peterson brush-cuts his famous mane.

Criticism: 'He wiggles about.'
Critic: Earnest teenager looking up from a chapter on 'The Subjunctive.'
Answer: Yes? And?
'Well, isn't this suggestive?'

No. Presley's violent movements may be coarse and vulgar. They are certainly not suggestive in the way that the jokes of many of the comics we hear on the radio are suggestive.

It is not true that Presley moves violently all the time – in the way that many of his half-baked imitators do. He seems to be in complete control of his performances – in the tradition of the finest artistes.

For his number 'Teddy Bear' in the film *Loving You*, he was static except for a very slight movement of the shoulders. The result was volcanic. Many singers don't move because they can't. Many more move continuously, because they wouldn't know what to do with themselves if they stopped. Presley not only knows how to move but also how to save up the movement so that when he uses it, it is really effective.

Criticism: 'His appeal is merely visual.'
Critic: The same earnest teenager.
Answer: Try to sell a million records of a sunset.

These are some of the negative comments on Presley. What can be said positively? First, Presley has succeeded dynamically in a way that only dynamic people can succeed. He has for three years almost towered over the pop-music scene like a Colossus and the outpouring of powerful critics have had as much effect as pea-shooters against a tank.

Ultimately, a man is only great if people think he is great. On these grounds Presley is great. But more than this, he bears other marks that identify outstanding men.

He took hold of many different, sometimes even conflicting influences and made something completely new from them. What he made was more than a personal style, it was a new mode of expression that had reference, not just to himself, but to millions of young people whom he grew to represent.

Since then he has been repeatedly imitated, but never successfully.

He is, therefore, something more than the sum of his parts – the voice, the looks and the wiggle. He is in fact an artiste, and like an artiste he continues to develop.

When Private Presley gets his demob he may not be the rage he is today but I am sure that he will steadily reinforce the reputation he has so hastily won.

HOW IS ELVIS MAKING OUT?

By Tom Ellis
Fort Hood, Killeen, Texas

It has taken me only three days to find out that Elvis Presley has warmed to the Army and, what is more important, the Army has warmed to him.

Elvis is happy. Really happy. This he told me without a hint of sarcasm.

'I've had it easier,' he said, 'but I'm meeting characters I never knew existed. I even found a couple of ex-University students who'd never heard of me. And, man, did I enjoy talking to them. Since I got here I can't remember one unpleasant incident, and that's more than I'd ever hoped for. Man, was I scared on that first day!'

Elvis's arrival at Fort Hood promised to be the Army sensation of the year. If war had broken out on the day he got to Fort Hood I doubt if the topic of conversation would have been switched from him.

Before he'd even kissed his parents goodbye the camp was electric with excitement.

Big newspapers boasted headlines like: 'Elvis Opens at Fort Hood For Eight Straight Weeks' – eight weeks being the time of basic training. The local newspaper, the *Killeen Daily Herald*, flashed: 'Elvis Will Train Here' across its front page.

His squad leader, Sergeant First Class William Fraley, told me: 'Many rumours reached the camp before he did … He was going to arrive by a special plane. He was coming in a white Cadillac driven by a chauffeur. Major-General W. Paul Johnson, our division commander, would be on hand to give him a personal greeting. A band would be playing. Girls would be posted along the road to throw flowers in his path … It was fantastic the stories that were going around.'

These rumours upset Presley fans. They were afraid that his enormous popularity would now backfire and cause resentment among Presley's fellow trainees. Indeed, many of the boys were, already, prepared not to like him.

'They must have been crazy to think I'd arrive in a special plane,' Elvis told me. 'If I had I'd have been asking for trouble.'

In fact, he arrived in the bus chartered for all 'new boys.' He stepped off the bus, his hair closely cropped – making him look ten years young – and his clothes creased after the long ride.

Waiting to greet him were a crowd of local reporters and photographers, women employees and a score of teenagers, most of them Army personnel.

'I was tired, dusty and nervous,' said Elvis, 'but that little welcome was just what I needed. I didn't expect anyone to be there at all.'

Sergeant Fraley told me that the rumours about Elvis's arrival being wrong helped him a lot.

'He made friends fast and there was no show-off about him,' he said. 'He soon showed real signs of leadership. That's why he was promoted to acting assistant squad leader so quickly.'

'So far everyone feels he has come through with flying colours. He's a big-hearted kid. He's ready to stand a treat if a buddy has run short before pay day. But the fellows don't take advantage of him. They know he's limiting himself as close to Army pay as he can. He doesn't try to buy his way or throw money around and play big shot.'

I heard an interesting story which backs up what Sergeant Fraley told me.

Lieutenant Melvin Meister said that in his indoctrination speech he pointed out that personal cars weren't allowed during the first eight weeks of basic training.

Said Lieutenant Meister: 'Then I asked the men to raise their hands if they were planning to send for their cars after this period. Elvis was not one of the boys who raised his hand. This was appreciated by a lot of the fellows who could not afford cars. I understand one of them said to him later, "Don't do without a car on account of us. Heck, you can always give us a ride!" '

Just as rumours preceded Elvis to camp so they dogged his steps while he was training.

The officer in charge of Elvis's Company, Company A, 2nd Medium Tank Bn., Captain Henry King, told me the one about Elvis not being able to sleep the first night because he was afraid of missing reveille.

'They tell the same story about every celebrity,' said Captain King. 'The fact is, trainees aren't wakened by bugle call any more. We have a soldier on duty in each barrack every night who wakes the boys at five a.m. From what I hear, Presley sleeps soundly but gets up as fast as the next one, grumbles just as much – but not more – and hustles out for roll call and the mess hall like everyone else.'

Captain King also confided that Elvis sneaks a few bars of chocolate in his pocket to tide him over the four hour study period or while out in the field.

'They're not allowed a snack break during those times and its an old Army custom to grab a quick bite while the instructor is conveniently looking the other way,' explained Captain King.

I asked Elvis how he felt he had progressed in the Army.

'I can't tell,' he said. 'I think I'm as popular as the next fellow and I'm trying very hard to live up the standards of the outfit.'

When I told Captain King this he said: 'He certainly is living up to the standards of the outfit. I think he'll benefit greatly by his Army experience. He's mingling with a wide variety of young men from varying backgrounds, and this is bound to prove useful to him later in life.'

I spoke to Master Sergeant Henry Coley about the amazing way in which Elvis has adapted himself to Army life.

He said he thought his career as an entertainer had a lot to do with it.

'A performer, if he's any good, has to learn discipline,' he explained. 'Putting on a show means you've got to follow certain basic rules and see them through. The Army's no stage show – but, in respect to discipline, it's the same. Everyone must do his part no more and no less, and pull together for the sake of the whole outfit. I think Elvis had good training in showbusiness for what's happening now.'

Lieutenant Malcolm MacLeod agreed with this, but put it the other way. He said: 'I have fifty young men under me here, and I've learnt that it's human nature to procrastinate. Given a chance, most people will put off an unpleasant duty. That's one of the toughest things to adjust to in the Army. An order given today must be carried out today. I imagine an actor or an entertainer gets plenty of training in that sort of thing. You have a list of scenes to be shot in a stated time, and a postponement of even one scene can cost many thousands of pounds extra. That's why Elvis is one-up on

men who have never had to deal with deadlines and on-the-dot action before.'

A day in the life of Elvis at Fort Hood is, I found, simply a duplicate of a day in the life of any G.I.

Said Elvis: 'I spend most of my time within the reservation of Fort Hood. There's almost every type of sport, and an assortment of hobby, craft, automotive-instruction and other shops in the self-improvement category. I'm never stuck for something to do.'

For relaxation Elvis and his friends usually wander to the nearest cinema or snack-bar.

'Films have always been my favourite pastime,' he said. 'We go quite often.'

At the cinema, Girl Guides often sell sweets and ice-cream to meet the expense of maintaining their clubroom on the base. It became quite a romp with them, each one pushing the other to get Elvis as a customer.

Elvis likes this and he won their hearts one night by buying sweets and ice-cream from every girl in the place.

As always his favourite form of relaxation is to 'phone his folks.

'Talking to them two or three times a week is like food and drink, a necessity,' he says.

Before relaxing, however, Elvis had to face the strenuous daily grind of learning to be a member of the American armed forces.

Elvis told me: 'Those first eight weeks were murder. It was work all the time without any leave. I ended up exhausted.'

Of this eight weeks of basic training much of the time was devoted to the study of individual weapons. Some twenty hours of his first week was given to military history, courtesy and justice. He also learned how to care for equipment.

During his second week he received his first practice on the firing range.

'Elvis was as jumpy as the rest,' said Sergeant Coley when I asked him about it. 'They have to make a certain score or they can't pass. Naturally they're a little strained. Elvis qualified all right, and when I told him he'd passed he took a deep breath and said, "I don't mind telling you I was scared." He's handy with a gun now.'

The seventh week of training is known as 'Bivouac Week.' It includes fifty-two hours of close combat work and personalised day and night field problems. He received instruction in code of conduct, first aid, map reading, guard duty, intelligence methods, infiltration, squad patrolling and firing.

'I didn't know there was so much to learn,' he said.

In spite of the Army's carefully planned diet Elvis lost eight pounds the first three weeks he was training.

'But I soon got it back in solid muscle,' he said, 'Let's face it, I've been using muscles I didn't know I had.'

Naturally, like all soldiers, not everything went well for Elvis. Not all the chores were easy, but he remained silent about the 'tough ones.' He blocked all questions I asked him about them with a laugh.

When I asked him what the worst part of Army life was he said: 'I can tell you that: Doing without girls! Like the other fellows, I say there's nothing like a nice girl to cheer you up.'

At the moment Elvis's career with the Army is not certain. Most of the trainees are being developed as replacements for the Third Army's division in Germany.

It has been rumoured that the Government, losing about half a million dollars in taxes for each year of Elvis's military service, will seek to make up for it by using his talents as a morale-builder for troops in America and other countries.

I asked Elvis how he felt about going into special service and what he planned regarding his career.

'My future?' he said. 'That's not for me to decide. My manager, Col. Tom Parker, has arranged for me to cut some more records if and when I get leave. As for special services, I reckon the Government will figure that out. I'm no better than any other soldier. I'm here to do what I'm told and to go where I'm told. If they want me to entertain I'll do it. I'm in their hands.'

Before I left Elvis I asked him if he had any regrets at all.

He said: 'Nobody wants to bust-up their everyday life and become a soldier. Nevertheless, I'm proud to be in the Army, and all I'm asking is to be given the same deal as any other American soldier. That's good enough for me.'

I only add that when I left Fort Hood at 10 o'clock at night, Elvis was singing to a bunch of his pals in one of the barrack rooms. And he wasn't singing rock 'n' roll. He was singing hymns.

Tom Ellis, *Photoplay*
October

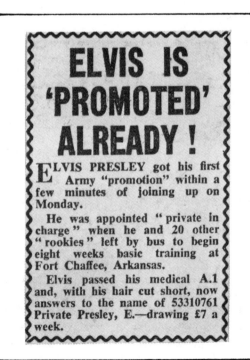

ELVIS IS 'PROMOTED' ALREADY !

ELVIS PRESLEY got his first Army "promotion" within a few minutes of joining up on Monday.

He was appointed " private in charge " when he and 20 other " rookies " left by bus to begin eight weeks basic training at Fort Chaffee, Arkansas.

Elvis passed his medical A.1 and, with his hair cut short, now answers to the name of 53310761 Private Presley, E.—drawing £7 a week.

Tragedy struck Elvis' life on 14 August when his much-loved mother, Gladys, died after a heart attack, aged just forty-six. Among many tributes penned to Mrs Presley, Keith Goodwin's perceptive article about her relationship with Elvis was given a prominent place in the scrapbooks. It is reprinted here from the New Musical Express *of 22 August. Two days after this, it was announced that Elvis was to be posted to Germany and planned to take his father with him. 'One of the last things Mom said was that Dad and I should always be together,' Elvis explained. 'Wherever they send me, Dad will go, too.' Would this at last bring the star to Britain, fans and headline writers began to wonder?*

WHAT MOM MEANT TO ELVIS

By Keith Goodwin

The influences in an entertainer's career are usually many and varied, but in most success stories, you'll find the constant advice, guidance and encouragement offered by a star's parents!

These are the people who help to shape the young life; who teach the potential artist to make the most of his talents; and who lend a helping hand when decisions have to be made.

They are the people, too, who share the heartbreaks, setbacks, and occasional joys that a new performer faces during his early career. In such times, their burden is a heavy one, for on their shoulders can rest much of the success or failure of a latent talent.

Few artists attempt to hide the depth of gratitude which they feel for their parents, and it's perhaps significant that the bond between artist and parents usually grows stronger as a performer conquers new pinnacles of achievement.

Devotion

Elvis Presley has never disguised his devotion for his parents. He has never been reticent about voicing his sincere appreciation for all they have done to make his way to stardom easier.

It's therefore relatively simple to understand and share the sorrow Elvis is bearing since the untimely death last week of the person closest to him – his mother, Mrs Gladys Presley.

A sensitive, highly strung youngster, Elvis had always looked to his mother for guidance. 'Mom is,' he once said, 'my best girl friend.'

It was Elvis's father, Vernon, who first bought him a guitar, but it was Glady Presley who encouraged her teenage son to persevere with the instrument.

Elvis's mother, too, was indirectly responsible for his first faltering steps in show business. He hadn't been singing or playing guitar very long, but the advent of Mother's Day prompted ambitious Elvis to surprise his Mom by privately recording her favourite song, 'My Happiness.'

He chose to make the record at the Sun Recording studios in Nashville. It was at the same studios that he waxed his first commercial records a few weeks later!

Elvis's ties with his family were extremely close. After a visit to their Memphis home, screen star Natalie Wood – then keeping company with Elvis – commented that she had never seen such a close-knit family. She also observed: 'His (Elvis's) mother fusses over him all the time.'

What was the reason behind this firm bond? The simple fact is that Elvis was one of twins, but his baby brother was born dead.

It's therefore natural to suppose that in an attempt to obliterate her shocking disappointment, Mrs. Presley lavished more love and affection on her only son than she

A poignant photograph of Elvis and his mother, published at the time of her death in August 1958

might have done had it not been for this tragic happening.

During his early childhood, Elvis grew to be largely dependent on his parents.

Vernon Presley has recounted the story of how Elvis excessively worried over the possibility of his father being hurt when he (Vernon) tried a high dive while the family were on a swimming expedition.

But Elvis wasn't a spoiled child and he encountered his fair share of childhood scrapes without escaping the consequences. And it might seem a trifle strange that Vernon Presley never spanked his young son – it was always Gladys who took care of the punishment!

Columnist Sidney Fields, of the *New York Mirror*, met Presley's parents and described them thus: 'Simple, neighbourly and unaffected by the fame and fortune of their son, or the furore he has created.'

Fields also observed:

'But they worry about the frenzy of their only child in his new life, his health, his driving, the mobs that besiege him, his future and the violent criticism hurled at him.'

Elvis quickly realised all this and did everything in his power to quieten his parents' fears. While filming in Hollywood or on tour, he dutifully telephoned his mother every day to set her mind at ease, but his greatest joys were his periodic visits home.

At home

It's been said many times that Elvis enjoys working. He does. But it's not the same sort of pleasure that he got from the simple family meetings held in the spacious surroundings of the luxurious 40,000-dollar home Elvis bought for his parents in Memphis.

He liked nothing better than to sit quietly at home, playing the organ and singing spirituals with his folks, both of whom, he contends, were fine singers. Sometimes he would escort his current 'date' home to meet his parents, and would eulogise about the eggs, bacon, potatoes and toast cooked by his mother that he earnestly claimed was his favourite food.

A non-smoker and non-drinker, Elvis is deeply religious and he accompanied his family to church whenever possible. Gladys Presley once said that, unlike some children, Elvis never needed any prodding to go to church.

When critics launched an all-out attack on Presley, asserting that his gyrations were 'sinful,' Gladys and Vernon Presley were quick to defend their son. Elvis maintained that his wiggling was 'natural,' resulting from a 'rhythmic impulse' born into him, and his parents rapidly silenced the critics as they stood by his side.

Though Elvis has fans scattered all over the world, his most important aim in life was to please his parents. 'More than anything else, I want the folks back home to think right of me,' he once told a reporter. Whatever anybody thinks, Gladys Presley knew that Elvis had achieved his goal.

The Presleys never pandered to their son – in fact, his childhood was governed by strict, unbreakable rules. Gladys taught him to play peaceably with other children; while Vernon was adamant that he would have to defend himself if he was picked upon.

His good upbringing is reflected in the 'Yes, sir,' 'Yes, ma'am,' 'Thank yous,' and other marks of respect and normal etiquette that punctuate his conversation.

Gladys Presley was always afraid that her son would get hurt – a fear that remained with her until the day she died.

During his youth, she wouldn't let him have a bicycle lest he should fall off, and later urged him to stop playing football in high school. When Elvis became a star, she feared the fans who mobbed him and the fast cars that he drove. Yet deep down, she knew that Elvis could always take adequate care of himself.

Typical of Presley's sincere concern for his parents was his persistent refusal to let his mother travel more than 100 miles to see one of his performances. He realised his mother's inability to travel long distances, and flatly refused to allow her to inconvenience herself.

Big debt

Whichever way you care to look at it, Elvis owes a lot to his parents, and he knows it.

It's to his credit that even at the peak of his sensational career, he was always the first to point to Gladys and Vernon Presley and say, 'Without them it could never have happened.'

There's no telling what effect Gladys Presley's sorrowful death will have on Elvis's future career. He has always been a shy and somewhat lonely person, and this won't help the situation any.

But today he is not alone, for in his grief there is some little comfort in the knowledge that his mourning is shared by millions all over the world.

HIS GRIEF IS SHARED …

Ann Hillier writes from Sheffield, Yorks:

As a long-time fan of Elvis Presley I read with great sorrow Keith Goodwin's article on the death of El's mother.

I couldn't be more deeply moved if it were someone very close to me. I know I speak for all his fans, his real fans, to whom he has brought so much pleasure and happiness these last few years. Perhaps the knowledge that his grief is shared all over the world will help just a little. I do hope so!

The question on everyone's lips will be, 'How will it affect his career?' I don't know,

and I don't very much care at the moment. To me he is no longer an idol on a pedestal, but a very human boy who has been hurt very deeply.

All I can say to El and his father is that we, who will be eternally grateful to Gladys Presley for bringing us El, will be sharing their burden.

(We have received many similar messages of sympathy from readers.)

New Musical Express
29 August

PRESLEY POSTED TO EUROPE!

Strong hopes of British concerts

The world's most dynamic and controversial vocal personality – Elvis Presley – has been posted to Europe! He joins an American tank corps in Germany on September 12, as part of his National Service with the U.S. Forces.

The comparatively short distance from Britain give strong hopes to the definite likelihood of him making his first appearances in Britain – during his leave while in Germany.

It is significant, too, that Lee Gordon, who has arranged many of Presley's U.S. concerts, is arriving in London this week-end – with the strong possibility that he will be joined here by Colonel Tom Parker, Elvis's personal manager. British fans will eagerly await developments – particularly as dates here would be quite logical for Presley, during leave from Germany.

He has completed his basic training course at the Fort Hood Army base in America; in a few weeks' time, Presley takes advantage of his first leave to record new titles for RCA. The session is scheduled to take place in Nashville, Tennessee.

After sailing across the Atlantic to Germany – via the English Channel – Elvis landed in Bremerhaven on 1 October. Following a rapturous greeting from five hundred German fans, he travelled by train to the US Army base at Friedburg, near Frankfurt, where he was stationed for the next seventeen months. He actually lived close to the camp in the small town of Bad Nauheim and among the first journalists to talk to him about this new phase of his life was Ray Nunn of Woman's Mirror *who wrote the following revealing report on 21 October. From October until the following spring, the Army denied the press access to Elvis in order for him to continue his military service.*

I DON'T BREAK WINDOWS SAYS ELVIS

Bad Nauheim, Germany

There is no one earth quite like Elvis the Pelvis – take it from me.

That's why I HAD to fly to Germany, to meet him for a frank, exclusive interview.

I found 53310161 Private Presley, E., in this small German health resort about 20 miles outside Frankfurt.

It is a place where aged invalids take thermal baths to ease their aching joints. Almost every other building is a health clinic.

Stylish

Elvis, 23, and I shook hands in his 'billet' – a sumptuous, four-star hotel, once patronized by the Czar of Russia. He's living there in millionaire style.

And why not? Because the lad IS a millionaire.

The most unusual soldier ever to wear a tailor-made Army uniform was resting when I arrived. He told me in a soft, dreamy Southern drawl: 'Ah'm on duty at 6 a.m. tomorrow, sir. Before Ah was drafted that used to be mah bedtime'.

Private Elvis reports for military training each day at a nearby camp – by taxi.

After we shook hands he told me: 'Ah'm glad to see you. Ah don't usually give exclusive interviews, but there's lots of things Ah want to clear up about mahself for mah fans in England. Ah want you to tell the British what Ah'm really like.'

Sharing Private Elvis' plush 'billet' were two members of his Hollywood staff and his father, whom he calls 'Mah Daddy.'

Guess who else was there?

His grandmother – but she was not feeling well enough to see me. Elvis explained to me: 'Mah Daddy is here because mah Mummy died recently. He's lonely and Ah wanted to cheer him up. And mah grandmammy too.' The night before we met, Private Presley, of the 32nd Armoured ('Hell on Wheels') Division had been driving dodgem cars at a nearby fairground.

'We had a lot of fun until Ah got hemmed in by the frauleins,' he explained. He was rescued by a passing Army truck in the nick of time.

Sapphires

He looked smart in his olive-green uniform. On his little finger of his left hand he wore a ring studded with black sapphires, a gift from Hollywood performer, Judy Spreckels.

'We've been friends a long time,' Elvis told me.

'Now Ah should like to make one thing quite clear, sir,' he said.

'Ah know Ah have a lot of imitators in your country, as Ah have a lot in the States.

Serious

'But Ah want to say that Ah don't break shop windows. Ah don't smoke or drink, and Ah always behave mahself in public.

'Ah'm not married because Ah take marriage seriously. Ah don't intend to get married and get out of it a couple of months later.

'If Ah thought,' he went on, 'that anything Ah might do would cause juvenile delinquency, Ah would return to truck driving.'

The moment Elvis sat down he began to vibrate his right foot. Next he started to shake a black, silver-knobbed cane, clutched between his fingers.

'It's an officer's swagger-stick,' he explained with a grin. 'Ah don't know if Ah'm allowed to carry one, but no one has told me not to – yet.'

Here's the first message I got from Private 'Hell on Wheels' Presley: 'Mah Daddy and me hope to visit England in January. Ah'd like to go there by train because Ah'm not keen on flying.'

The rest of the interview went something like this:

Do you intend to shimmy, gurgle or swivel while you're over here?

No sir, Ah'm here to serve mah country. And Ah don't like to appear without mah own band, which is in Hollywood.

Is there a guitar in your kitbag?

A small one, sir, Ah play it when Ah want to let off steam – in mah hotel room.

Why are you wearing two medals?

One is for tankmanship, sir. The other is for marksmanship with a pistol.

At least

What do you want with a pistol? You're not a cowboy.

It's impossible to use a rifle inside a tank, sir.

What about rock 'n' roll? (I asked). Will you continue singing it after you leave the Army in 16 months?

Yes, sir. *(Elvis didn't hesitate.)* Ah must not forget that this is what made me famous. Ah will always sing at least one song in every picture.

Do you clean your own shoes now?

Yes, sir. Ah spit on them and then shine 'em.

Do you like the Army?

It has its points. If Ah did not have mah own profession Ah would seriously think of signing on as a regular. It's better than truck driving.

How old were you when you left school?

Eighteen, sir. And Ah'm not stupid.

Kisses

Not long ago a girl complained that you bit her hand. Do you do it all the time?

No, sir. Ah just kissed her hand. Maybe that's the way Ah kiss. Maybe Ah can't help biting.

You like to sign your name on girls' bare arms, legs and ankles. What sort of pen do you use?

A ballpoint, sir – it doesn't scratch.

You used to look mean and moody, Elvis. Lately I've seen you smile. Are you happy now?

Ah take each day as it comes. Of course, Ah worry sometimes. No one knows the pressure a star has to face.

Haircut

When are you going to have another haircut?

Very soon, sir. It's beginning to grow again.

Don't you think your fans might forget you by the time you leave the Army?

Ah hope not. Ah have signed to start four big pictures in a row the moment Ah leave the Army. Ah'd like to play a mixed-up, tough character like the hero of a film called 'Somebody Up There Likes Me.'

ELVIS PRESLEY may only be a private in the U.S. Army, but he had full command of the big Press reception given him before he sailed from New York to Europe.

This is the most evident feature of an unusual and exciting all-talking Presley EP, the sleeve of which is reproduced alongside.

The disc begins and ends with a blast from the ship's fog horn. In between we have Elvis gay, Elvis grave, most polite (punctuated with 'sirs' and 'ma'ams') answering, in clear, attractive Southern drawl, questions about...

* * *

FANS: "They have been very loyal and sent me presents of such things as cookies and other things you appreciate in Army life."

* * *

FUTURE: "Pick up where I left off, sir . . . be a good actor . . . I get out of the Army March 24, 1960, sir . . ."

* * *

ARMY LIFE: "Treated well . . . great time . . . (referring to odd characters in Army. **In civilian life I got harassed at times, too.**"

* * *

IDEAL GIRL: "Female, sir" (big laugh, one of many, plus applause).

* * *

GET MARRIED IN SERVICES: "Don't think so, sir . . . I don't want to be rushed."

* * *

COULD FUTURE WIFE BE IN SHOW BUSINESS?: "No difference to me if a girl is in show business or driving a truck."

* * *

WHEN WAS THE LAST TIME YOU WERE IN LOVE?: (This was one of the few questions Elvis hedged by replying): "Many times, ma'am."

* * *

CLOSEST TO MARRIAGE: "Before I started singing. My first big record saved my neck."

* * *

ABOUT MOTHER (Here Elvis's voice changes from gay lightness to deeper tone and slower pace): "I'm an only child . . . I lost a companion and friend who'd help me . . . even in the middle of the night she'd come

to hear my problems . . . I'd angry with mom someti (over restrictions), but she right (to restrict him)."

* * *

WILL ROCK 'N' ROLL APPE DIMINISH?: "Don't know hope not."

* * *

BEING IN THE ARMY, YOU HAPPY NOT TO ASKED FOR AUTOGRA SO MUCH?: "No, ma When no one asks me for autograph, then I start worry ma'am."

* * *

TAKING WIGGLE OUT R'N'R: "If you feel it gotta move around. I hav anyway."

* * *

HAVE YOU BEEN LUCK "Very lucky. I came along w there was no trend in music people were looking for one

TALKS *(on his latest extended-play)* AS ~~SINCE~~RELY AS HE SINGS

se questions and many more
...ired at him at the general press
...ence. Then a single interviewer
... him other questions in the
... of the library of the USS Ran-
...he liner he sailed across the
...c in, just before the ship sailed.

    ★   ★   ★

...N DID YOU EAT LAST?:
... breakfast, but I couldn't eat
..." (it was 2 p.m.).

    ★   ★   ★

...T THOUGHTS BEFORE
...VING AMERICA? : "I want
... honest about it . . . I'm look-
...forward to Germany . . ."

    ★   ★   ★

...AGE TO FANS : "While I'm
...of your eyes, I hope I'm not
...of your minds."

... fog horn sounded and the
...w—and disc— ends.

...l summing up : this is a
...or's piece, and I found that
...et more from the disc each
...you play it. Presley is as
... when he's talking as he is
...he sings. **ALLEN EVANS**

Will he ... won't he ... come to Britain? Speculation about a possible visit to Britain by the world's most famous GI was rife in the winter of 1958

The field

Do you think anyone down here hates you?
Some folk have written unkind things about me. But as Ah've already said, Ah let off steam in solitary. Ah don't make a nuisance of mahself when Ah'm off the stage. Ah was properly brought up.
Your name has been linked with many girls. What say you?
Ah play the field, sir. Ah've no special girl friends.
If you can't sing or dance when you come to England, Elvis, what else can you do?
Ah can play football on roller skates, sir. Back home Ah have a roller-skating football team.

Nice

FOOTNOTE: I should like to place on record my opinion that Elvis is a nice, friendly guy.
It's a pity that some of Britain's so-called rock 'n' roll stars don't behave themselves as well as Private Presley does.

Ray Nunn

Despite the news blackout on Elvis' Army service in Germany, the thought that the singer was just across the Channel was almost too much for British fans to bear and there was speculation that some of them might travel to Germany to try and see him as the cutting hereunder reveals. And a month later, on 5 December, there was even talk of Elvis visiting London at Christmas to appear in a special television show!

BRITISH 'ASSAULT' ON PRESLEY IS HELD BACK – FANS WAIT PATIENTLY

The 5,000 members of the official Elvis Presley Fan Club – who breathlessly followed the news last week of their idol's arrival in Germany – are unlikely to launch a mass invasion of the Continent.

Discreetly holding them in check are Jeanne Saward and Doug Surtees, president and co-president of the Club. Commented Jeanne to the MM: 'Elvis is trying to be a soldier and an ordinary guy. It wouldn't be fair to him for us all to rush over.

'In any case, it would be very difficult to arrange a party. Anything less than 500 in number wouldn't be worthwhile – and the fares would be prohibitive.

'Doug and I may possibly go over some time before Christmas – but only if we get the permission of Elvis and his manager, Colonel Parker, first.'

Britain? – not yet

Will Elvis come to Britain? 'Possibly, if he can get leave – but that won't be likely for some while,' adds Miss Saward.

'His work as a Tank Corps Commander will keep him busy. He's in the 3rd Armoured Division – their motto is "Hell on Wheels." '

PRESLEYMANIA – 1958

TWIXT ELVIS AND PAT. Colonel Tom Parker has reportedly purchased the screen rights of Pat Boone's book, *Twixt Twelve and Twenty*, to be filmed by Elvis Presley. The Colonel plans to film this book by Elvis' great rival in the pop charts when Presley completes his Army service.

Hollywood Reporter, 5 January

☆ ☆ ☆

ELVIS BY A GIRL FRIEND. Dolores Hart, co-star with Elvis Presley in *Loving You* and *King Creole*, says, 'Despite all Elvis' high spirits and his rushing about, he's the most relaxed person I know. Often while he was waiting for a scene to be shot, he'd pick up his guitar, loll on a chair and start to sing, and everyone within earshot would fall under his spell. The Elvis I knew – my friend, the man – is shy meeting people for the first time, and so sensitive to the other person's shyness that he makes the effort to put you at ease as he did me the first day we met.'

Screen Stars, February

☆   ☆   ☆

ELVIS AND POLITICS. Elvis Presley's record 'Hound Dog' was played to the Louisiana House of Representatives when it was debating a Bill to allow the training of hunting dogs during the closed season. The Bill was passed!

Glasgow Sunday Mail, 11 February

☆   ☆   ☆

SOLDIER ELVIS. Fans pleaded in vain for locks of Elvis Presley's hair when he was reduced to a crew cut on joining the Army on Monday. Among those present was Colonel

Tom Parker – making the singer the only private in the U.S. Army to employ a Colonel! Apparently Presley leaves very little in the can at RCA-Victor as he goes into the Army. Victor plan to follow him wherever he's stationed when they need sides. Meanwhile, Elvis' recording 'Don't' currently riding high in the charts on both sides of the Atlantic has now exceeded two million sales ...

Billboard, 25 March

☆   ☆   ☆

CHANGE OF PLANS. Elvis Presley's basic training site has been changed to the 2nd Armoured Division at Fort Hood according to a decision made in Washington. He will be there eight weeks. Presley did not take the officer candidate test along with other aptitude and classification tests. Only a rookie who scores above a certain mark on certain tests is permitted to take the test. 'I never was good at arithmetic,' Presley said jauntily, 'That's Colonel Parker's department.'

New York Post, 5 April

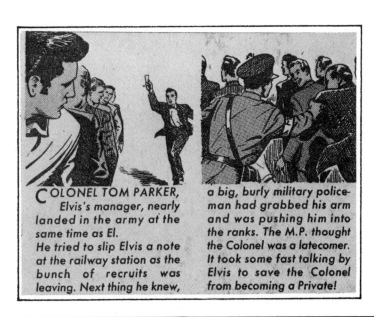

COLONEL TOM PARKER, Elvis's manager, nearly landed in the army at the same time as El.
He tried to slip Elvis a note at the railway station as the bunch of recruits was leaving. Next thing he knew, a big, burly military policeman had grabbed his arm and was pushing him into the ranks. The M.P. thought the Colonel was a latecomer. It took some fast talking by Elvis to save the Colonel from becoming a Private!

GARY CROSBY WARNS ELVIS. Interviewed recently, Gary Crosby, son of Bing Crosby, who has just left the Army, said of Presley and the Army: 'My deepest sympathies are with him at this time, and believe me, I don't even know him. If they want to get you, there are a million little ways they can do it. I was lucky to stay out of serious trouble, but it wasn't easy. And I was a nobody, nothing, compared to what he was when he went in.'

Hollywood Reporter, 16 April

☆ ☆ ☆

SHAKING A LEG! Elvis Presley told journalist David Ragan about some of his Army experiences and recounted how the troops had ragged him about his inability to sit still. 'Like the other day,' he related, 'when I was sitting on a foot locker and my leg was moving while some music was playing. And a sergeant said to me, "Private Presley, I wish you'd stop shaking that leg." I said, "Sir, when that leg stops shakin', I'm finished!"'

New Musical Express, 1 May

☆ ☆ ☆

SNAKES ALIVE! Tragedy nearly struck Elvis Presley during a week of his basic training which he spent in the field under actual combat conditions. A venomous copperhead snake got into his tent one night and it took until 3 a.m. to remove the snake and restore the tent to order. 'All the exercise I got has sure improved my physical condition,' Elvis said later.

Disc, 5 May

☆ ☆ ☆

ELVIS TIRED. Latest report on Elvis Presley in the Army comes from his good friend, Anita Wood: 'Elvis sure needs his rest after that eight weeks' basic training. He looked very tired when he came home and said he'd like to sleep for a week. He said the training was brutal.'

Picture Show, 13 June

☆ ☆ ☆

DOG TAGS FOR SALE. Merchandised from 2 July are these articles bearing Elvis Presley's endorsement – dog tags, bracelets, key chains and anklets – all containing his signature, army serial number, blood type and an etched portrait! In announcing these products, Colonel Tom Parker said, 'My business while Elvis is away will be to make sure his millions of fans won't forget him. If I didn't work for him all the time he is gone I would be pretty ungrateful.'

Cashbox, 19 June

☆ ☆ ☆

ANOTHER SINGING PRESLEY! Jesse Presley, 61-year-old grandfather of Elvis Presley, has been signed by a Kentucky record label to wax the songs he remembers from his youth.

Billboard, 27 June

☆ ☆ ☆

A NIGHT WITH ELVIS. A U.S. magazine is being sued by Hollywood actress Natalie Wood for libel. One complaint concerns spending a week-end at Elvis Presley's home 'unchaperoned.'

New Musical Express, 4 July

☆ ☆ ☆

RISE FOR ELVIS. Elvis Presley has received a promotion and a raise. It's an automatic promotion, making him a private second class. He now gets $85.80 instead of

$83.20 per month. According to the Army, Elvis merits the increase. He is currently serving in the temporary rank of acting assistant tank leader. An Army spokesman said, 'That suggests very strongly he is doing a very good job as an individual soldier.'

New York Post, 1 August

☆ ☆ ☆

FANS AT ELVIS' MOTHER'S FUNERAL. The funeral of Elvis Presley's mother at Forest Hills Cemetery, Memphis was startlingly similar to the funeral scenes in the Tommy Sands film, *Singing Idol*. The services were open to the public. Women fans of the singer made up 95 per cent of the crowds in the chapel. Spectators lined the sidewalks along the three mile route from the funeral home to the cemetery. About 700 persons were at the graveside. They talked and craned their necks to catch a glimpse of Presley.

New Musical Express, 29 August

☆ ☆ ☆

POETIC SEND-OFF. Singer Anita Wood saw Elvis Presley off at Fort Hood. When he arrived at the Brooklyn Army Terminal *en route* for Germany, he carried a book, *Poems That Touch The Heart*. Before embarkation, the Army band played 'Hound Dog' and other Presley hits. Explained the Chief Warrant Office, 'I felt we should make it a Presley field day. Any man who takes care of his father the way he has, and took care of his mother, I admire.' Presley is still very broken up over his mother's death …

New Musical Express, 20 September

☆ ☆ ☆

ELVIS PRESLEY JUNIOR. A letter received by Elvis Presley in his new German home reads: 'Dear Herr Presley, We have just given birth to a magnificent young son, and we think his little voice sounds a bit like yours. Of course, he is only one week old, but we shall name him Elvis Presley Schmidt and hope that some day he will made us as proud as you have made your father and mother. God Bless you, Mr and Mrs Franz Schmidt.'

Woman's Mirror, 30 November

☆ ☆ ☆

FANMANIA. One of the most hilarious incidents involving G.I. Elvis Presley now serving in Germany has been revealed by a camp sentry. Apparently a young German fan of the singer managed to get hold of an Army uniform and hoping to see her idol approached the camp gates with the cap pulled down over her eyes. But as 'he' saluted the guard, 'his' moustache fell off!

Picturegoer, 12 December

1959

ELVIS the KING RETURNS

WIN · A WO[...]
· DATE

ELVI[...]

EVEALING
S SHOCK[...]
CRET

appearan[...]
of Elvis

ELVIS PRESL[...]

STAR OF STAGE, SCREEN, RADIO, RECORDS AND T[...]

ELVIS PRESLEY MAY VISIT LONDON
"Evening News" Reporter

AMERICAN rock 'n' roll king, Elvis Presley, may come to London next year. He has been offered about £250,000 [...] Johannesburg [...] make 25 per [...]ces in Euro[...]

ELVIS

kissed me

PRESLEY — that's all we had h[...] at the ele[...] on ELVIS P[...]

ELVIS 50th ELVIS PRESLEY

CHART ENTR[...]

The first the general public heard of Elvis in person again was on his birthday, 8 January, when Dick Clark, the host of the top-rated TV Show, American Bandstand, *spoke to him live in Germany over a telephone link. Clark informed Elvis he had been voted 'Singer of the Year' in the USA, Canada, Britain, Australia, Africa, Egypt and Iraq and 'King Creole' had been adjudged 'Best Record of the Year'. Elvis was especially gratified to be told by the television host, 'The folks at home certainly haven't forgotten you. If anything they're more and more interested in your activities and the things you're doing and anxiously await your return.' The following month Colonel Parker's office issued an article bearing Elvis' signature about his life in the Army which was reprinted on both sides of the Atlantic. 'My Army Life Is Fine' is reprinted here just as it was pasted into the scrapbooks.*

MY ARMY LIFE IS FINE

By Elvis Presley

Well there's one thing you can say for being in the Army. I've had more time to relax and think about life a bit. More time than I've had in the whole of the past couple of years.

In fact, I'm only now beginning to realise just how fast the pace has been since I got my big break in show business. Not that I have any regrets. From the start I knew that a break such as I got only comes once in a lifetime and I'd be a fool not to work as hard as I could while the chances were there.

But that meant giving up things. There isn't much chance of getting out to enjoy yourself when you're hopping about all over the country, or you've got lines to learn for a new movie.

Now that's all over for the time being. Whether I like it or not, I'm having to take things easier. When the day's parades are over, the evening is all mine to do what I like with. And, from my experiences of the past couple of months, I like this new life fine.

I can sit back now and think of some of the things I've been missing. Girls, for instance. Now that I stay put in one part of the country, it's quite a novelty for me to take the same girl out more than once.

WHO KNOWS, PERHAPS I'LL EVEN FIND TIME TO GET MARRIED DURING MY TWO YEARS IN THE ARMY!

Not that I have any serious romantic interests at the time of writing. But I can never guarantee about tomorrow!

Sure, I've felt close to falling in love a couple of times before now. Did you know I almost got engaged twice before I got into show business? But something prevented me from getting involved at the last moment.

It's funny, but if you don't care for a girl, it'll come out in the long run. I discovered that I didn't care as much as I thought I did. In a way, it's lucky I didn't get tied up.

Nowadays I just let things ride. I don't care enough for one girl to be identified with them. I just prefer to date them all until I find the right one.

I know the press have done their best to marry me off a couple of times. Once a newspaper described Anita Wood as my 'number one girl friend.' But there was no truth in it.

THAT'S ABOUT ALL WE COULD DO. WE'D HAVE BEEN MOBBED IF WE'D GONE TO A BALL GAME OR OTHER PUBLIC PLACE. THAT'S ONE OF THE LIMITATIONS OF BEING IN THE PUBLIC EYE.

I guess some of the girls have just come for the publicity. But you can't really blame them. Entertainers need the press. If the papers didn't write, no one would know what you're doing. Everyone needs the press.

Mind you, some press reports I read sound pretty crazy. Like the ones that said the Tommy Sands film, *Sing, Boy, Sing*, was kind of based on my life story.

Well, from what I can see, the only similarity between the guy in the film and me is that we are both singers. My grandfather isn't dead yet. I only heard from him a little

What happened was that Anita was seeing me off at the station. The cameraman told me to kiss her, and a reporter said: 'Number one?' I said: 'Yeah, sure,' and boarded the train.

I was halfway to California before I realised what he meant. But by then it was too late. The papers had all printed that she was my number one girl friend.

Before I joined the Army, the only time I could really relax was when I had a few hours off and headed home for Memphis. Most of my friends are there. Folks have known me since I was a kid and don't pay too much heed to my success. It's easier to be myself there.

Sometimes I'd invite a girl friend home for the evening. I'd introduce her to my folks and we'd have dinner in my apartment. Then afterwards we'd just ride around, go to a drive-in for a hamburger or see a real late movie.

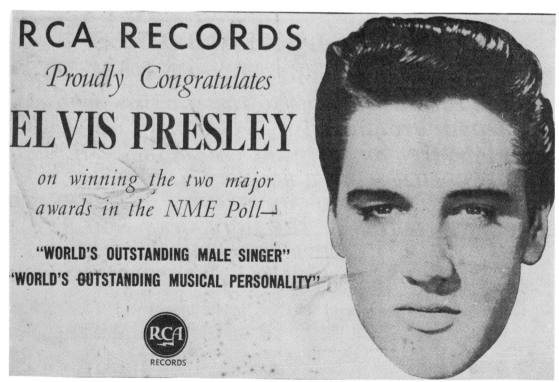

A BIG
HUNK
O'
LOVE

RCA-1136

while ago. And that manager was nothing like the Colonel!

It's amazing the number of people who think Colonel Parker is some kind of Svengali who tries to run my private life as well as my professional career. In fact, he only advises me on business matters. My private life is my own affair.

But I guess I've always done what he says as far as my show business life is concerned. Being in the Army has given me the chance of looking back over the past couple of years and realising how fantastic they've been.

Perhaps some of the most hectic times for me were the personal appearances I made in various parts of the country. I've usually been very nervous when I go onstage, but I'd always stop shaking once I start singing.

Sometimes I'd forget one of the lyrics of a song when I was in the middle of my act, but no one ever knew. I guess they couldn't tell what I was singing anyway!

The same thing happened once in the middle of a recording session. When the time came for me to wax 'Blue Moon,' I didn't know all the words. When I got to the middle eight I just started yelling!

Always one of the big excitements of a personal appearance was getting out the theatre without causing a riot. All the plans would be laid on beforehand, and I'd just carry out orders like a robot.

What happened was that it was always fixed for me to leave before the audience

Even though Elvis was in the Army he was still winning awards galore – as the RCA advertisement for January 1959 opposite reveals. His records too, like 'A Big Hunk O' Love' also sold extremely well

Private Presley spends his evenings serenading the lovely Margrit

Bardot-like Margrit Buergin, Presley's new friend

From COLIN LAWSON

BAD NAUHEIM, Sunday.

IN front of what Paw Presley calls his old jalopy — a barely used Mercedes 300—stands the £3,000 B.M.W. owned by his son Elvis, America's gift to teenagers.

And, by what I saw outside his hotel here, a gift to quite a number of middle-aged German spinsters too.

They sighed " Ach, how beautiful " as the sound of Presley's voice drifted from his room.

Last night the U.S. Army's wealthiest P.F.C. (Private First Class) sang to his newest girl friend. 16-year-old Margrit Buergin.

Elvis reckons she is sure some girl and the nearest thing in Germany to Brigitte Bardot.

The music

I was permitted to listen as he sang. The famous pelvis swayed and the voice rang through the hotel like an air-raid siren.

Paw allowed it sure was a good song. He thought it was a religious song called " Stand By Me."

He was wrong. It was " Don't Be Cruel "—which helps to swell his disc royalties of around £100,000 a year.

The U.S. Army is doing its best to ignore P.F.C. Presley. They reckon it does no credit to the toughest, roughest fightin' unit in the famed 3rd Armoured (Spearhead) Division to be saddled with the rock 'n' roll king.

Elvis lives with his retinue on the first floor of the Green Wood Hotel.

There is Paw, Grandmaw Elvis, and his two companions, Rex West and Lemar Fike.

What do they do? Says Paw: "They act as travelling friends —get railroad tickets, keep him company, and that."

They seem to like it. They should. They live free and get more money than Presley's army pay of £33 a month.

Two girl secretaries complete the household.

The words

At 6.30 Elvis gets up, eats egg, bacon, toast, and peaches out of a tin. Off to barracks at 7.30.

Back home at 12 for pork chops or Southern fried chicken, peas, beans, and ice cream.

Into barracks by car and safely home again at 5.30 for the evening session—listened to, of course, by Margrit.

Paw allowed the couple kissed quite a lot. They certainly do. Last night Elvis said: "She's more sexy, more attractive, and more charming than ever."

Conversation is a bit difficult. She speaks no English, he no German. But everybody assured me they find it mighty fun with a dictionary, g e t t i n' the meanin'.

I asked Paw if Elvis liked the army.

"Well, now, sir, that's surely the question," he replied. "Guess he don't very much. But he puts up with it.

"He sure ain't lookin' for promotion to sergeant."

even guessed I was out of the building. They'd tell me to be at a certain point as soon as I came off the stage, and I was.

THERE WERE NO BOWS. NO CURTAIN CALLS. I'D JUST FINISH THE LAST NUMBER AND AWAY I'D GO!

Well, those days are over for a while, though I guess I'll still be doing some personal appearances during my furloughs. Anyway, the Army has called a halt to that side of my career for a time.

Despite Elvis' protestations that he had no serious girl friend, he actually dated two German girls during 1959 – a pretty blonde 16-year-old typist named Margrit Buergin, and later the 22-year-old dark and sultry film actress Vera Tschechowa. Colin Lawson of the Daily Express *revealed Elvis' friendship with Margrit in a story published on 18 January, and within two months, Magrit herself was telling the inside story in* Photoplay *magazine. Shortly after, America's most famous serving soldier was reported to be escorting the brunette Vera around Bad Nauheim and Frankfurt. A number of newspapers and magazines tried unavailingly to make both these romantic episodes into full-blown love affairs. What was to prove the big romance of Elvis' life, with the even younger 15-year-old daughter of an American Air Force Captain named Beaulieu also stationed in Germany, was still six months ahead …*

Stories of Elvis appearing in a British-made film before he left the Army provided some controversial copy for the press – the music papers in particular – in February 1959. No sooner had these plans been revealed, however, than agents acting for Elvis protested about the project and attempted to block the use of any film footage featuring the star – as this cutting from the New Musical Express *reveals …*

ELVIS' AGENTS PROTEST TO BRITISH COMPANY

Elvis Presley's U.S. representatives, the William Morris Agency, are protesting to Border Films regarding their intention to include newsreel shots of Presley in their film *Climb Up The Wall*. Starring Jack Jackson, it is due for release here shortly.

The reel in question shows Presley boarding the liner USS Randall, then talking to fellow draftees as he sailed from America to Germany last year.

The news shots were taken in America and flown over to Associated British-Pathe, who included them in their newsreel. Associated British-Pathe were approached by Border Films.

A spokesman of AB-Pathe said: 'The extract was sent to us with no restrictions. It was treated like any other item in the newsreel.

'When Border Films approached us, their request was dealt with on the same basis as any similar request received to include newsreel material in a feature picture.

'Providing Presley's name isn't used in the billing and the shot is used solely as a flash-back, we feel no objection can be raised.'

In June, Elvis was given a fourteen day leave from the Army and after a few days in Munich crossed the German border into only the second foreign country he had ever visited: France. In Paris he tried to play the typical tourist but soon discovered that his face and fame were as well known in the French capital as anywhere else when hordes of fans pursued him. He still managed to enjoy the visit, though, as an account in Melody Maker *by Alex Drummond, billed as 'the only British reporter to interview Elvis Presley during his Paris visit', reveals ...*

ELVIS PRESLEY'S VERY UN-SECRET VISIT TO PARIS

By Alex Drummond

The world's richest corporal sat on the edge of a chair, twirled his black peaked cap and said: 'Ah gotta git adjusted.'

Elvis Presley, rock-'n'-roll idol of more than half the world's teenagers, was talking about his future: 'Ah just dunno,' he said. 'Ah just gotta go back and find out fo' myself.' Elvis, serving with the 32nd Tank Regiment in Bad Nauheim, near Frankfurt, had sneaked into Paris last week with two Service friends to spend a rip-roaring five days' leave before he leaves the Army and goes back to America, in March.

For four days he had remained hidden in the discreet, dignified Hotel de Prince de Galles, in Paris's famous Avenue George V.

Teenagers

Then after a round of the bright spots and a visit to the Lido, the news of his arrival got out.

Next day, three French teenagers, duffle-coated and ponytailed, arrived to collect his autograph. They were unlucky. 'Mr Presley is not here,' they were told.

But before he returned to his unit on Sunday night, he finally agreed to see me – after much ado and a five-hour wait.

In his suite, with its green plush chairs, its shaded lights and red carnations, he talked about the future, the Army – and Paris.

As he talked the soft strains of Chopin came from the radio. There wasn't a record player or disc in sight.

A waiter brought in a tray of coffee. 'I never touch alcohol. Never in my life – not even in Paris,' he said, as he poured me a cup.

Live it up

He went on: 'Paris reminds me of Hollywood and the kinda life I led there. You know, sleep all day and live it up at night.'

Elvis, pale and sleepy after four nights in Paris, yawned and said: 'You know, I've only had a few hours' sleep since I've been here. But it's been worth it.'

Girl friends? 'I like girls, but there's no one special.'

'The only Mrs Presley who will be going back to the States will be my grandmother, who is living in the house I've rented at Bad Neuheim.'

Great future

The future? 'I still think there's a great future in rock-'n'-roll, but maybe it will need to be adapted slightly to modern ideas. Maybe I'll have to find a new technique, I just don't know.

'It will take a little time to get the feel of things when I get back to the States, but I've learnt to adjust myself – the Army taught me how.'

'How about a British trip?' I asked.

'I've got three films to do for Paramount first. Then, maybe, I might come to England.

'The nearest I've ever got to England is seeing the White Cliffs of Dover from the deck of a troopship on the way to Germany. But I want to come as an entertainer, not as a sightseer.

'I've got a huge fan club in England and I'd love to meet some of those fans. But it will be about a year before I can manage to get over.'

Then he talked about the Army: 'It was tough at first, but I wouldn't have had it any other way. Maybe I could have got into the special service or something, but then' – he nodded towards his two Service pals, Joe Espiela and Airman Currie Grant – 'I wouldn't have met real guys like them.

Last night

'If I'd dodged it I just couldn't have lived with myself. These are real guys. If there was trouble, maybe they would get killed. I couldn't sit back and let that happen.'

He put on his cap and pulled on his white gloves.

'I'm not used to this high living but it's my last night in Paris and I'm going to make the most of it,' he said.

As Elvis' military service drew to a close in the autumn of 1959, speculation grew as to what the future held for the rock 'n' roll star who had not performed for almost two years. Film producer Hal Wallis visited Elvis in Germany to discuss a come-back film and plans were also announced by Colonel Tom Parker for recording sessions to be held once the singer was back in America. In Britain, with their idol just across the Channel, British fans tried desperately to get Elvis to perform in the country before his return – over 1,000 Yorkshire fans signing a petition with this objective in mind. At the end of October there was even speculation, if not much hope, that Presley might be a last minute addition to the all-star cast of the Royal Variety Performance the following month ...

1,000 PLEAD FOR PRESLEY

More than a thousand people in Yorkshire have signed a petition organised by two Elvis Presley fans appealing to America's most famous soldier to perform in Britain.

In a letter accompanying the many pages of closely written signatures, Elizabeth Budrey and June Dinsdale, of Harrogate, say:

A REMINDER FOR ALWAYS
The photograph that led to it all

ELVIS kissed me

ELVIS PRESLEY– that's all we had been talking about for weeks at the electric store where I work as a typist. Not only was Elvis in my country, but he was in Bad Homburg, a few miles from my hometown Frankfurt.

I wasn't as crazy about Elvis as my girl friends were. I liked him fairly well. In fact, I had six of his records, but he was not my favourite singer. I much preferred Frank Sinatra.

I became more enthusiastic about Elvis after I saw his film *Love Me Tender*. His voice was sweet, and his is a shy, boyish smile, and he was so sincere.

One day I was coming home from work to our flat in Frankfurt, where I live with my mother, my two brothers, Rolf and Pieter, and my grandparents. I met Bruno Waske in the hallway.

Bruno is a photographer for a German weekly picture magazine, and he lives on the fourth floor in our building. I have known him almost all my life. His son, who is just on my age, seventeen, is a very good friend of mine.

"How would you like to come with me to Bad Homburg tomorrow?" Bruno asked me. "It's Sunday, and you don't have to work. I am going to take some pictures of Elvis Presley at his hotel, and you could ask him for his autograph."

"How wonderful," I cried. "Elvis Presley in person! My friends will all be jealous!"

I couldn't sleep all night. I had never seen anyone famous, and Elvis was something super-special. All the girls in Germany were mad for him. His autograph was even selling on the black market. That's how popular he is! What a story I would have to tell Inga, my best girl friend, and everyone else at the office.

Bruno came to pick me up right after lunch. I hadn't eaten *(Continued overleaf)*

24

Continued from overleaf

He held my hand so tight

a bite myself, I was so excited.

All the way to Bad Homburg, I chattered at Bruno. But I was nervous. It did not seem real that I was about to see Elvis Presley.

Then I began to worry. After all, how was Bruno so sure I could even get near to Elvis to ask for his autograph? There would be many people crowding around his hotel. Maybe we would not see him.

"Never mind, you will see him," Bruno said. "I have to take some pictures of him, and I have never missed an assignment yet."

At Elvis' hotel in Bad Homburg, we learned that Elvis would be taking a walk with his father in a park nearby at 4.30. There were a lot of photographers around, who were waiting, like Bruno, for him to come out.

My eyes were glued on the door of the Ritter's Park Hotel. Suddenly I grabbed Bruno's arm. "There he is," I screamed, and I dashed across the street.

Elvis was followed by several men. I noticed them without seeing them. I saw only Elvis. He looked very handsome in his American uniform.

I squeezed through the photographers, who were beginning to crowd around him. I held Bruno's visiting card up to him. It was all I had. "Please, may I have your autograph?" I asked him in German.

Unable To Speak

He smiled, and I thought I would melt. "*Wie Geht Es Dir?*" (How do you do?) he said to me, also in German, and he looked straight into my eyes, as he signed his name.

"How about a picture with the girl, Elvis?" all the photographers began to shout. Elvis smiled again and looked at me questioningly. I could only nod my head, I was unable to speak.

He took my hand in his, right there in front of everyone, and we began to walk towards the park. He asked me my name, and he repeated it after me. "Margrit," he said softly.

We did not say much. It was difficult, as I do not speak much English. For the last two months, I had been going to night school twice a week to learn English. That was because I hoped to go to America one day. I understand a little but I speak only a few words. But I found it easier to understand Elvis than my English teacher. Elvis spoke English slowly, so softly, spacing the words carefully to make it more easy for me.

"*Autogramm* . . . autograph. It is the first German word I have learned," Elvis said. We were still walking, hand in hand, followed by hundreds of people.

"How about a little kiss?" one of the photographers asked.

I blushed a deep crimson and Elvis looked

'WITH SUCH A CROWD I DIDN'T THINK HE'D NOTICE ME.'

embarrassed too. Then he laughed. He tosses his head like a little boy when he laughs. He looked at me for permission, and I nodded my head.

He took me very gently into his arms and kissed me lightly on the cheek. "Again, again," cried the photographers. Once again he kissed me, holding me closer.

This time I closed my eyes. No more photographers milling about. No more crowds watching us. No cameras clicking, no people pushing. *Just Elvis*. . . . hugging me, his lips warm against my face—kissing me again and again and again. (Later Bruno told me there had been sixteen kisses.)

Finally, I opened my eyes. Elvis put his hand gently against my cheek. He smiled at me and said, "Thanks a lot."

Then he took my hand, and we walked back to the hotel. Elvis bent down and kissed me on the cheek. Then it was all over. He waved and went into the hotel.

The crowds of people began to cheer and scream, "Elvis, Elvis." They were staring at the second storey balcony. I did too.

Elvis was standing on the balcony. He looked straight at me and blew me a kiss. I blew one back. Then he disappeared.

The people began to leave, but I stood in a daze. I kept looking and looking up at the balcony. Bruno finally brought me back to the real world.

"Do you know what just happened?" Bruno cried.

"Elvis kissed me," I answered.

"Not *that*," Bruno said, "something *else*. I was just talking to Lamar Fikes, Elvis Presley's secretary, and he said that Elvis wanted your address and phone number. What do you think of that?"

I could not answer. I just gulped and looked up at the balcony.

For the next several days, I did not think of anything except Elvis. I hoped and hoped he would call me, but deep in my heart I did not think he would.

Two weeks went by and there was no call from Elvis. I gave up hope. But just the same I kept looking in the paper for news of him. I read that he had moved (Continued on page 1)

'These are the names of a thousand of your Yorkshire fans who beg of you to come to this country. Please take pity on us and make the trip. This plea comes because we have heard you won't perform in Britain. Oh, why won't you? Do you hate us that much? I'm sure we're not all that bad. When you get to know us you'll find this out for yourself …'

Unfortunately, this passionate plea – like so many arriving daily at the offices of the now undisputed official Elvis Presley Fan Club of Great Britain and the Common-wealth – is not likely to alter the situation unfolded to me by co-presidents Jeanne Saward and Doug Surtees.

Said Mr Surtees: 'Frankly, I cannot see Elvis coming here at all. Apart from the news that he'll come if he can make it some day our guess is as good as anyone else's. After all, why should he visit Britain any more than go to any other country to see his fans? If he did spend a leave here time would only permit him to play two or three big cities at the most.'

'It must be remembered Presley has army commitments and has asked to be treated the same as any other serving man,' added Jeanne.

'The BB, ITV, RCA Recording Company, Radio Luxembourg and several national newspapers and magazines have offered to fly us over to Germany to meet Elvis, provided we could fix up the necessary arrangements.

'We wrote to Elvis' manager, Colonel Parker, in the States. He 'phoned Presley. You can imagine just how disappointed Doug and I were when Elvis' father refused on the grounds that it was impossible, having had so many requests already. Rather than do it for us it was wiser to do it for no one.'

Further information from 24, Clarendon Flats, Mayfair, London, W.1. (Member-ship fee 11/6d. Junior section, 3/6.)

FOOTNOTE: Advertisements in the American World Wide Elvis Presley fan club magazine: *'Have you sent for your calendar? I mean our special calendar to mark the days till Elvis gets out of the service? It shows how long he has been gone, the number of days he has left to serve and a marking system to keep it up to date.'*
What a glorious waste of time!

ELVIS PRESLEY … SURPRISE STAR?

Will Elvis Presley be a last-minute 'surprise' star performer at this year's Royal Variety Performance at the London Coliseum on November 3?

Strong rumours circulated on both sides of the Atlantic this week, suggesting the likelihood of this idea becoming a reality – especially in view of the fact that Presley is so close to London. For an event of this nature a high-level request would not be unsympathe-tically treated by the U.S. military authorities.

In the official announcement of artists taking part, unlike previous years, only two American stars have been named as opposed to four in 1957, five in 1955 and four in 1954. With tickets priced up to £21, it is widely believed that every effort will be made to add excitement to the event by securing the world's most famous and controversial vocal personality.

Even if U.S. Army chiefs gave their approval, the final decision would still be Presley's to make – but for a Royal occasion of such an auspicious nature, it is most unlikely that he would refuse.

Meanwhile, news from America has been received revealing approval for release of the extended-play disc by Elvis Presley – an edited version of the press conference prior to his departure from New York to Germany. RCA in Britain await the completed present-ation for release here at the earliest opportunity.

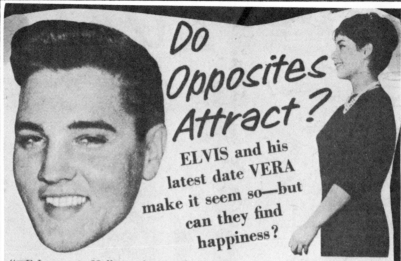

Do Opposites Attract?

ELVIS and his latest date VERA make it seem so—but can they find happiness?

"IF I come to Hollywood to work near you, what will your friends say? Many of your fans would hate you to get tied up with a German girl."

Dark-haired German actress Vera Tschechowa traced a pattern with her fork on the restaurant tablecloth. These words were difficult to say.

And her boy-friend—Private Elvis Presley—hated hearing them. Because he knew there was no answer.

Gently he stroked Vera's hair. "Nobody could hate you, baby."

But it seemed funny, all the same, to think how close they had got when they came from such different backgrounds.

Elvis and Vera certainly are a case of that old saying, "opposites attract."

Let's trace their history:

1937 Elvis, descendant of English emigrants, is growing up in a broken-down farmhouse at Tupelo, Mississippi.

1937 Vera, descendant of genius Russian writer Anton Chekhov, is growing up in Berlin where her doctor father owns a medical clinic.

1954 Elvis, now working as a truck driver, is studying at night school to become an electrical engineer. As a gift to his mother, he makes a private recording of "My Happiness". A recording company executive hears him, and makes a note Elvis Presley is someone to watch!

1954 Vera has just left her exclusive convent school, is now training as a fashion artist. But she has another idea—to be an actress.

1958 Vera is a successful film actress—has made films in Austria, Germany, Italy.

1959 A German journalist thinks it would be a good idea to photograph Elvis with the kittenishly-pretty Vera. This turns out more than a business appointment.

Vera invites Elvis to meet her family. Elvis invites Vera to meet his Army buddies. Friendship blooms into something more. Elvis and Vera go for long drives in the country together, exchange keepsakes.

1960 Elvis and Vera must now face the future. He is returning to America. And Vera?

"You're a talented actress—and a lovely one," Elvis told her that evening in the restaurant. "You speak English well. If you get work in Hollywood, we can be together."

Well, Vera is still thinking over Elvis's suggestion. But so far she has not decided whether to follow him to the States. For she realises that, once back home, there'll be other girls in Elvis's life . . . American girls . . . the girls Elvis grew up with.

Vera is wise. She knows only too well that opposites attract. But having a background, an upbringing in common, can often, in the end, prove more important.

During his summer leave in June 1959, Elvis took a trip to Paris where, as always, he was soon surrounded by beautiful girls!

PRESLEYMANIA – 1959

ARMY OF CORRESPONDENTS. Since Elvis Presley has been in the Army, his manager, Colonel Tom Parker has had to put an extra three secretaries on his pay-roll to handle all the star's additional fan mail.

Billboard, 12 January

☆ ☆ ☆

PRESLEY QUITS. Jesse Presley, Elvis Presley's grandfather, is quitting show business. He's not making enough money. 'I've gotten nothing out of my singing career,' said Jesse recently in Louisville, Kentucky. 'Guess I ought to give it up.'

Cashbox, 20 January

☆ ☆ ☆

LOREN ON PRESLEY. Actress Sophia Loren likes jazz but not rock 'n' roll she told Elvis Presley. Elvis was visiting her on the set of *The Black Orchid*, made a year ago, but the story has only just been revealed. 'I don't mean to be rude,' Sophia told him, 'but I don't see why you sing that stuff. I think you have a wonderful voice, but you are wasting your talent with that music … As a matter of fact when you come out of the Army I don't see why you shouldn't make a dramatic picture in which you wouldn't have to sing. You are a fine actor, and I'd like to make a film with you. But you'd have to cut your hair – I don't like long hair!'

Music Scene, February

☆ ☆ ☆

POPULAR G.I. Hedda Hopper writes after a trip to Germany: 'Lt.General George Thomas Vannatta told me Elvis Presley minds his own business, does every job assigned to him well without griping, and is the most popular boy in his outfit.'

Los Angeles Times, 4 March

☆ ☆ ☆

SINGING BAN. Elvis Presley's promoters have warned him that he may well lose his fans if he persists in not going into the Army's Special Entertainments Section. But Elvis has insisted that until March 24, 1960 he is going to be 'just a soldier'.

New York Post, 26 March

☆ ☆ ☆

BROADWAY OFFER FOR ELVIS. Elvis Presley has been offered a Broadway show when he gets out of the Army. Colonel Parker, meanwhile, continues to turn down TV series for Elvis, but may do – either on TV or in the movies – a western-with-music for Presley …

New Musical Express, 4 April

PREDICTING THE FUTURE! Pop music expert Atra Baer predicts what may happen to Elvis Presley when he leaves the Army: 'It'll be many years before Elvis is ready for pasture, but if he sticks to the shout-wiggle style, his time on top is necessarily limited. The Presley future lies in his ability to broaden his scope, make more and better movies, improve his voice on ballads, and lay down the law when it comes to some of Colonel Parker's strange (to me) notions about not doing personal appearances on TV unless for astronomical sums.'

The Journal American, 10 April

☆　☆　☆

UNREFINED ELVIS. French sex kitten screen star Brigitte Bardot says that Elvis Presley is 'not refined' and she would refuse to appear in movies with him. Anita Wood, a close friend of the star, commented on this, 'She's crazy! Brigitte will flip when she sees him, like everybody does. There's nothing like a nice southern boy to change your mind.'

Weekend Mail, 1 May

☆　☆　☆

COMICS ON ELVIS. Bob Hope on US TV: 'Elvis Presley's the guy who lost his hula-hoop but hasn't found out about it yet!' And according to English comedian Derek Roy, 'Elvis Presley is a worried man – he has receding sideburns.'

Tit-Bits, 19 May

☆　☆　☆

ELVIS IN CAR CRASH? Rumours spread in Germany this week that Elvis Presley had been killed or badly hurt in a car accident. When contacted by this paper, the singer said, 'I'm very much alive! Don't believe these sensation-seekers who are out to harm my name by spreading these untrue stories about me.'

Melody Maker, 29 September

☆　☆　☆

PRESLEY TO RECORD IN BRITAIN? It is virtually certain that Elvis Presley will record in Europe – with every likelihood of the sessions taking place in Britain. RCA in New York said this week, 'Depending on the time Elvis is allowed by the Army before he leaves Europe we will wax titles by him there – preferably Britain to Germany.'

New Musical Express, 3 October

☆　☆　☆

TERRIFIC HOMECOMING. Colonel Tom Parker, Elvis Presley's manager, has some special plans for his star's return from the services. Says the Colonel, 'When my boy comes marching home to Hollywood I aim to give him a real welcome home party. It'll make any other clambake, catfish fry or blowout look puny.' Colonel Parker says he has a request for a closed circuit telecast from the Ellis Auditorium, Memphis to about 200 cities across the country when Elvis goes back to his home town. Other plans include four films to be made one after another …

Billboard, 4 December

1960

ELVIS
the KING RETURNS

WIN · A WOR
· DATE

ELVI

EVEALING
S SHOCKI
CRET

appearan
f Elvis

ELVIS PRESL

TAR OF STAGE, SCREEN, RADIO, RECORDS AND T

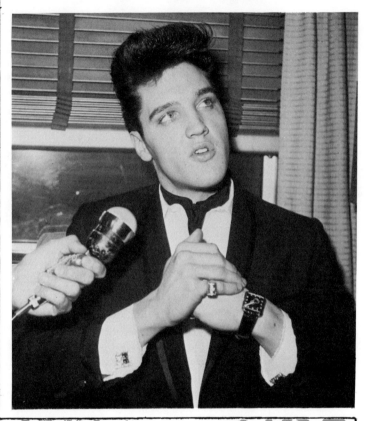

ELVIS PRESLEY
MAY VISIT LONDON
"Evening News" Reporter

AMERICAN rock 'n' roll
king, Elvis Presley, may
come to London next year. He
has been offered about
£250,000 Johannesburg
make 25 per-
ces in Euro

ELVIS ARMY

kissed me

ELVIS

ESLEY— that's all we had
at the ele on ELVIS

ELVIS 50th ELVIS

HART PRESLEY

On 2 March, Elvis finished his Army service, having attained the rank of Sergeant and completed his tour of duty with a fourteen-day training mission in the Black Forest called 'Operation Snowshield'. Before leaving Germany to fly back to America, Elvis held a press conference at Friedberg at which he revealed for the first time his friendship with Priscilla Beaulieu, later to become his wife. The most revealing report in the scrapbooks is by Peter Hopkirk of the Daily Express which is reprinted here. (As a matter on note, on Elvis' return flight to Fort Dix, New Jersey, the aircraft made an hour-long refuelling stop at Prestwick airport in Scotland, and the star walked on British soil for what was to be the one and only time in his life.) Hordes of fans and newspapermen were also waiting for Elvis when he reached Memphis on 7 March, and Malcolm Adams' report the following morning for the Commercial Appeal is also reprinted here. This, too, revealed another of Elvis' new fascinations – with karate …

ELVIS WANTED 'TO GET HOME' BUT 'KIND OF LIKES' UNIFORM

Extra Stripe Added By Tailors Bothers Singer –
He Couldn't Sleep Last Night Away From
Memphis – Wants To See Old Gang
By Malcolm Adams

Elvis Presley, back in his favorite city at last after two years in the Army in Germany, talked with reporters as the Southern Railway's Tennessean pulled his private car the last few miles in to Union Station.

About a dozen cars and taxis were at Buntyn Station, across from the Memphis Country Club on Southern, as his train stopped briefly there. Only two or three, however, appeared to be there to see the king of rock and roll.

Elvis went to the platform on the rear of the Pullman and waved to several boys and girls.

'I hope none of them plan to play hookey today,' he laughed. 'They still have time to get to school.'

Seated beside an Army buddy, Sgt. Rex Mansfield of Dresden, Tenn., the Memphis singer appeared to be tense as he talked with newsmen.

Q. – Elvis, you look a little tired?

A. – I couldn't sleep any last night.

Q. – What did you do?

A. – We just talked and kidded around most of the night. I guess it will take a while to realize I am out of the service. I'm still tense inside.

Q. – You look a little thin. What's your weight now?

A. – I'm down to 170 pounds and want to stay at about that weight. I weighed 182 when I went in. Guess it was the Army life … and it's not a bad life, you know.

Elvis said he had studied long hours for nearly a year to try and master the ancient Japanese method of defense and offense without the use of weapons. He explained he took Judo lessons for a while but shifted to Karate.

'I took four lessons a week,' Elvis said. 'Each lesson was for three or four hours.'

Q. – How did you have time for all that study since we read over here that you went out a lot when you were off Army duty?

A. – I didn't go out much. I couldn't. That's why I had time to study and read some. I developed a real feeling for Karate.

Fans greet the newly demobbed Elvis when he steps from the train in Memphis

Elvis was introduced to the sport of karate while in the Army and continued to practise the sport for the rest of his life

Presley bids f

THE PERFECT SOLDIER PACKS UP TO
AND HE LEAVES BEHIND PRISCILL

From PETER HOPKIRK

FRIEDBERG, Germany, Tuesday.

ELVIS PRESLEY flies back to the United States tomorrow, leaving behind an "outstanding" military career and a new 16-year-old American girl friend.

The rock 'n' roll sergeant, about to be demobbed, today gave a "farewell to arms" Press conference in Ray Barracks, Friedberg. There has been nothing like it since the D-Day briefings.

Floodlights lit a mess hall of Harringay proportions as 25 - year - old Presley, immaculately dressed in the khaki-green uniform of the Third Armoured Division, held court over 200 reporters and cameramen.

'Great experience'

Said Presley, who came out to Germany 18 months ago as a private: "The army has been a great experience for me. I wouldn't have missed it."

The army has presented him with a certificate of achievement for his "service as an outstanding soldier."

THE GIRL FRIEND: She is 16-year-old schoolgirl Priscilla Beaulieu, eldest daughter of an American Air Force captain stationed at Wiesbaden.

Said Presley: "We have been dating for the last three to four months. She is a very mature girl. She's got beautiful blue eyes—a very pretty brunette, and I like her very much.

"We've been meeting in her father's home. We've been going to the movies together, and we've been going for rides together. That's all."

He added: "There is nothing serious really."

Questions were shouted from all parts of the hall. The army handled the situation like a military operation.

Press kit

Every reporter had been issued with a "Press kit." These comprised a "fact sheet" on Presley, and "action" pictures —Presley with Jeep, Presley with Tank.

Some American reporters became shirty when they found that the "Press kits" had run out.

Presley, who wore on his chest two rows of shooting and proficiency medals, answered the questions easily. About :—

GIRLS. How did German girls compare with American?

He said: "They are both females. Other than language there isn't much difference."

HIS CAREER. He last made a record in June 1958.

He said he had no firm record commitments, but would like to make some records because

A wonderful experience

The future

"people soon forget you in this business."

His first engagement in the United States will be a television show with Frank Sinatra on May 1.

"I hope I can do more acting though," he said. "I want to be more of an actor and

PRISCILLA BEAULIEU
I shall cry

less of a singer and I'm not going to let my sideburns grow. I've outgrown that bit."

He talked of his films. Three are planned in Hollywood this year. The first: called "G.I. Blues."

"I don't think they are going to be rock 'n' roll pictures," he said. "I've done four and you

can't get away with too much of it . I want to make a career in acting."

PRISCILLA was in class at a Wiesbaden high school while Presley was giving his Press conference.

She said: "He is very intelligent. He's wonderful. He's charming. We became very close friends. He's just great."

But then she added: "You shouldn't think there is anything serious."

A promise

"I know I shall cry when he has gone. Elvis is every girl's dream of the perfect boy friend."

But she and Elvis have promised to write. "And I hope," she added, "that Elvis will still want to see me when I go back to the States."

Said her mother: "Elvis is just the kind of boy every mother would like her daughter to go out with."

Priscilla will be at the Rhine main airbase tomorrow when Presley takes off for New Jersey. He will be demobbed a few hours after landing.

| Acting comes first | Serious, of course | And sideburns are out |

Elvis stood up to explain more about Karate. He said blows are delivered with the open hand – the exterior edge of the hand which is hardened by exercises.

Waving his half-clenched fist, Elvis said that 'I can break a one-inch board with one blow with my hand.'

'I went to Paris to see a Japanese instructor in the art and took a couple of lessons.'

Someone in the railroad car volunteered that he believed all Elvis was saying and that he didn't want any blows sent in his direction.'

Q. – What have you missed most about being away from Memphis?

A. – Everything. I mean that ... everything.

Q. – What's the first thing you want to do?

A. – I want to get home. And I may stay right at home for a couple of days. Then I want to get around and meet some of the old gang. It's been nearly two years since I have seen any of them. That's a long time.

Q. – Are you anxious to get out of the uniform?

A. – No, not that. You know I don't have to be wearing it now. I sorta like this uniform.

(Later in the afternoon Presley was in civvies.)

Ex-sergeant Presley was wearing an Army dress uniform. The yellow stripes on his blue jacket were those of a staff sergeant. Actually Presley had a lower rank – 'buck' sergeant.

'I'll probably get put in jail about that,' he commented. It's not supposed to be here, that bottom stripe. It's not issue but something I bought in Germany and in the mad rush the tailors made a mistake.'

Q. – You plan to take off the bottom stripe?

A. – Hadn't thought much about it. Don't suppose they would send me to jail for having it?

Q. – Do you have any romantic interest waiting in Memphis?

A. – I won't know until I get around a bit. Two years is a long time, you know.

Elvis shifted the conversation from possible romances here to making records for RCA-Victor. RCA representatives aboard the train were Bob Kotlowitz and Henni Dauman.

'Somehow the word got around that I made some records while in the service,' Elvis volunteered. 'It is true that some of the records were released while I was in Germany, but they were cut before I started my hitch.'

Q. – Since you didn't make any personal appearances while in service, have you kept up with your singing?

A. – I sure have. I had plenty of time for it when I was off duty. I would play records and sing. I guess I got in more singing than I would have if I had been working at it.

Q. – What about your style of singing. Planning any change?

A. – No, sir. I just do what comes naturally.

Q. – Does that mean you will do what some folks call 'wiggle' when you sing?

A. – I still get butterflies when I go on. Will I still shake when I sing? I let it come naturally. If I stood still I would be lost.

Q. – What are your plans for the movies?

A. – My ambition is to develop as an actor.

Q. – It has been reported that you have stated that you want to pattern your movie career after Frank Sinatra's.

A. – I have great respect for Mr Sinatra as an actor. I never made the statement, however, that I want to pattern my career after Mr Sinatra. I want to do it my own way. It will take time and experience.

(Elvis will appear on the Sinatra nationwide television program from the West Coast May 12. The 25-year-old internationally-known Memphis singer will receive $125,000 for his appearance. He is expected to sing three songs.)

HERE'S HOW AN IDOL AFFECTS DEVOTEES

One in the small sea of faces pressed against the iron barrier waiting for a glimpse of Elvis Presley at Union Station early yesterday morning belonged to a dark-haired girl of about 20, a little short and plump, and wearing glasses.

As he came out of his private car and walked in her direction, resplendent in his blue dress uniform and surrounded by uniformed police officers, her face shone with anticipation and she began to tremble slightly.

He was only about six feet away from her when he signalled to his escorts that he would stop for a few minutes to greet the crowd that had come down on this chill morning to see him come in.

The young woman pressed her face tightly against the bars and reached out a hand. The young man smiled her a gentle smile, took her hand briefly in his, and passed on.

For a second her eyes followed him. Then she closed her eyes, pressed her lips tightly together, and stood trembling. For maybe half a minute she stood like that, then she began to cry.

First duties for the new civilian were a recording session in Nashville on 20 March followed a week later by his first public appearance on the Frank Sinatra Spectacular *from Miami. A Nashville music writer, Pat Twitty, was on hand to report Elvis' first session in two years.*

ELVIS WAXING AGAIN

By Pat Twitty

Spell the name backwards and it was Sivle Yelserp who recorded at Nashville's RCA-Victor Studio on Sunday, March 20. But turn the letters around and it was Elvis Presley – and therein lies a story.

Though the office of Elvis' manager, Col. Tom Parker, performed some tricks to shroud the singer's first post-Army session in 'cloak-and-dagger' secrecy, local radio and TV announcers were divulging news of Presley's presence in Nashville into their microphones at the same time Elvis was singing songs into his.

There was, however, no stampede. Most of the citizens in Nashville and outlying areas accepted the news with quiet dignity, and were able to go on to bed and get a good night's sleep as usual!

The few youngsters who were seen around the studio on 17th Avenue South were the same ones who are likely to be looking for 'something different' to do on any Sunday night.

Two policemen who stood guard at Victor Studios' front door did just that and little else, though they were called upon to dispose of one intruder who got as far as the reception room inside the building. Ironically, he was not the typical fan, but a personable member of Elvis' own profession whose courage had been temporarily

enlarged and he tried to join Elvis in song.

The Presley session got underway around 8 p.m. Nashville time, and lasted until 7 a.m. Monday. With the exception of one or two, the musicians and singers who were contracted for the session thought they were coming to one by RCA-Victor's Jim Reeves.

Reeves, who had agreeably consented to go along with the deception, uses many of the same people on his sessions as were used on Presley's.

In this instance, the people included bass man Bobby Moore, guitarist Hank Garland, drummer Buddy Harman and pianist Floyd Cramer. Vocal backing was by The Jordanaires, composed of Gordon Stoker, Hoyt Hawkins, Neal Matthews and Ray Walker.

Elvis' own electric guitar man Scotty Moore and drummer D.J. Fontana were present, along with one of his personal friends. Steve Sholes, Bill Bullock and a publicity man arrived from RCA-Victor's New York offices, and, of course, Nashville's a-and-r chief, Chet Atkins.

Local Victor engineer Bill Porter and studio staffer Jackie Niseley were present, and last – but not least – of those present was 'The Colonel,' Tom Parker, with his assistant, Tom Diskin.

Despite the fact that all 'official' Presley publicity is released through Parker's office, the story of Elvis' recording session here is told in a chain of reactions reaching from those who were in the heart of the session to others not directly involved.

For example, the girls behind the Crystal Hamburger counter don't make up orders for one hundred hamburgers every Sunday night. Neither do they pour as many cups of sweetmilk 'to be taken out.' Add 'a heck of a peck' of French fried potatoes to the order given them by three young men and you've aroused their feminine curiosity!

'It was the fat boy who said, "We might

Elvis in dinner jacket and bow tie for his appearance on the Frank Sinatra Show *in which Sammy Davis jnr. was among the stars*

as well go on and get a hundred. Victor's paying for 'em anyway." ' The counter girl filled the order listened and figured: 'A hundred hamburgers, plus "Victor" equals Elvis.'

While the usual tone of a Nashville recording sessions is one of urgency, since running into overtime makes money for musicians and expenses for record companies, the Presley session was long and leisurely and 'expense no object' in tone.

Last week, when some people in on the session were engaged in casual conversation about it, one of them remarked: 'When Elvis stops singing and does something else, don't nobody say anything to him.'

Another added, 'He must've played around on the drums for ten minutes or more.'

But the musicians who participate in Presley sessions find him to be one of the easiest artists in the business to work with. And this opinion might well please Elvis more than anyone else in the world.

'He never tries to tell you how to play or what to do,' one musician said. 'He tends to his singing and lets you tend to your playing.' And then, this note was added: 'He's just a nice guy … a gentleman.'

Elvis cut six songs in his most recent session, clad in black pants, black and gold cumberbund, tux-type, fancy white shirt with ribbed tucks down front, and black cardigan sweater.

After the eleven hours spent in the studio one observer said, 'He was just getting started good around 6.30 (a.m.).' From Victor, he was whisked to a private railroad car (which had also aroused suspicions) at Nashville's Union Station for rest and a short Press conference before departing late Monday for Florida.

Elvis Presley commented briefly on his first recording session in Nashville. 'After two years,' he drawled, 'it was sorta strange at first. But after singing a couple of hours it all came natural again.'

He was questioned about rock 'n' roll and replied: 'It has to be natural. The audience can tell if it's faked. If I couldn't feel it, I wouldn't do it.'

The Presley tape left Nashville early Monday (March 21) and records were pressed and back in this city by Wednesday. By last Friday, Elvis' first release had already over a million and a half firm orders – a Gold Disc before it is issued!

Both songs on the release are published in America by the Elvis ASCAP publishing firm, Gladys Music, named in honour of his mother who died while he was serving in the Army. This is significant because, as one observer pointed out, 'Maybe it's more than money responsible for both songs being in

Gladys Music. Maybe it's Elvis' feeling about the loss of his mother … his sentiment.

Of all the crazy questions he was asked when he came home, seems like nobody considered: here was a kid coming back home for the first time since his mother died.

Cashbox, 25 March

The third of Elvis' immediate tasks was to complete the filming of his 'comeback' film, GI Blues *which he did in Hollywood in April–May 1960. Director Norman Taurog described Elvis as 'a natural' who reminded him of Bing Crosby and Perry Como. When the film was released later in the year it was universally praised, and in Britain became the first of Elvis' movies to be reviewed by that most prestigious of newspapers,* The Times – *and favourably too, as the review reprinted here recalls. In July it was announced that Elvis' father, Vernon, was to marry again – which resulted in a flood of stories that the star was allegedly upset that another woman was to take his beloved mother's place. Elvis answered these charges in the August* Screen Stars *magazine reprinted here.*

Music writer Pat Twitty with Elvis and the Jordanaires at the star's first recording session since joining the Army

MR PRESLEY SHEDS SOME MANNERISMS

Style of his own in G.I. Blues

The young popular entertainer, especially if he is a singer, is apt to be judged less by reason than by prejudice – and prejudice derives its impulse largely from the accident of age. A large and enthusiastic tick will be placed opposite his name by the vast majority of those who have yet to experience the joy of being 21; crabbed middle-age, and all on the wrong side of it, will draw through it a thick line, eloquent of disgust and disapproval.

Mr Elvis Presley has had considerable experience of both kinds of treatment, but even those most determined to condemn must, if they are at all fair-minded, have

second thoughts after seeing *G.I. Blues*, directed by Mr Norman Taurog and now to be seen at the Plaza Cinema. The film itself, one of those American service comedies which so painfully stress the licentiousness of the soldiery, is nothing, and serious criticism would soon lose itself in the vast wastes of vulgarity that are its natural home, but Mr Presley himself is a different matter.

As Tulsa, a tank gunner serving in western Germany, he is an acceptable person. Gone are the 'side-boards' that were such an offence to the conservative, and gone, too, are those convulsive jerks of the body, making him resemble a jelly in a high wind, which used to accompany his singing. He has in this film a considerable number of songs, some of them above the average in tunefulness, to sing, and he sings them pleasantly. He has an unmistakable style of

Fan photograph taken in the Beverley Wiltshire Hotel in Hollywood with Elvis dressed for filming GI Blues

his own, yet there are moments when the ghostly image of the youthful Bing Crosby flickers across the screen.

The Times

The summer produced a new challenge for Elvis when he worked on his sixth movie, Flaming Star, *in which he played a half-breed Indian, Pacer Burton. The picture was filmed at the sprawling Conejo Ranch in the San Fernando valley near Los Angeles, noted for being unspoilt by power lines and other installations. Elvis himself brought such authenticity to the role that in December he was given a special award by the Los Angeles Red Indian Tribal Council for his 'constructive portrayal of a man of Indian blood'. The critics, too, liked* Flaming Star – *foremost among them Clancy Sigal of* Time & Tide, *who revealed who had been originally intended to play Elvis' role ...*

BRINGING THE WESTERN UP TO DATE

Elvis straddles the colour bar

By Clancy Sigal

It is not often a pure-bred Western comes into town knowing how to take care of itself. Credit for *Flaming Star* must go to the director Don Siegel, and to that old screenwriter pro, Nannally Johnson, who is listed as co-writer of a novel by Clair Huffaker. Out of their experience with the tight, medium-budget picture (unhappily almost extinct), Siegel and Johnson have contrived to do what Huston, Zinnemann, Ford and Kubrick have so signally failed at, the creation of a well-shaped, logical, frequently convincing, occasionally moving picture in coloured wide screen consisting of some of the most archaic strands of film myth and corn.

That they also succeeded in getting us to want to believe that the leading player, Elvis Presley, is what the script says he is, an inscrutable, likeable, faintly dislocated half-Indian boy raises conventional accomplishment to the level of a feat. The part was originally written with Marlon Brando in mind, and though Elvis might not do as brilliant a job as the turbulent, moody, Brando, he handles well a role designed for an actor he admires.

The story is about the half-breed son of a full-blood Kiowa (Dolores Del Rio) and her white husband (John McIntire) who also has a white son (Steve Forrest). The heart of the story is the way in which the relationship between the half-brothers is stated, economically, and with a consistently reined-in romanticism which I find difficult to fault. *Flaming Star* is an Owen Wister Western with an up-to-date race angle in which 'we', of course, are the villain, and the violence is

Elvis Answers Those Stories That He Hates His Stepmother

ELVIS doesn't hate his new stepmother.

Despite all the rumors to the contrary, Elvis gave his blessing to his father, Vernon Presley, and Vernon's new bride when they announced that they had wed secretly in Huntsville, Ala., on July 3. *1960*

Though Elvis wasn't told just when the wedding was to take place, he hadn't intended to be present at the ceremony in any case. He felt that his presence might cause a public clamor, and he wanted nothing to spoil the sanctity of the day for his dad and the former Mrs. Davada Stanley.

El has certainly shown in more ways than one that he bears no malice toward blonde, 31-year-old Dee. He made his feelings toward her quite clear in an interview he gave in Memphis during a brief rest between filming "G.I. Blues" at Paramount and "Flaming Lance" at 20th Century-Fox.

When he was asked if he had any resentment about his father marrying someone just six years older than himself, Elvis replied without hesitation: "Absolutely none!"

He continued, "I read a few things in fan magazines which aren't true. Here's the real story: Daddy was with my mother for 26 long years. He never left her side as far as I know. Now she has passed away and he is all alone. If he can find happiness in some way, I'm all for him. All of the time he was in Germany with me, he was a miserable, unhappy, broken man.

"She (the new Mrs. Vernon Presley) seems to be a pretty nice, understanding type of person. She treats me with respect just as she does Daddy. She realizes she could never be my mother. I only had one mother, and that's it. There will never be another. As long as she understands that, we won't have any trouble.

"Daddy has had some pretty terrible letters since this thing came out," Elvis admitted. "But he is my father, and he's all I have left in the world. I'll never go against him or stand in his way. He stood by me all these years and sacrificed things he wanted so I could have clothes and lunch money to go to school. I'll stand by him now, right or wrong."

Some reports had said that Vernon and Dee would occupy the little cottage behind Graceland after their marriage. But Elvis explained that the cottage has been remodeled to store souvenirs that he and his father brought back from Germany.

"Daddy and his wife will live in the house with me," he stated.

As a matter of fact, Elvis noted, he has had part of his large enclosed garage at Graceland, his $100,000 mansion, converted into a play room for his stepbrothers.

An informal photograph on the set of GI Blues.
Elvis with co-star Juliette Prowse

slightly excessive and logical. It beats hands down anything else of its type in town.

There was considerable anxiety among British fans in July when it was announced that the first record Elvis had cut for a single release since he had left the Army, 'It's Now or Never', was to be banned from sale in Britain because of copyright restrictions! Although the number was already a huge seller in America, the song had to be dropped as one side of a disc with 'A Mess of Blues' and substituted by 'The Girl of My Best Friend.' However, negotiations between RCA and the other interested parties finally resulted in 'It's Now or Never' being cleared for release in November. Perhaps because of all the publicity, the number became the fastest-selling record in British music history and an instant number one in the pop charts. The record also earned Elvis his

first Gold Disc from British sales alone, and to mark the achievement, top DJ Jimmy Savile was sent to America to present the award to Elvis in person. The two men met while Elvis was filming another dramatic role in Wild in the Country, *his last movie for 20th Century-Fox. Jimmy Savile's account of his meeting was published in the* New Musical Express.

PRESLEY'S U.S. TOP DISC CLEARED FOR ISSUE HERE

Next Month, not in Seven Years!

Copyright difficulties surrounding release in Britain of Elvis Presley's 'It's Now Or Never' have been overcome! The disc may be on sale here within a month – instead of RCA waiting seven years before they could issue it!

The waxing – a straight vocal with new lyrics of 'O Sole Mio,' made famous by Enrico Caruso – was banned from sale in this country because copyright clearance could not be obtained.

These restrictions did not exist in the U.S., where the waxing rocketed up the charts to No. 1 position, but it seemed that RCA would have to wait until the copyright expired in seven years time before they could issue it here.

The final clearance became absolute on Monday, after some weeks of negotiations, believed to have involved not only British Decca, who are responsible for issuing the disc, but the Italian publishers, their British counterparts, and top executives of RCA-Victor.

No release date has been set for the record and no coupling has been planned, but RCA will make arrangements to rush-release it when 'Mess Of Blues' shows signs of moving substantially down the charts.

PRESLEY MAY TAKE OVER SINATRA ROLE
Three new film parts lined up

AN unusual casting may feature Elvis Presley as a jazz pianist in a forthcoming Hollywood production, cables Nat Hentoff. There is a possibility that he will play the lead in the film "Solo," originally planned as a starring vehicle for Frank Sinatra.

Presley reportedly will star in another Hal Wellis production next spring. Provisionally titled "Hawaiian Beach Boy," it will feature Presley as a dancer as well as a singer.

Work has now finished on Presley's first post-demob film, "G.I. Blues" and, in a fortnight's time, he starts on his next picture—for 20th Century-Fox. Tentative title is "Brothers of Flaming Lance," a humorous Western in which Presley will play a half-cast.

Elvis received a special award from the Red Indian Tribal Council for his portrayal of an Indian in the film Flaming Star

Gold Disc in Double Quick Time –

PRESLEY'S 'NOW OR NEVER' BREAKS ALL SPEED RECORDS FOR SALES!

Dealers Overwhelmed by Crowds Demanding Disc

Elvis Presley – the undoubted king of record stars. That is how his latest British disc triumph has been hailed. The sales in this country of 'It's Now Or Never' have been faster than any previous hit anywhere in the world. It is virtually certain he will get a gold disc within a month of issue – his first from British sales alone.

Less than two weeks after it had been released, sales exceeded three-quarters of a million and the waxing is selling in such quantity that by early next week, demand could have boosted sales to a million!

Presley broke all records with an advanced order of more than 548,000 for the disc by its issue on October 28.

On Wednesday of this week, just twelve days later, Decca, who distribute Presley's label RCA, had received orders from dealers for 771,100 copies.

One dealer in a London suburb reported selling twelve times more copies of 'It's Now Or Never' than any other disc last Saturday.

Another, in an effort to cope with the fantastic crowds thronging his shop for two hours, only admitted those who wanted the Presley disc.

The previous fastest-selling disc was Harry Belafonte's 'Mary's Boy Child' (another RCA issue) which between mid-October and December, 1957, sold a million copies in this country alone.

MEMPHIS MEADOWLARK

Wild in the Country (20th Century-Fox) casts Elvis Presley, the well-to-do Memphis meadowlark, as a farm boy who fears he bears the mark of Cain because he clonked his brother with a milking stool. The parole board takes the broad view, however, and soon Elvis is out haylofting with two chicks, brown-haired Millie Perkins, a long way from *The Diary of Anne Frank*, and Tuesday Weld, a 17-year-old who is going to look a great deal like Saturday night before she is 20. Afternoons he spends with Hope Lange, a widowed psychologist.

Once that's accomplished, Elvis turns out to be an author possessed by – as Clifford Odets, who wrote the film, puts it – 'beauty and power and excitement.' Hope and Elvis motor up to the state university to bag a scholarship from the friendly old white-haired English professor. On the way back it rains, and, perhaps a bit too cautiously heedful of the fact that the car has bald tires, they take lodging (separate rooms, of course) at a motel. But love blooms through the plasterboard, and some lowlife spreads the news. Scandal breaks loose. Elvis sings

'FABULOUS!' exclaimed ELVIS to me as I gave him his Gold Disc

At the Gold Disc presentation ceremony are (l to r) JIMMY SAVILE, W. W. BULLOCK, vice-president of RCA-Victor (record division), ELVIS PRESLEY, GEORGE MAREK, vice-president of RCA and general manager of the record division, and Col. TOM PARKER, Presley's manager.

Says JIMMY SAVILE

Host of the 'Teen and Twenty Disc Club' and Warner Bros. disc jockey

NMExclusive

I HAD flown more than 6,000 miles to present Elvis Presley with his first British-earned Gold Disc—and there I was, speeding across Hollywood, an hour behind schedule for my appointment with the man whom I call the greatest.

Elvis was due to shoot the closing sequences from his latest movie, "Wild In The Country," and I was supposed to be at the 20th Century-Fox studios at 1.30 pm.

The chances were that if his filming had finished, he wouldn't be able to wait around for me.

But, after battling my way through studio security men, I was introduced to his manager, Colonel Tom Parker.

I breathed a sigh of relief. Work on the film was a little behind, and Elvis was still on the set.

My mission, of course, was to present him with the Disc for the phenomenal sales of "It's Now Or Never," now over one and a quarter million !

Work on the film stopped while the presentation was made. As you can see from the picture, El walked straight from the set to meet me. The clothes he is wearing are those he wears in "Wild In The Country."

UNEXPECTED

I told him about the huge sales of "It's Now Or Never," and handed him the Disc.

He said : " Gee ! Isn't it fabulous?" And then did something quite unexpected.

You see, I knew that he already had 34 Gold Discs, so another one might not make any difference to him. I was so wrong !

He danced around the set, clutching the latest trophy in his hands and showing it to everyone—artists, technicians and studio hands.

Even as we chatted he wouldn't put it aside, or give it to someone else to take to his dressing-room.

Now here's something else that I think proves El's sincerity.

As you know, in addition to hosting the Warner Bros.' disc-jockey programmes on Radio Luxembourg, I run another 208 series—the Teen And Twenty Disc Club.

Elvis, of course, is member No. 11321—and he was fully aware of this, as his conversation showed !

The membership hadn't been completed by one of an army of secretaries—no, El knew all about it, and was extremely thrilled when I told him the programme had an unofficial listening figure of 20 million. I call that real interest !

We chatted about Europe, and El told me that he would dearly love to come over here, but stressed that his business affairs were managed completely by Col. Parker.

" It's like this—I do my job, and he does his," he drawled.

As we were talking, a photographer was snapping away at us—much to my surprise, for I had heard all sorts of stories about Elvis, the Colonel and cameras.

Indeed, it's a fact that few pictures of Elvis are ever taken, and I learnt later, that I was the first d-j to be photographed with Elvis, an honour of which I am particularly proud.

When the presentation was over, the Colonel and I retired to his private room just off the set and we discussed all manner of subjects.

He gave me some presents, by the way, and like the photographs I have of my trip, they rank as treasured possessions.

Among them were a box of cigars and a shirt that Elvis wore ! Boy, I know a few cats who'd give anything to own the latter !

In all, I spent about twelve days on the trip. As well as presenting Elvis with his Disc (which, of course, was my main object), I met many fabulous personalities, and I'll do my best to tell you briefly about them.

I made many tape-interviews for future Warner Brothers' and Teen And Twenty Disc Club programmes—not least the Everly Brothers and Edd " Kookie " Byrnes.

In fact, when I went to Burbank, California, to tape the Everlys, I misjudged the distance to the Fox studios —and that's why I so nearly missed meeting Elvis !

While in the film city I visited my old friend, Diana Dors, who is there with her husband, Dickie Dawson.

Do you know they are one of the most popular couples in Hollywood ? Absolutely everyone is just crazy about them.

WONDERFUL

Dickie and Di have a wonderful circle of friends from all branches of show business. When I tell you they range from Mr. and Mrs. James Mason to Nat " King " Cole, you'll have some idea !

Well, the trip that I shall remember for the rest of my life is over.

How can I forget the polite, quiet-spoken, smartly dressed, sincere Elvis Presley, so completely different from the caricatures of him ?

Or that fantastic showman, Colonel Tom Parker, complete with pink nylon coat, bowler hat and cigar ?

I'm a Yorkshireman (don't tell me you didn't know !) and I'm blunt by nature.

If I like a person I tell them so. If I don't, I still tell them. Call it rudeness, if you like. I prefer to call it sincerity.

Elvis and the Colonel are sincere, all right, and I value their friendship.

several mournful ballads. It all turns out well. At fadeout, Elvis gets all three girls and the scholarship too.

The absurd side of this nonsense is that Elvis is much too good for the show. He is, in fact, the best actor in the film. The deep-pile sideburns have been clipped slightly, and something – perhaps German umlauts learned in the Army – has strengthened the rosebud mouth. He behaves with considerable authority, and shows his dramatic ability by containing his laughter when Hope Lange says (to the lad who was buying Cadillacs before he was 21): 'Don't try to tell me you're just a barefoot country boy.'

PRESLEYMANIA – 1960

COLONEL PARKER'S GAG. Colonel Tom Parker, Elvis Presley's manager, printed up a special newspaper to send to friends as a joke. The headline reads: ELVIS RE-ENLISTS. HAL WALLIS SUFFERS TOTAL COLLAPSE. COL. PARKER JOINS CIRCUS.

New Musical Express, 14 January

☆　☆　☆

HOME FIT FOR A HERO? At the Academy Award presentations, Bob Hope commented on movie strike, 'Hollywood agents starving in streets – is this the world we want Elvis Presley to come home to?'

Billboard, 14 February

☆　☆　☆

PRESLEY IN UK. Unexpectedly Elvis Presley made his first visit to Britain last week. For an hour he signed autographs at Prestwick, Scotland, while waiting to change planes for home to the States ... Asked if he felt it would be difficult to settle down into

civilian life, Elvis said, 'Well, I guess it won't be too difficult to adjust myself from $180 per month to about $1 million per year!'

Melody Maker, 12 March

☆　☆　☆

PRESLEY TOUR? Reports in show biz circles of a US and European tour by Elvis Presley, Fats Domino and Fabian later this year for which British fans will be asked £5 per seat.

Photoplay, March

☆　☆　☆

ELVIS' DIARY. US magazine, *The Post*, has announced that it is paying $250,000 to serialise a diary that Elvis Presley kept during his time in the Army. The singer has denied this claim, 'I kept no diary,' says Presley; and his manager, Colonel Tom Parker has added, 'If such a diary had been written we'd certainly have known about it and we certainly don't!'

Daily Telegraph, 20 March

☆　☆　☆

FAN MAIL. During his Army hitch, rock 'n' roller Elvis Presley received an estimated 15,000 letters a week from his admirers. At Christmas he received 400,000 cards from well-wishers who wanted him to know he hadn't been forgotten.

Screen Life, April

☆　☆　☆

RUBBISH IS OUT. Returning to recording in Nashville, Elvis Presley said: 'Rock 'n' roll is not fading from the scene, most of the sellers are still rock. But I tell you this: the day is over when a singer could take any rubbishy song, record it with a rock beat and get a hit. During the two years I've been in the Army, music has got better. There wasn't so much wild stuff, and artists started adding strings and getting better arrangements. The sound is now of much better quality than when I first started recording.'

Nashville Banner, 26 April

☆　☆　☆

ROYAL FANS. When the King and Queen of Nepal visited a Hollywood studio, the autograph they most wanted and – and got – was Elvis Presley, filming *G.I. Blues*.

New Musical Express, 3 May

Elvis acted with 'considerable authority' in Wild in the Country *according to critics. His co-star was Tuedsay Weld*

MR WONDERFUL. Under consideration for Elvis Presley – a screen version of *Mr Wonderful* which starred Sammy Davis jnr., on the Broadway stage.

Variety, 18 May

☆　☆　☆

BE KIND TO ELVIS. Sacramento disc jockey Bill Stewart sponsored a national 'Be Kind to Elvis Day' last week, playing records by the rock 'n' roll star for solid 24 hours.

Cashbox, 3 June

☆　☆　☆

DIME A DOLLAR. Colonel Parker, Elvis Presley's manager, said recently, 'Elvis relies on straight income and so do I. When he

Ricky Nelson to play Elvis in film?

A FILM of the life of Colonel Tom Parker, manager of Elvis Presley, with Bob Hope playing Parker and Ricky Nelson or Fabian playing Presley! That is the fantastic news that has reached DISC from Hollywood this week, but at press time the story was still unconfirmed.

Apparently it is unlikely that Elvis Presley will play himself in the film if it materialises. One reason given is that his fee would be too high. Another is that his film commitments are already too heavy for him to be able to undertake any additional parts.

Fabian and Ricky Nelson are two names mentioned for the Presley role in the film, with the latter the favourite.

Parker is one of the most enigmatic star-builders in the history of show business, and has asked, and got, fantastically high fees for the services of his protégé. The Colonel is apparently a courtesy title only, bestowed upon prominent people who live in the southern states of America.

PRESLEY—fee too high?

works, he knows that about 90 cents out of every dollar he earns goes to the Government and a dime to him. Even when he was in the Army, earning first $120 a month and finally $145.24 as a sergeant, he was taxed on his Army pay in the 87 to 91 per cent bracket because of his outside income. I guess he was taxed heavier on his Army pay than any soldier in history.'

Disc, 17 July

☆　☆　☆

HITTING THE JACKPOT. While in the Sahara Hotel, Las Vegas, Elvis played the fruit machines for three hours. Netted thirteen jackpots, one worth $312!

Melody Maker, 9 September

☆　☆　☆

TEETOTAL. Louella Parsons reports: Elvis Presley, who has never tasted a drop of liquor, confessed to Philip Dunne when he had to play a mean drunk in *Wild in the Country* that he didn't know how a drunk would act. Director Dunne provided him with a coach who did.

New York Post, 15 November

☆　☆　☆

MOVIE BANNED. Elvis Presley's film, *Flaming Star* has been banned in South Africa because Presley plays the son of a white man and an Indian woman.

Daily Express, 1 December

☆　☆　☆

SOUR APPLE AWARD. The Hollywood Women's Press Club has nominated Elvis Presley as 'the least co-operative actor of 1960'. In answer Louella Parsons wrote, 'How far afield can they get, giving an official "sour apple" to a boy who served his country with distinction for two years, who suffered the tragedy of his beloved mother's death, and who has gone from picture to picture without intermission since his release from the Army?'

Los Angeles Times, 19 December

1961

ELVIS
the KING
RETURNS

WIN · A WOR
DATE

EVEALING
S SHOCK'
CRET

appearan

f Elvis

ELVIS PRESL

STAR OF STAGE, SCREEN, RADIO, RECORDS AND T

ELVIS PRESLEY
MAY VISIT LONDON

"Evening News" Reporter

AMERICAN rock 'n' roll
king, Elvis Presley, may
come to London next year. He
has been offered about
£250,000 ... a Johannesburg
... to make 25 per
... ces in Euro
... in

ELVIS

kissed me

ARMY

RESLEY – that's all we had
at the ele   on ELVIS

ELVIS 50th ELVIS PRESLEY

HART ENTR

Elvis immediately followed the success of 'It's Now or Never' with another classic, 'Are You Lonesome Tonight?' which Al Jolson had first sung years before Jaye P. Morgan made it a hit in 1959. Elvis' version with its throaty, spoken section in the middle, became a smash hit in both America and Britain – where it was released on 13 January with advance orders of over 500,000 and again went straight to number one in the hit parade. Thereafter it was to be a staple in Elvis' repertoire for the rest of his career. This transition of the wild rocker into a powerful ballad singer attracted considerable comment in Britain – leading pop singers and DJs contributing to a special feature in Disc magazine. The fascinating and revealing comments of three personalities, Cliff Richard, Marty Wilde, and Pete Murray are reprinted hereunder. The enormous success of 'Are You Lonesome Tonight?' promoted a number of 'answer' records including 'Yes, I'm Lonesome Tonight' recorded by no fewer than five girl singers, Thelma Carpenter, Dodie Stevens, Linda Lee, Ricky Paige and Glenda Collins; 'Oh, How I Miss You Tonight' by the reply specialist, Jeanne Black; a comedy response by the Hillbilly singers, Homer and Jethro; and an all-instrumental version by a Mr Saks!

Cliff Richard

'As soon as Elvis came out of the Army his voice improved. It's now much stronger and much more powerful. He has a fantastic way of controlling his voice which he proved in "It's Now Or Never".

'He seems to have a lot more warmth, and judging by *G.I. Blues* his acting has gone up by 100 per cent. I think his voice on records such as "It's Now Or Never" and "Are You Lonesome Tonight?" is far better than on his rock numbers, namely "Stuck On You" and "King Creole" and so on.

'I've always been a fan of Elvis but now I am a bigger fan than ever.'

Marty Wilde

'I don't like the new Presley. First of all I want to make it quite clear that I am his number one fan. I worship the ground he walks on. He is the greatest. BUT I don't like what he is doing now.

'I don't like his new thick, deep tone, the old standards he is recording and the very poor backings that are accompanying him.

'I think "It's Now Or Never" was atrocious compared with his early smash hits like "Jailhouse Rock" and "Treat Me Nice". These were great.

'I can't even say that I like Elvis's new LPs. Again the backings are corny. The sooner he gets back on to his old kick, the better, as far as I'm concerned.

'Mind you, I think his voice has improved tremendously. And without any doubt he is going to appeal to a much wider public and in so doing is going to attract many, many more fans, which is exactly what he wants – an all-round market.

'Personally I don't blame him for what he has done. It was a smart move.

'But I think whatever Elvis does, he is great enough to get away with it.

'If he recorded "Auld Lang Syne" I'd still rush out and buy a copy.

'But I wish he would get back to his old

style and give us a good-class rock number. He seems happier singing this kind of material anyway. Rock is far from dead!'

Pete Murray

'I think the man who has guided Presley into this new style is the most brilliant man in the business today. For I feel sure had Elvis continued to record the kind of stuff he was doing before his army days he would most certainly have had it.

'Now, he can only go up and up. His old fans have grown up in the two years he has been away. To be a continued success an artist must grow up with his fans. I've got a theory about all this. I think the kids between 13–17 go for the beat and rock, after this they go for traditional jazz and then after this they turn to Sinatra. They obviously get maturer in their tastes. I believe the kids wanted a maturer Presley.

'As for these two new Presley records, personally I wouldn't buy them. They're not my cup of tea. As for that dramatic little speech Elvis gives on "Are You Lonesome Tonight?" well I thought it was sickening, but what a fabulous selling gimmick. A brilliant idea!

'The message of the lyrics is so important, too. Take the song "Are You Lonesome Tonight?" I bet 75 per cent of women who buy a disc with a title like this are frustrated.

Steve Sholes, famous RCA a-and-r manager, talks about

PRESLEY'S LATEST RELEASE

Hello folks! I sure hope you're going to enjoy the new Elvis disc that's coming your way this week. Maybe I'm kinda biased in its favour, but I've got a hunch that you will enjoy it as much as 'It's Now

Or Never' – and you sure received that one warmly.

My close interest in the disc is, of course, due to the fact that I was co-producer, along with Chet Atkins, of the session. Both Chet and I honestly feel that Elvis has handled 'Are You Lonesome Tonight?' in really outstanding fashion. It's an old ballad which has now become something of a standard, and I reckon that Elvis excels himself on it.

In many respects it's similar to 'It's Now Or Never,' and it has a particularly well-handled recitation on it.

Yes, I hope and believe that the youngsters will go for this in a big way.

The other side is in complete contrast. As distinct from Presley's rich, warm and mellow tones on the ballad, he really swings on the coupling. Titled 'I Gotta Know,' it's an out-and-out rocker, sung in sizzling style by E.P.

This number was the product of an all-night session in our Nashville studios, and again Chet and I were supervising.

As always, the Jordanaires were as good as ever – and the accompanying musicians backed Elvis up in great form. In fact, I think it's only fair to switch the spotlight on to the backing group.

There's Moore and Garland on guitars. Fontana and Harman on drums, Bob Moore on bass, Boots Randolph on sax and, of course, Floyd Cramer at the keyboard.

All of us at RCA hope you will get as big a kick out of this disc as with previous Elvis Presley recordings – and you know something tells us that you will!

DECCA REPLACE 'LONESOME' DISCS

Complaints from record buyers who bought Elvis Presley's, 'Are You Lonesome Tonight?' and thought it was faulty, flooded into dealers at the weekend – and resulted in Decca sending out huge supplies of fresh pressings.

Owing to an unusual amount of bass sound in the recording, a worn stylus tends to jump over a section of the disc, but for the repressing much of the bass was cut.

Decca offered to replace all records returned to dealers, but in many cases buyers bought a new stylus instead!

YES, I'M LONESOME TONIGHT

Thelma Carpenter

DODIE STEVENS

Yes, I'm Lonesome Tonight

Elvis' achievements in the music world were marked by two special events in his home state of Tennessee early in 1961. On 25 February he returned to Memphis as the guest of honour on 'Elvis Presley Day' – giving two charity concerts during the day – and on 8 March was made an 'Honorary Colonel' for his charitable work and the fame he had brought to the area by the Tennessee State Legislature in session at Nashville. In being made the 'equal' of his manager, Elvis told the packed gathering: 'God bless all of you, as he has blessed and guided me through my career.' He then returned to Memphis in his new black Rolls-Royce!

On 25 March, Elvis made a rare flight out of mainland America to Hawaii to appear in another charity concert and give what was to be his last live performance until 1969. He also did some location filming for his eighth movie, Blue Hawaii, with Joan Blackman. The concert was to raise funds for a Pearl Harbor memorial and over 5,500 wildly enthusiastic fans packed the Bloch Arena near the Harbor where Elvis sang nineteen

songs accompanied by Scotty, D.J. Fontana, Floyd Cramer and the Jordainaires. Among the supporting acts at the concert was the comedienne and singer, Minnie Pearl, a long-time friend of Elvis from his days on the Louisiana Hayride, who gave the following report of the concert to the British Elvis Presley Fan Club Magazine.

LIKE SOMETHING FROM A GANGSTER FILM!

Co-star Minnie Pearl recalls Elvis' Hawaii Charity Concert

The reception that Elvis got in Hawaii – both on and off stage – was fantastic! I seriously worried for the boy's safety as the fans surged from all sides to try and get to him from the moment he landed on the island.

The police in Hawaii did a fine job, but they really had their hands full! There was an estimate 3,000 fans at the airport, plus the ones lining the streets as we drove to the hotel where another 500 nearly mobbed him.

The show, that night, was packed and the gross takings were $52,000. This amount went towards the building of a monument over the USS Arizona which was sunk by Japanese aircraft on Pearl Harbor Day in 1941 with over 1,100 men on board.

Elvis was at his best that night and the crowd gave him one encore after another. He wore a gold lamé jacket, heavily sequined, and among the numbers he sang were the Johnnie Ray hit, 'Such A Night', one of his first Sun recordings, 'Somethin' Blue', and he climaxed the show with that all-out rocker, 'Hound Dog'.

The trickiest part of the show was getting Elvis from the building without being torn apart. 'Operation Exit Elvis' had to be executed with split-second timing, Elvis dashing from the stage to a fast car which was already moving as he jumped in. It was a bit

CITY OF MEMPHIS
PROCLAMATION
BY THE MAYOR

WHEREAS, Elvis Presley has distinguished himself in the fields of popular music and moving pictures; and

WHEREAS, Elvis Presley has unselfishly served his country honorably in the military service; and

WHEREAS, Elvis Presley has set an outstanding example for young people; and

WHEREAS, Elvis Presley has maintained a dignity and humility that has inspired the admiration of millions of people, both youth and adults; and

WHEREAS, Elvis Presley has received world wide fame and acclaim; and

WHEREAS, even though his career has required Elvis Presley to be away from Memphis for long periods of time, he has continued to maintain his home here and comes back home as often as possible; and

WHEREAS, Elvis Presley has shared his good fortune, fame and success generously with his fellow Memphians and each year has contributed thousands of dollars to many worthy Memphis charities; and

WHEREAS, Elvis Presley has demonstrated a devotion to Memphis which has made Memphis known throughout the world as the home of Elvis Presley; and

WHEREAS, a tremendous number of Memphians and other people through-out the world have expressed a desire that the City of Memphis recognize Elvis Presley by naming the Coliseum in his honor; and

WHEREAS, the Coliseum provides a place for wholesome and all-around entertainment and recreation which is characteristic of Elvis Presley:

BE IT THEREFORE PROCLAIMED that the Coliseum shall be named

ELVIS PRESLEY COLISEUM

IN WITNESS WHEREOF, I have hereunto set my hand and caused the Seal of the City of Memphis to be affixed this 4th day of January, 1967.

William B. Ingram, Jr. - Mayor

City of Memphis

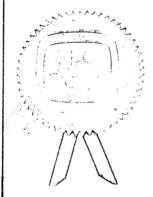

Copy of another citation given to Elvis by the City of memphis in 1967 recognizing his achievements

Elvis' last live performance for almost a decade – a charity concert in Hawaii on 25 March

like watching a get-away scene from one of those gangster movies!

Although we did not know it at the time, Elvis and the Colonel paid for all the supporting artists and also purchased a block of tickets in the auditorium worth $21,000!

Elvis is a very talented boy, I believe, and will be recognised for his talent more and more as he continues to mature and develop. All in all, Hawaii was a truly wonderful and exciting experience for me and I loved every bit of it. You can take it I'm an Elvis fan all the way!

Although newspaper interest in the Presley Phenomenon invariably focused on Elvis, the character of Colonel Parker always loomed large in any story. And despite the fact that the Colonel was always ready with a quote or a statement for the press, he shrouded his own career and origins in considerable secrecy and it has only been since Elvis' death that anything approaching the true story of the Dutch-born former carnival sideshow operator, described as a mixture of the born gambler and hard-nosed negotiator, has come to light. One of the earliest and most interesting pieces about the Colonel was Dave Cardwell's pen portrait for the New Musical Express *of 26 May which was also pasted into the scrapbooks.*

The hearts of Elvis' millions of fans around the world missed a beat on 12 July when newspaper headlines hinted that the star might be recalled into the Army! Elvis was busy filming Follow That Dream *(initially called* What A Wonderful Life*) and could do no more than say he was quite willing to fulfil his military obligations if called upon. The threat came to nothing, however, and Elvis completed work on the picture. Co-starring with him was the teenage actress, Anne Helm, who in October came to live in London in a modest little flat and talked about Elvis and the making of* Follow That Dream.

DATES WITH ELVIS

Presley's Follow That Dream *co-star Anne Helm talks to Alan Smith*

She's no ordinary person, the girl who co-stars with Elvis Presley in *Follow That Dream*. **For, while she was in Britain recently, Anne Helm chose to live in a modest little side street near Earl's Court tube station … just a few doors away from a fish-and-chip shop.**

She poured me a cup of tea as she told me: 'I can't stand hotels. I like it this way. It's quiet. And much, much better than staying in some stuffy place where the service might be bad. Here, I can come and go as I choose.

'Apart from that, I've had the family staying with me. Can you figure us all trying to get together in a hotel room? This way we've got freedom.'

I asked her about Elvis and she looked up, thoughtfully. 'What can I say except that he's a wonderful person, easy to get along with? He's very sincere.

'I've heard stories about him going to fantastic lengths to avoid his fans, but as far as I'm concerned they're exaggerated. Quite often he strolls round the film studios, or he might stop at the main gate to chat to the gateman.

'He can't see everybody, naturally. Filming is taking up a lot of his time and he likes to concentrate. But he always tries, as he did when two girls spent all their holiday money coming all the way across the country to visit him.

'What does he like to do when he's not busy?'

She smiled. 'Play with cars, I guess. He's got all kinds … a Chevvy, a Rolls. He's like a baby with cars.

'Then he likes gambling. He often plays cards with the boys on the film set.

Clothes are another of his hobbies. He's always trying new styles.'

Anne's mother walked in. 'Anne's been out on dates with El,' she said, 'but she says it wasn't much fun. He may not be troubled much round the studios, but when he gets into a crowd he's recognised at once.

'That way they can't go out places like an ordinary couple, they've always got to keep hiding. I guess that's one of the disadvantages of being famous.

'Elvis has a tremendous following in your country, hasn't he? I was having my hair done in a shop in Bedford recently, and I don't know how it came up, but I mentioned Anne was my daughter.

'I swear that those girls got so excited they were trembling!

'They were asking me all kinds of questions about Anne and Elvis. I'd no idea there was such an interest in him. Heaven knows what it would have been like if he'd been there himself!'

I gave her a rough description. Her eyes popped.

Anne took over: 'You know, I'd always thought Elvis had appeared in Britain. I remember him saying something to me about the London Palladium. I can't recollect what it was now, but I thought he'd done a show here while he was doing his Army service in Europe.

I asked her if there was anything she didn't like about Elvis.

'Well …' she said, hesitating, and giving some thought to it, 'I didn't like those terrible sideburns he used to have. He doesn't have them that long now and I think he looks better for it. And you know, I think his voice is much, much better than it used to be.

'I've always liked his singing – I think I've got every record he's ever made – but I prefer the smoother sound he gets today. I'm not so keen on his old country style.

'I've always studied acting myself, but Elvis doesn't bother. It just seems to come instinctively to him. It's the same with his singing. I mean, he hasn't had vocal lessons and the results are pretty fine.

'The Colonel keeps a pretty close watch on his affairs when he's making a film, but don't let that give you the wrong impression. He isn't an interfering busy-body or anything like that. If he thinks anything is wrong he just says so. And more often than not he's probably right.

'I love the Colonel. He's a wonderful, good-hearted man, lots of fun to talk to.

'He's shrewd, though. He's been the guiding light in Elvis' career, and nobody can deny he's kept him right there at the top.'

Anne's mother took up the conversation: 'A lot of sensational things are written about Elvis, but he just ignores them. That doesn't mean they don't sometimes hurt him, but I guess he has to take the rough with the smooth.

'I remember not long ago I was passing a bookstall and I saw a magazine with a headline, "Presley's Baby."

'I don't mind telling you I bought the magazine, but inside were a few lines about Elvis' step-mother having a child I thought it was a pretty tasteless way to sell copies.'

Added Anne: 'Not long ago a reporter interviewed me and when the paper appeared there was a headline about "The girl who slapped Elvis' face with a fish." El and I had just been playing about on the set. A bit of fun. To the casual passer-by the headline made it look like I'd attacked him or something!

'While we're talking about it, I'd like you to deny all those stories you probably heard about me having terrible rows with Elvis. I read one story about how I was supposed to have gone to a studio official in tears, asking to be taken out of the picture.'

Elvis enjoying himself on location in Hawaii with co-star Joan Blackman while filming Blue Hawaii

Colonel Parker protects Elvis by asking a fortune for him

POWER and publicity for Presley—these have been the aims of Thomas A. Parker, who likes to be called " The Colonel." Despite the fact that he says he doesn't want any limelight on himself, he has become almost as famous as Elvis—by making Presley famous.

There's no doubt about it, Parker has guided E.P. with great skill. His demands for almost prohibitive fees have not only protected Presley from too much exposure either on TV or stage, but have brought headline publicity for the star throughout the world.

Presley has complete faith in Parker's judgment. " Better ask Colonel Parker," is what Presley tells reporters who ask him about his future activities. In the beginning, it was Elvis who asked Parker to be his manager.

Always a colourful salesman, brought up in the rough-and-ready carnival world, he had managed such country-and-western singers as Hank Snow, Gene Austin and Eddy Arnold, and Presley wanted Parker to handle him.

Fat share

At that time, Presley was nothing more than a promising rock singer, but Parker must have seen some future in him because he accepted—and has since built Presley's talent into a reputed 2,000,000 dollars a year asset.

Parker takes a fat share of this, but even so he was spotted selling autographed pictures of Presley outside the Cotton Bowl in Dallas, Texas, while Elvis was working inside.

When asked why he, a millionaire, was doing this, he replied : " Don't want ever to get so big I won't sell pictures."

Selling photographs is nothing to his bold effrontery when reporters complained that their seats at an Elvis concert were too far away to see him properly.

Parker told them to wait, and hurried away. Everyone assumed that he had gone to arrange seats nearer the stage. They couldn't have been more wrong !

Back came the Colonel carrying pairs of binoculars for the reporters. To add insult to injury, he charged them two dollars each for the hire of them.

Parker's title of Colonel comes not from military promotion but from the Governors of the states of Kentucky and Louisiana, who made him an honorary Colonel for his efforts in the entertainment profession.

It was quite an honour for a man who was orphaned as a child and was brought up by an uncle who ran a pony circus in a travelling fair.

Parker drifted in and out of many jobs, from running a merry-go-round to a town dog catcher.

It wasn't until the '40s that he started to become a star catcher instead. He brought cowboy Tom Mix to London in 1947, and although Mix had been the king of the westerns for many years, Parker knew he needed to prod the memories of the post-war British public with an unusual stunt.

He soon had one. He booked Mix into the swank Savoy hotel, and the next evening the plush dignity of this famous hotel was interrupted by the sight of Tom Mix riding into the foyer on his horse !

The resultant publicity—because the Press was tipped off by Parker in advance—was world-wide.

From his tough early experiences one might get the impression that Parker is only interested in making as much money as he can as quickly as possible. This is not true.

For charity

Both he and Presley give away large amounts of money to deserving charities, and only recently Parker helped to organise big charity performances, starring Elvis, in Memphis and Hawaii.

When it comes to acts of this kind, Parker seeks no publicity. One instance of his kindness came to light (after he'd hidden it) following the Memphis concert. A 73-year-old fan,

What manager of any other world-famous star would display an advertisement for his protégé's latest picture on his back ? That's Colonel Parker for you !

Miss Murray Hooper, found that she hadn't saved enough money to make the round air trip from Houston, Texas, to Memphis, and buy a ticket as well.

Parker heard of this. He knew Miss Hooper, who attended many Presley concerts, would be sadly disappointed, so he paid for a charter plane to bring her to Memphis, bought her a seat and paid for her place at a special 100 dollars-a-plate lunch later.

Parker has helped many artists since taking over Presley. One young man approached him for help and was given a small spot on a TV show. Today even Parker must be surprised to see the progress this boy has made in films and on TV. His name—Tommy Sands.

On many occasions Colonel Tom has joked about the fabulous sum of money that he and Elvis gross each year. The easy way he demands hitherto unheard of " asking prices " for Presley's services has caused world-wide comment.

But Parker just grins and shows a great sense of humour about it illustrated recently when the 20th Century-Fox company asked him if Presley could sing two songs in the screen version of the musical " Do Re-Mi."

The executive was astounded when Parker replied : " Maybe — for 100,000 dollars."

The studio official replied : " We don't want Elvis to be in the whole picture, just to sing two songs. Won't take more than two days at the most."

Smiling, the Colonel said mildly " We'll flip for it. Heads, Elvis sings two songs for **200,000 dollars** ; tails he sings **four** songs for nothing ! The executive refused the " kind offer."

Autobiography

Parker threatens to write his autobiography, but even here he will introduce a gimmick as eccentric as his favourite taste in outdoor wear—shocking pink overcoat, black bowler and purple spats !

He plans to have one chapter of reading matter and one of advertisements alternately throughout the book.

An enterprising literary agent read about this and got in touch with the Colonel, offering Parker 100,000 dollars for the rights to publish the work, a colossal price for any book publisher to pay.

Imagine his surprised dismay to hear Parker's retort : " I guess could let you have the back cover for that much."

Parker was once asked what would happen when, and if, Presley ever fades out of the public eye. Parker just shrugged and drawled : " Elvis could always go back to driving a truck—his own truck. And I could always go back to being a dog catcher—head dog catcher."

She laughed. 'Actually, it was quite the reverse. I had a wonderful time making *Follow That Dream*. We spent all last summer doing it. It was fabulous!'

Aged 22, Anne has been in England making a film comedy, *The Iron Maiden*, at Pinewood studios. Michael Craig has another of the leading roles.

Although this makes her second comedy in recent months she actually prefers strong dramatic parts, as in *The Internes*, which has just been released in the States. Comedy films are her preference when she goes to the cinema herself.

Her professional ambition is to appear in a film with Marlon Brando or Elia Kazan, with whom she studies acting in Hollywood.

'I've missed the sun in England,' she told me before leaving for America, 'but I'll miss Marks and Spencers when I get back to the States. I've been doing all my shopping there.'

I walked up the narrow street, past the chip shop and over the road to the station. And again I thought: 'Can Elvis have ever had a more intriguing leading lady than Anne Helm?'

She was certainly one of the most down-to-earth stars I've met.

The year ended for Elvis with news of one film that would never be made – a screen biography of the great country-and-western singer, Hank Williams – and with him playing the part of a boxer in another called Kid Galahad. *Co-starring tough-guy actor Charles Bronson, the picture, when it was released the following year, generated a lot of discussion in boxing circles about Elvis' expertise as a boxer. British boxing writer, Peter Wilson of the* Daily Mirror, *was less than impressed and found himself deluged with letters from fans; while the English heavyweight, Billy Walker, an Elvis fan, had some much kinder*

remarks to make. Both these contrasting reviews were pasted into the scrapbooks.

ELVIS TO PLAY HANK WILLIAMS IN FILM

Half-a-million musical role set for 1962

Hollywood – After a delay of almost four years, MGM is going ahead with plans for Elvis Presley to play the title role in the screen biography of America's most famous country-and-western star – the late Hank Williams, cables Dane Marlowe.

This plan was first revealed in the NME during October, 1957. It was shelved when Presley began his two-year spell in the U.S. Army the following year and since his discharge, he has so far been tied up with other film commitments.

Shooting on *The Hank Williams Story* is scheduled to begin next year. Presley's co-stars in this exciting production have not yet been named.

The film will be the second under Presley's new five-year contract with MGM, the terms of which call for at least one film a year, each guaranteeing the singer $500,000. The first movie, which begins later this year, is *Chautauqua*.

Alabama-born Hank Williams achieved world-wide fame as the leader of the Drifting Cowboys prior to his death on December 31, 1952.

He has many albums released here by MGM and composed such as 'Your Cheatin' Heart,' 'There'll Be No Teardrops Tonight,' 'Cold Cold Heart' and 'Jambalaya.'

Presley is now working on his first film for Mirisch Productions. Originally titled *Pioneer Go Home* it is now being called *What A Wonderful Life*.

Shooting is taking place on location at Crystal River, Florida. Produced by David

ELVIS PRESLEY ALERTED FOR U.S. ARMY RECALL

HOLLYWOOD—ELVIS PRESLEY has been alerted for recall into the U.S. Army. His career, at present committed to the tune of more than $4 million, is seriously endangered by this threat, cables Dane Marlowe. Although he was demobilised more than 18 months ago, Presley is on the U.S. Government's list of reservists who have been warned to stand by prepared for any extended military moves over the Berlin crisis.

His Army unit, the 32nd Armoured Division stationed in Germany, has checked his address and imminent movements so that he can be easily contacted.

He is currently shooting "What A Wonderful Life," which is now being made in Hollywood—location shooting in Florida having proved too difficult.

Providing Presley remains a civilian, a unique TV deal is being negotiated for him — which will earn him a million dollars for one appearance, but the show cannot be screened until his present film commitments are completed.

They include his next for Mirisch — which may be "They're Playing Our Song," switched with the originally mooted "Kid Galahad" remake, and four under MGM auspices.

For each of these six films, Presley is being paid an average of $500,000 plus 50 per cent. of the profits — with the TV pact if it materialises, a total of at least $4 million.

Until most of these commitments are completed it is unlikely that Elvis will undertake many stage engagements, although negotiations are beginning.

Another bid to arrange an Elvis Presley appearance in Britain has been turned down. Birmingham promoter Brian Delorme offered him £89,000. He promised to arrange jet transport so that Presley need not be away from Hollywood for more than 24 hours.

Referring to the suggestion, Col. Tom Parker's office stated that, when Elvis was free to visit Britain, first consideration would be given to those seeking to book him four years ago.

Elvis back in the Army? The thought sent shivers round the fan world!

Weisbart with Gordon Douglas as director, it will have Anne Helm starring with Elvis.

This will be only her fourth film, and in the previous three she had minor roles. She was spotted while appearing in a *Route 66* TV show.

ELVIS K.O.'D

By Peter Wilson

All I can say is that if *Kid Galahad* is the way Elvis Presley fights, it's just as well he's got a voice – if only to call for help!

He's wider open than a barn door and the way he holds his right hand cocked ensures permanent injury – for himself.

And there is no need to worry about the terrible gash seen over his right eye in one scene. It looks to me as though his mascara has run!

THE FANS COME OUT FIGHTING!

In defence of Elvis

● I think Wilson's remarks about Elvis are disgusting, humiliating, outrageous and insulting.

It amazes me that someone so ignorant can criticise someone who is so talented. Not to put too fine a point on it ... I'M FURIOUS!
(Miss) H. Van-Roose, Leicester.

Elvis serenades co-star Anne Helm in Follow That Dream

MGM had plans for Elvis to play the legendary cowboy singer Hank Williams in a film around the time this photograph was taken in 1961

• We are very, very annoyed to read the criticism of our dream man and hero, Mr. Presley. If Mr. Wilson had half Elvis's looks, physique, talent and sex-appeal, we would not object to his remarks.

Elvis Admirers, Kettering, Northants.

• In hitting Elvis below the belt, Peter Wilson left himself wide open to the wrath of the greatest pop singer's fans.

Eleven Girl Fans, London, S.W.4.

• I think Elvis has got a bit of pluck to go into the ring. Other stars would employ a stand-in.

(Miss) I. Jones, London, S.W.11.

• I don't think it was very nice of Mr. Wilson to write the way he did about Elvis. You can't expect wonders from him.

(Miss) C. Hodgson, Woodford Green, Essex.

• We don't like the remarks about Elvis's mascara running. It doesn't run like that. We know. We are girls.

Three Loyal Fans, London, E.17.

• He may not be the world's best boxer, but even David Charnley and Henry Cooper have been known to leave themselves wide open. And they can't sing!

(Miss) S. Ives, Laindon, Essex.

Elvis the boxer in Kid Galahad

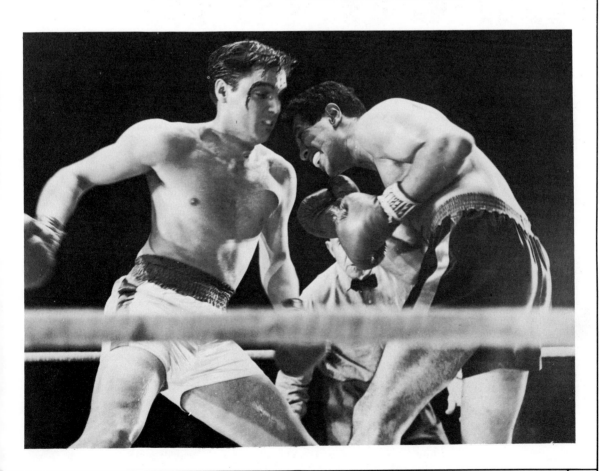

WE asked KO specialist, Bill Walker, to comment on th performance of Elvis as screen boxe Kid Galahad. It was a case of no hold barred. Billy supplied our phot captions and some frank comment

BILLY WALKER
HAS A RINGSIDE SEAT FOR
KID GALAHAD

I "Elvis has the build of a handy fighter but I can't say he looks like a boxer. He's too 'refined'. His nose is too straight and slim for a typical boxer—usually a boxer has a fleshy face and a pretty broad nose!"

HIS blond head bowed over a stack photos from the new Elvis fil Kid Galahad, rising young heav weight boxer Billy Walker pronounced : " This is one film I have to see."

Billy has the sort of looks which kno the girls for six. Televiewers have fall in a big way for this quiet-spoken six-foot with the frank open face and honest gr eyes. He has a smile which would sco heavily with Dr. Edith Summerskill. Sl is, of course, the MP who has conduct her own private " Ban the Boxing " car paign on the grounds that it is a cru sport. Billy's fresh-complexioned, unmark face and perfect teeth, hardly advertise h claims. He may be in a rough, tough wor but Billy is very much the boy next door, the boy next door happens to resemble Greek god !

If Billy Walker is risking his good loo to concentrate on good hooks, Elvis r similar risks during the filming of Galahad. The famous profile emerged u scathed only because The King prov more than able to defend himself. T local boxing pros., the De La Fuente brothe can still feel the humiliation of their fi ever ring defeats—at the hands of Elvis !

Elvis insisted on doing a boxer's quo of roadwork, punchbag, workouts and prote dieting during filming, helped by Mus Callahan, a former junior world welterweig champion.

Billy likes Elvis. It was natural th we should go to him for some commer

2 "Elvis' training equipment is authentic. The headguard and gloves are exactly the same as those I use. Incidentally, if you watch TV you might be interested to know that amateur boxers use 8 oz. gloves, while a professional fighter uses the lighter 6 oz."

3 "When I have a workout with the punchbag it isn't long before my hair is absolutely soaked with the effort, and it straggles over my forehead. Since Elvis has longer hair than I have, I assume that he's discovered some secret grooming method!"

the advance pictures from the film in ch Elvis enters Billy's world. What we 't expect to find was a gentle Billy ker at the home of his brother George, ling a toy poodle pup in the palm of his l! Its name was even more un-cted—Boo Boo! But Billy restored balance by pointing out that his own at home in Ilford, is more in keeping his profession—it's a boxer, natch! vis' weakness for poodles matches 's, but how does he compare with in the beefcake stakes? He has a er frame than the champ, weighing t thirteen pounds less than Billy's pact fourteen stone. But as far as nt goes, the boys are on level terms at foot. Whether they are level-pegging he romance stakes is another point. e Billy is ordered to forgo dating g training, Elvis met more than his e of lovelies on the *Kid Galahad* set. t it's Elvis' film all the way. Apart his acting and boxing, he fits in half ozen El-ectrifying numbers: *King of Whole Wide World, Riding the Rainbow, histlin' Tune, Home is Where The Heart Is, Lucky,* and *This Is Living.* And Elvis really *A Lotta Livin' To Do,* lately! ese two kids, Billy and Elvis—would change places? According to Billy, ing short of a million-dollar film con-would lure him from the square jungle ollywood. As for Elvis, he would find ry hard to sacrifice leisure hours with guitars and cars . . . in that order.

4 "This is the way to prepare for a fight—get out of town. When I'm in strict training, I often go down to a farm at Stanford-le-Hope in Essex. It's owned by my brother's father-in-law, and he lets me keep in shape felling trees and helping out with the livestock."

OVER ▶

BILLY WALKER
HAS A RINGSIDE SEAT FOR
KID GALAHAD—*cont.*

5 "The final pep talk, before you enter the ring, begins as your gloves are laced up by your manager. He tells you to watch this and watch that. By this time you're fed up with the long weeks of training, and can only think 'I'm free tomorrow'!"

6 "This could be the moment you've been thinking about through those long hours of training. At this point, Elvis looks much more like a fighter. If he's thinking like one, too, he'll be praying that the other fella doesn't get up!"

7 "Elvis wins, of course! The man on the left is obviously his 'second.' You probably recognise the swab and gum shield in his hands. The objects in his mouth are antiseptic eye swabs which are to stop blood flowing from cuts around the eyes."

8 "Elvis with co-star Joan Blackman. I can tell you that this is something a boxer rarely has the opportunity to do! While in strict training, this cosy sort of get-together is right OUT. And believe me, it's tough!"

● ● ● ● ● ● ● ● ● ●

more
ELVIS

This week FREE in *Valentine* there's a full colour portrait of Elvis specially painted by the great Continental artist Noiquet. It's fab. Get a copy at your newsagent now . . . if they're not all sold out!

PRESLEYMANIA – 1961

BAD SCRIPTS? Colonel Tom Parker gave this reasonable explanation as to why Elvis Presley never objects to his movie scripts: 'For the $500,000 a picture they're paying him, plus $5,000 a day overtime – they're going to offer Elvis a *bad* script?'
New Musical Express, 4 January

☆　☆　☆

TOUR OFF. Elvis Presley was supposed to do a 100-city personal appearance tour to ballyhoo his picture, *G.I. Blues*, but Paramount reluctantly cancelled the tour because so many local police officers refused to guarantee Elvis' safety. There are just so many fans who want to tear him apart in sheer adoration.
New York Journal American, 8 January

☆　☆　☆

DIAMOND STUDDED WATCH. RCA-Victor have presented Elvis Presley with a diamond-studded wrist watch. The back of the watch is engraved with Presley's combined sales figures for the past five years – 76 million discs.
Billboard, 20 January

☆　☆　☆

PIRATE TAPES. RCA-Victor could not understand why dealers in several States started to order the film album of *Flaming Star*, starring Elvis Presley, after saying they had heard it on their local radio stations, because as yet no copies of this LP have been pressed. They then found out that so great was the demand for this album that people had been taking portable tape recorders into the cinemas and taping the sound-track, which in turn they were selling to the small stations. This has now been stopped and anybody found doing this will be sued at once. Victor intend to bring out the album, but not until the sales of *G.I. Blues* have cooled down.
Disc, 24 January
[It was released in April, 1961.]

☆　☆　☆

PRESLEY & CROSBY? Producer George Stevens in huddle with Colonel Tom Parker for Elvis Presley to make cameo appearances in new Bing Crosby Film, *How The West Was Won*.
Variety, 4 February

☆　☆　☆

NO TELEVISION. Colonel Parker says he will keep Elvis Presley off TV screens as much as he can, although he gets fantastic offers every day. He feels that if Elvis's fans see him free on TV they won't be so anxious to pay at theatre box offices. Colonel Parker also got an offer of $50,000 a week for Elvis for the Dunes Hotel in Las Vegas. He didn't even bother to reply ...
Los Angeles Times, 11 February

☆　☆　☆

HAT-TRICK FOR ELVIS. Elvis Presley has at last scored the elusive British hit parade hat-trick which had previously eluded every artist. As his latest British release 'Wooden Heart' moves into the number one slot this week, Elvis clinches his third successive top-seller here, the previous two being 'Are You Lonesome Tonight?' and 'It's

Now Or Never'. Several artists have secured two consecutive No.1 hits – including Cliff Richard, Adam Faith, Russ Conway, Lonnie Donegan and Anthony Newley – but the third has eluded them all, until Elvis.

Melody Maker, 24 March

☆ ☆ ☆

NO VILLAIN ROLE. Colonel Tom Parker has vetoed MGM's idea that Elvis Presley should star in Tennessee Williams' *Sweet Bird of Youth*. The Colonel didn't think the role – definitely not a virtuous one – would be good for Elvis' reputation.

Billboard, 7 April

☆ ☆ ☆

THE THINGS KIDS DO. Elvis Presley finally had to arrange for a 24-hour guard for his hotel room when filming in Hawaii. Some fans pretended to be mail messengers with registered letters and others climbed into his room through the fire escape.

Daily Express, 12 June

☆ ☆ ☆

ELVIS THE PILOT. While in Memphis, Elvis Presley took a short flight in a Piper Comanche, passing over his home, Graceland, and handling the controls. After the landing, Elvis' instructor said, 'If he was afraid, he certainly didn't show it and he handled the plane nicely for the first time up.' Elvis himself commented, 'I might as well buy an airplane – I've got one of everything else!'

Memphis Commercial–Appeal, 26 June

☆ ☆ ☆

ELVIS AT YANKEETOWN. Despite reports that Elvis Presley was filming *Follow*

That Dream at Crystal River in Florida, in actual fact he was at a place called Yankeetown – playing a Southern Hillbilly!

Cashbox, 19 July

☆ ☆ ☆

ELVIS' TAXES. Asked recently why he didn't form a Corporation to avoid paying such enormous taxes, Elvis Presley said he felt the US government was entitled to what it got from him. He added, 'You can only spend so much – you can only live so much.'

Dallas Times, 7 August

☆ ☆ ☆

SUSPICIOUS CHARACTERS. On August 8, Sergeant W.L. Maley of the Memphis police force was called to the vicinity of Elvis Presley's home, Graceland, to check on some 'suspicious persons' reported loitering in the area. Sgt. Maley found the persons on Old Hickory Road, east of the Presley home, where they turned out to be men from the U.S. Department of Agriculture's Pest Control Division checking an outbreak of white-fringed beetles that feast on soybeans!

Memphis Press-Scimitar, 9 August

☆ ☆ ☆

PRESLEYTIZING. Parents of young people in Pakistan have taken to using the word 'Presleytizing' to describe the boisterous activities of their sons and daughters when dancing to Elvis Presley records or watching his films in cinemas …

Daily Telegraph, 14 September

☆ ☆ ☆

FLOOD AID. Elvis Presley's mentor, Colonel Tom Parker, offered the singer's services to the Governor of Louisiana for two large benefits being held to help flood victims in the state. Parker has also been negotiating for Presley to play the Seattle World Fair next year for $250,000. During negotiations, Parker was asked, 'Is there any room to negotiate on this price? 'Sure,' the Colonel answered, 'but only one way – up!' In case of rain, the Colonel says, he and Presley reserve the right to sell their one-dollar plastic umbrellas.

New York Times, 19 October

☆ ☆ ☆

PRICELESS CAR. While filming Elvis Presley's latest movie *Kid Galahad* on location in Hemet, about 100 miles from Hollywood, an assistant director tried to buy a 1923 Model T Ford from a local resident who refused all offers. But, said the owner, if her 14-year-old daughter could have lunch with Elvis Presley it was a deal. Watch for the Ford with Elvis on board chugging through Hemet!

New Musical Express, 29 November

☆ ☆ ☆

ELVIS – PRIZEFIGHTER! Colonel Tom Parker, Elvis Presley's manager, says boxing promoters have been calling him every day offering fights for his star since stories have leaked out about Presley's prowess in the ring in *Kid Galahad*. 'One guy in New York is offering $200,000 for one fight,' says the

One of the Christmas cards sent by Elvis and Colonel Tom Parker in 1961

Colonel, 'and a wrestling promoter in Miami is sending me registered letters by every post offering $150,000 for a one-night exhibition.'

New York Post, 5 December

☆ ☆ ☆

PRESLEY II. Competition for Elvis Presley? The name of a new recording star just launched in America is Gaylon Presley (no relation) …

New Musical Express, 7 December

☆ ☆ ☆

CHRISTMAS GREETINGS. According to reports, Colonel Tom Parker has ordered one million Christmas cards for himself and Elvis Presley to send out this Christmas …

Melody Maker, 19 December

1962

ELVIS
the KING
RETURNS

WIN : A WORL
DATE

EVEALING
S SHOCK
CRET

appearan
of Elvis

ELVIS PRESL

STAR OF STAGE, SCREEN, RADIO, RECORDS AND T

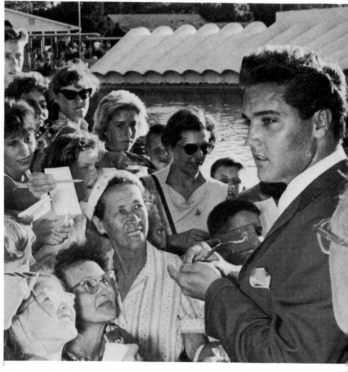

ELVIS PRESLEY MAY VISIT LONDON
"Evening News" Reporter

AMERICAN rock 'n' roll king, Elvis Presley, may come to London next year. He has been offered about £250,000 a Johannesburg to make 25 per ces in Euro

ELVIS

kissed me

ELVIS 50th ELVIS PRESLEY

CHART ENTR

The spring of 1962 found Elvis busy again in Hollywood recording and filming his next movie, Girls, Girls, Girls. *A visitor to Elvis' recording sessions was the British composer Bunny Lewis, who had written the singer's 1960 hit, 'Girl Of My Best Friend'. What he saw and heard while in Elvis' company formed the basis of the rather caustic article he wrote for* Reveille *in March 1962.*

WITH ELVIS IN HOLLYWOOD

By Bunny Lewis

While I was staying in Hollywood I met Elvis Presley. He sent his town and country sedan to meet me at the airport. Had I been a girl I would have merited the Rolls, he said.

His chauffeur-valet, Lamar Voigt took me to the studios where he was recording the sound track of a new picture *Girls, Girls, Girls,* to be made this month in Hawaii.

With him were the Jordanaires, Boots Randolf, a terrific honking tenor player, and D.J. Fontana, a not-so-terrific drummer – all from Nashville, Tennessee. The rest of the musicians included one of the world's great guitarists, Barney Kessel from California.

Presley had been recording solidly from midday to midnight for three days and I was most impressed by his perseverance after the right sound. Even in the recording studio I could easily tell what a terrific performer of this kind of music he is.

He alters things, tries new sounds and okays all takes.

He knows the sound he wants although not always coherent enough to get his message across.

Incidentally he has been dieting, has lost twenty pounds and looks terrific.

Whatever else I think about Elvis I bow to his professionalism in the studio.

The number of hangers-on is fantastic. There are never fewer than twelve in the recording booth, plus four superfluous characters in the studio itself.

In the corridor another eight of Elvis's entourage sat playing blackjack.

Two days later I went up to meet him in his home in Bel Air. It is like an annexe of Buckingham Palace. In the courtyard stood fourteen cars. If Elvis ever fails as an artist he can go straight into the second-hand car business.

The more notable of his models are: Rolls, Thunderbird, Lincoln, Chrysler and a new white Cadillac.

This last contains a TV set, a radio, a refrigerator, a make-up kit, two telephones and a record player – all gold plated. (NOW will you practice?)

Elvis has a personal entourage of about twelve, all on the payroll. These were all in the house at Bel Air.

With the exception of Lamar I never saw any of them doing anything other than play cards or shoot pool. They are there to keep Elvis company.

Also in attendance were a dozen or so of the most unattractive young girls it has been my misfortune to meet.

Average age about seventeen, scruffy and almost speechless, they sat around vacantly, presumably awaiting the arrival of the lord and master.

The boys ignored them.

We were joined by Elvis's father and stepmother who proved about the only sensible people in the whole set-up, charming and unaffected.

By this time it was 10 p.m. and as Elvis had not got up – he sleeps all day unless filming and never rises before 6 p.m. – I wandered around the house.

I was horrified to hear demoniacal screams coming from the bowels of it.

I wondered if it had all been too much for one of the girls, who had flipped her lid. But

Alan, one of the entourage, assured me all was well and took me down to the cellars.

Here we found a poor gibbering chimpanzee crying with loneliness and screaming its head off. This was the newest addition to the household.

It obviously loved Alan and was most friendly until we left when it started screaming again.

Since, by now, it was ten-thirty and I had to catch a plane at midnight. I retired from this crazy household.

Making some great sounds – Elvis with musicians on the Hollywood set of Girls, Girls, Girls

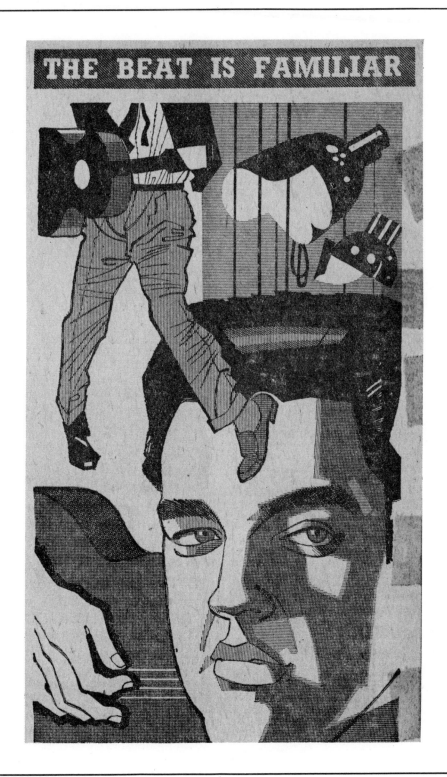

Even before Elvis had finished work on Girls, Girls, Girls *speculation was again rife about future projects for the star. Perhaps the most unusual of this or any other period of his life was the idea of him playing the part of his manager, Colonel Tom Parker, as suggested in this report from the* New Musical Express *of 5 May!*

ELVIS PRESLEY MAY FILM MANAGER'S LIFE STORY

MGM wants Elvis Presley to star in a film based on the colourful life of his manager, Colonel Tom Parker. The project is being discussed in Hollywood with the studio, which recently signed Elvis for four films.

Called *Right This Way Folks*, the story would be a dramatic one tracing the colonel's career since he was a fairground barker in Tampa, Florida.

Parker is this week doing research for *Right This Way Folks* at the Florida State Fair.

A similar event – at Seattle – will be the scene of another Presley film which goes into production this year, *Take Me To The Fair*. Ted Richmond will produce.

Presley's first film under the MGM deal will be a romantic comedy, *Mister, Will You Marry Me*.

Producer Jack Cummings is now working on the script in co-operation with Luther Davis.

Production will begin this summer, and several new songs will be featured. The setting will cover the harbour, night clubs and beach resorts around San Diego, California.

Busier than ever, Presley also has a commitment this spring for the Paramount romantic comedy, *Cumbo Ya-Ya*. This is one of a number of projects for which he is under a long-term contract to Hal Wallis.

'Cumbo Ya-Ya,' a Creole expression meaning 'Everybody talks at once,' will have Elvis playing the skipper of a fishing boat. Like *Blue Hawaii* it will give him ample opportunity to sing and dance.

On 22 May, the Daily Mirror *published the results of a nationwide poll it had conducted among younger readers to find out the person they would most like to meet – and thereby started a series of stories that ran for the rest of the year about whether or not Elvis would ever visit Britain. The poll revealed that Elvis had taken third place behind the Queen and the Duke of Edinburgh. But when the Mirror's sister paper, the* Sunday Pictorial, *followed up this verdict and demanded in a banner headline,* ELVIS WHY DO YOU SNUB US?, *tempers and pens flared throughout the country for several weeks. Nor was this the end of the controversy. For in September it was announced that a package deal had been put together to try and lure Elvis across the Atlantic – followed by news that he had actually been invited to appear on the* Royal Variety Show. *Though neither deal materialized, they further emphasized the passionate desire of fans outside America to see the King in person, as the cuttings here underline ...*

Left: Cartoon tribute to Elvis from the Daily Mirror, *24 March*

THE ROYALS ARE YOUR FAVOURITES

With 'The King' Third!

One of the questions in the *Mirror's* massive inquiry to discover the verdict of youth on the Royal Family was:

'Which of this list of people in the news would you most like to meet?'

This was the result:

		Per cent.
1	The Queen	21
2	Prince Philip	15
3	Elvis Presley	13
4	Albert Schweitzer	12
5	President Kennedy	9
6	Acker Bilk	4
7	Bertrand Russell	4
8	Elizabeth Taylor	3
9	Lord Montgomery	3
10	Helen Shapiro	2

Daily Mirror 22 May

ELVIS, WHY DO YOU SNUB US?

Elvis Presley has just given Britain a king-sized snub. He refuses to set foot on these shores.

And that's in spite of the fact that he has just been voted by thousands of Daily Mirror readers as the personality they would most like to meet after the Queen and Prince Philip.

Elvis also refused to meet two winners of a nation-wide Presley popularity competition that was to have been organised by the British representatives of his latest film, *Follow That Dream*.

Plane trip

United Artistes Film Corporation offered the winners a plane trip to Hollywood, coinciding with the West End release of this film, followed by a luxury weekend which including a meeting with Elvis.

But Elvis, it seems, couldn't be bothered.

Tom Diskin, the Pelvis's representative, told me by phone from Hollywood:

'You gotta realise that Elvis is a very busy man.

'**Maybe he could spare a few moments later in the year to see somebody from Britain, but at the present he's kinda tied up.**'

I told Mr Diskin that British pop fans were also very busy people, but they find time to join the Presley Adoration Society and go out to buy his records by the million.

So why can't Elvis spare a few moments to say hello to a couple of prizewinners, or come over here and say thanks?

'Waal,' said Diskin, 'Elvis sure is busy.'

Hope?

I pointed out: 'Frank Sinatra is busy, but he's due here next week to give charity concerts for the people who helped to make him rich.'

'Waal,' came the reply, 'Sinatra isn't making so many films as Elvis.'

'**Elvis hasn't time for personal appearances. He's real busy.**'

'Is there any hope of Elvis coming to Britain, if only for a fleeting visit?'

'Waal,' said Mr Diskin, 'he's real busy.'

I asked Mr Diskin to give me a straight answer to a straight question.

'Waal,' he replied.

'Yes or no?' I insisted.

'Waal,' said Mr Diskin.

'Oh waal,' I said – and hung up.

Sunday Pictorial
27 May

ELVIS – HERE SOON?

Mystery 'Phone Call

Here's a startling tip-off suggesting that Elvis Presley may shortly make a concert appearance in Britain. It comes not from London's Tin Pan Alley pundits, but from Elvis himself via the *South Wales Echo*!

This newspaper publishes an account of a telephone call Elvis made to a Cardiff girl,

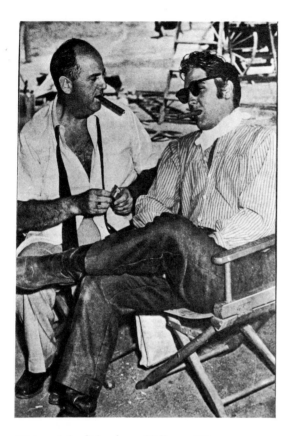

Elvis and the Colonel on a Hollywood film set

Elizabeth Davies. Elvis was apparently recording telephone conversations made at random with British fans for an American radio broadcast.

In the course of the conversation, Elvis is reported as saying he was coming to London's Albert Hall 'in the near future.' He said he would send Elizabeth complimentary tickets.

Elizabeth has since received a parcel containing all of Elvis's recent recordings.

So far, there has been no confirmation that Elvis intends to sing in Britain. He has previously said he won't sing here for several years.

New Record Mirror
10 November

ELVIS PRESLEY WAS INVITED TO ROYAL SHOW

Elvis Presley was invited to take in next Monday's *Royal Variety Show*, but had to refuse because of his film commitments for MGM's *Take Me To The Fair*.

The company stand to lose heavily if anything happens to Elvis' life or fitness.

The invitation to Presley – at one time denied by a spokesman for the organisers – was confirmed this week by Arthur Scott, secretary of the Variety Artists' Benevolent Fund, the benefiting charity.

According to Dorothy Romero, editor of the Hollywood-based *Elvis Mirror*, Presley received a telegram from London on September 24, and replied that he would have been willing to appear had circumstances permitted.

His manager, Colonel Parker, said: 'We have pointed out to newspapers that call us that it is true we have not been able to make personal appearances in Britain, but it is also true we have not appeared elsewhere.

'Through a motion picture, millions see Elvis; through a personal appearance a very small fraction would see him. We are thinking in terms of the many rather than the few.'

Presley's film boxing drama, *Kid Galahad* may have its West End showing delayed. This is because of the success of *Dr. No* at the London Pavilion.

The Presley film may not open now until November 16.

Far away from all the controversy, working in Hollywood, Elvis ended 1962 filming his twelfth movie, It Happened at the World's Fair. *This moment, in fact, was to mark the start of a new era in stylish dressing for Elvis who had a whole new line of clothes designed and made for him by the famous Hollywood tailor, Sy Devore. The*

IF EL CAME?

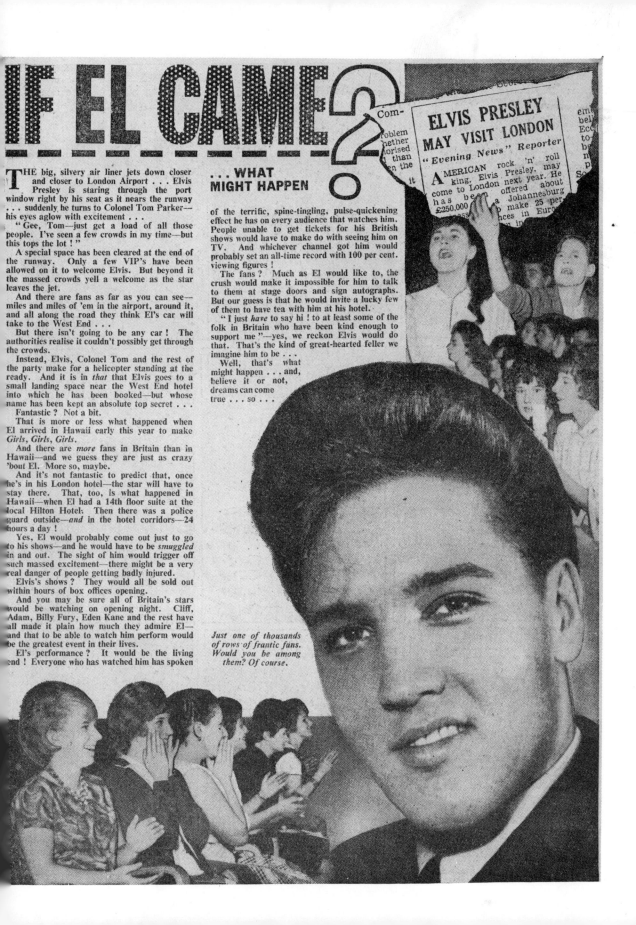

THE big, silvery air liner jets down closer and closer to London Airport ... Elvis Presley is staring through the port window right by his seat as it nears the runway ... suddenly he turns to Colonel Tom Parker—his eyes aglow with excitement ...

"Gee, Tom—just get a load of all those people. I've seen a few crowds in my time—but this tops the lot!"

A special space has been cleared at the end of the runway. Only a few VIP's have been allowed on it to welcome Elvis. But beyond it the massed crowds yell a welcome as the star leaves the jet.

And there are fans as far as you can see—miles and miles of 'em in the airport, around it, and all along the road they think El's car will take to the West End ...

But there isn't going to be any car! The authorities realise it couldn't possibly get through the crowds.

Instead, Elvis, Colonel Tom and the rest of the party make for a helicopter standing at the ready. And it is in *that* that Elvis goes to a small landing space near the West End hotel into which he has been booked—but whose name has been kept an absolute top secret ...

Fantastic? Not a bit.

That is more or less what happened when El arrived in Hawaii early this year to make *Girls, Girls, Girls.*

And there are *more* fans in Britain than in Hawaii—and we guess they are just as crazy 'bout El. More so, maybe.

And it's not fantastic to predict that, once he's in his London hotel—the star will have to stay there. That, too, is what happened in Hawaii—when El had a 14th floor suite at the local Hilton Hotel. Then there was a police guard outside—*and* in the hotel corridors—24 hours a day!

Yes, El would probably come out just to go to his shows—and he would have to be *smuggled* in and out. The sight of him would trigger off such massed excitement—there might be a very real danger of people getting badly injured.

Elvis's shows? They would all be sold out within hours of box offices opening.

And you may be sure all of Britain's stars would be watching on opening night. Cliff, Adam, Billy Fury, Eden Kane and the rest have all made it plain how much they admire El—and that to be able to watch him perform would be the greatest event in their lives.

El's performance? It would be the living end! Everyone who has watched him has spoken

... WHAT MIGHT HAPPEN

of the terrific, spine-tingling, pulse-quickening effect he has on every audience that watches him. People unable to get tickets for his British shows would have to make do with seeing him on TV. And whichever channel got him would probably set an all-time record with 100 per cent. viewing figures!

The fans? Much as El would like to, the crush would make it impossible for him to talk to them at stage doors and sign autographs. But our guess is that he would invite a lucky few of them to have tea with him at his hotel.

"I just *have* to say hi! to at least some of the folk in Britain who have been kind enough to support me"—yes, we reckon Elvis would do that. That's the kind of great-hearted feller we imagine him to be ...

Well, that's what might happen ... and, believe it or not, dreams can come true ... so ...

Just one of thousands of rows of frantic fans. Would you be among them? Of course.

stylist to the stars talked about his work to Jonah Ruddy in an interesting article reprinted here. Equally interesting was the news published by the New Musical Express on 21 December that Elvis' latest disc, 'Return to Sender' had become his fiftieth chart entry. The publication applauded the fact that he had now achieved thirteen number one hits – nine of these in the two years since he had left the Army! – and had occupied the top spot for a total of fifty-two weeks, the equivalent to having been on top of the charts for a whole year of the seven years in which he had been in show business. No mean achievement, the NME concluded, for an artist who had never been seen in person in Britain!

A very stylish-looking Elvis facing a father with a shotgun during a scene in It Happened at the World's Fair

PRESLEYMANIA – 1962

ELVIS RIPS IT UP! Thailand may ban Elvis Presley movies as a result of a ruckus that occurred at a recent screening there of *Blue Hawaii* …

New Musical Express, 5 January

☆   ☆   ☆

CAR CHARGE. Colonel Tom Parker is charging admission to an exhibit of the fantabulous car he gave Elvis for Christmas. The car has everything from TV to phone to a record player to a bed in it! The money taken in will be donated to charity.

Melody Maker, 6 January

☆   ☆   ☆

ELVIS ON CENSORSHIP. Asked about censorship, Elvis Presley said recently: 'Censorship is a joke, although I have obeyed it. The movement I did – that everyone who is supposed to know what's right objected to – was eliminated from my early movies. Now everyone is doing it, only more exaggeratedly, and they call it 'The Twist'! Some of the people I have seen doing it should not be doing it – they are vulgar.' (Elvis apparently watched twisters at Las Vegas Thunderbird Lounge, but wouldn't join in.)

Billboard, 12 January

☆   ☆   ☆

PERFECT RELATIONSHIP. Columnist Hedda Hopper reveals: 'Colonel Tom Parker and Elvis Presley have a perfect working relationship. When the day's work ends, they go their separate ways. They've had dinner together twice in the last six years. The colonel doesn't check on Elvis' private life.'

Los Angeles Times, 19 February

Friday, November 9, 1962

JONAH RUDDY sends more information about

NEW WARDROBE FOR ELVIS

"WE'LL give Elvis a new wardrobe for this film, and have him look like a smart, well-dressed young business man. It's a switch from sports shirt and blue jeans and sports jackets," said the producer of "Take Me To The Fair" at Metro-Goldwyn-Mayer Studios, Mr. Presley's third movie for 1962.

Accordingly Sy Devore, the master-tailor of show business stars, was given the assignment of equipping Elvis with his new wardrobe.

For the last Presley film, "Girls! Girls! Girls!", the Devore organisation had provided Mr. Presley with three raw-silk jackets and several pairs of black silk trousers.

"It was decided to make this wardrobe as a sort of surprise for him," Sy Devore told me.

"I had his measurements and I engaged an actor who is his exact size and weight to stand in for his fittings.

"We then took the wardrobe to the studio and all I can say is that Elvis flipped when he saw it. He tried on the clothes and they were almost a perfect fit. He looked marvellous in them and I'll tell you why. He has a natural flair for wearing well-fitting clothes."

Mr. Devore gave me the cost of the clothes in dollars, but to bring it to Savile Row standards, I've calculated the equivalent in guineas.

There were, therefore, ten suits at 100 guineas each; four sports coats at 75 guineas each; 30 specially designed shirts with a deep collar and narrowed cuffs, at eight guineas each; 15 pairs of slacks at 25 guineas a pair, and six dozen ties at three guineas each!

The trousers Elvis Presley wears have to be specially designed. It seems that he wears no underwear, not even briefs.

All his jackets have to be designed to allow for freedom of movement.

He wears boots, not shoes. They are of the short Wellington kind, called Continental Gaiters in Hollywood.

In "Take Me To The Fair," Elvis plays a pilot who gets romantically involved with a lovely girl at the

——— BY SPECIAL REQUEST ———

LETTER TO THE EDITOR.—A little while ago, in Nat Hentoff's column, we read a little about Elvis' new wardrobe. Could you get us more information?—10 EP Fans, Hackney.

*　　　　*　　　　*

MEMO FROM EDITOR TO JONAH RUDDY IN HOLLYWOOD: Please send more information on Elvis' wardrobe.

ELVIS (in part of his new wardrobe) signs autographs at the Seattle World Fair, watched by Colonel TOM PARKER.

Seattle World Fair.

So Mr. Devore designed a special black leather jacket which he wears while piloting his plane. It is probably the world's most expensive leather jacket. It cost 80 guineas, and is entirely hand made.

Mr. Devore considers this film marks the beginning of a new era for Elvis Presley. "He will take his place amongst America's well-dressed men," he assured me. "I consider

this is my greatest styling achievement since I persuaded Bing Crosby to give up his incredible, chromat sports shirts and trousers whic didn't match at all."

The nice thing is that Sy Devo. uses the finest British materials fo his suits, jackets and trousers.

Thus Elvis is sporting fine suitin from Huddersfield, Bradford and West of England in "Take M The Fair."

ELVIS 50th CHART ENTRY!

1. Heartbreak Hotel...2nd
2. Blue Suede Shoes..9th
3. I Want You, I Need You, I Love You.............................14th
4. Hound Dog...1st
5. Blue Moon...9th
6. Love Me Tender...11th
7. I Don't Care If The Sun Don't Shine............................23rd
8. Mystery Train..25th
9. Rip It Up..27th
10. Too Much...6th
11. All Shook Up...1st (7 weeks)
12. Teddy Bear...3rd
13. Paralysed..8th
14. Party..2nd
15. Got A Lot O' Livin' To Do....................................17th
16. Loving You...24th
17. Tryin' To Get To You..16th
18. Lawdy Miss Clawdy...15th
19. Santa Bring My Baby Back To Me.................................7th
20. I'm Left, You're Right, She's Gone............................21st
21. Jailhouse Rock...1st (3 weeks)
22. Jailhouse Rock EP...18th
23. Don't..2nd
24. Wear My Ring Around Your Neck..................................3rd
25. Hard Headed Woman...2nd
26. King Creole..2nd
27. I Got Stung/One Night.......................................1st (3 weeks)
28. A Fool Such As I/I Need Your Love Tonight...................1st (5 weeks)
29. A Big Hunk O' Love..4th
30. Strictly Elvis EP...26th
This marked the end of the first phase of Elvis' career, when he was drafted into the Services. The remaining 20 best-sellers are from his post-Army period :
31. Stuck On You...2nd
32. Elvis Is Back LP...17th
33. A Mess Of Blues...3rd
34. The Girl Of My Best Friend....................................6th
35. It's Now Or Never...1st (9 weeks)
36. G.I. Blues LP..25th
37. Are You Lonesome Tonight...................................1st (5 weeks)
38. Wooden Heart...1st (3 weeks)
39. Surrender..1st (4 weeks)
40. Wild In The Country..1st (1 week)
41. I Feel So Bad..20th
42. His Latest Flame..1st (3 weeks)
43. Little Sister..18th
44. Rock-A-Hula Baby...2nd
45. Can't Help Falling In Love....................................3rd
46. Good Luck Charm..1st (5 weeks)
47. Follow That Dream EP...11th
48. She's Not You...1st (3 weeks)
49. Kid Galahad EP...15th
50. Return To Sender...1st

☆　☆　☆

MONKEY BUSINESS. If 'Scatter', Elvis Presley's pet chimpanzee, doesn't give the okay nod to a date, the lady is never asked for a return engagement. 'Scatter' rides along with Elvis in his new car in a seat made specially for him.

Hollywood Reporter, 30 March

☆　☆　☆

PRESLEY'S FAN-AMPLIFIER. Elvis Presley's new Cadillac has a loudspeaker on the outside so that he can address his fans as the spirit moves him.

Daily Express, 13 April

CRICKET RACKET. Crickets, thousands of them, made life miserable for director Gordon Douglas on location during the filming of Elvis Presley's latest movie *Follow That Dream* for United Artists. Each time Presley started acting, the crickets, almost in unison, would set up a loud buzzing noise, entirely drowning out the dialogue. 'What's making these crickets act like this?' asked exasperated director Douglas. 'Maybe they're Pat Boone fans,' grinned Presley.

Daily Mirror, 25 May

☆　☆　☆

BYE, BYE ELVIS. Colonel Tom Parker has asked £750,000 for Elvis Presley to star in film, *Bye, Bye Birdie*, reports Mike Connolly. 'You must agree Presley puts everything in writhing [sic],' the columnist adds.

Hollywood Reporter, 18 May

☆　☆　☆

UNDERSTANDING ELVIS. Elvis Presley says: 'To understand me, I guess a person would have to know how I grew up. For instance, I remember my first pay cheque and how I spent it. I used it to pay a bill at a clothing store. After school I worked as an usher at a theatre and even before I'd been paid the first time I went into a store and charged some clothes. Fancy shirts.'

Movie Life, June

☆　☆　☆

NO PART FOR FATHER. Elvis Presley's father, Vernon Presley, wanted a small part in his son's new picture, *Follow That Dream*, now shooting. Colonel Tom Parker handled the negotiations. 'How much do you want?' the producer asked. 'Fifty thousand dollars,' the Colonel answered. Consequence: no appearance by Presley snr. in the movie.

Cashbox, 19 July

SCHOLARSHIP DONATION. Once again this year, Elvis Presley is making a $1,000 scholarship donation to a deserving child at the annual charity field day for handicapped children at Boston, Massachusetts.

Daily Mail, 2 August

☆ ☆ ☆

READING POLITICS. Elvis Presley, who used to describe karate as his main hobby, has recently been reading extensively, and is particularly interested in politics ...

New Musical Express, 29 August

☆ ☆ ☆

ELVIS IN THE UK. Recording star Roy Orbison, a close friend of Elvis Presley, says, 'When Elvis became popular he got so big that by the time the offers came round from England he couldn't take them. Once you get into the movie star category it's a different situation. You are working to a tight schedule and very little free time is allowed. But with

Elvis I think it is a sincere thing and I believe he will come for a visit – though I don't think he will perform, because he doesn't even perform at home.'

Record Mirror, 6 September

☆ ☆ ☆

THE PRICE OF BEING ELVIS. A short while ago, Elvis Presley and his manager, Colonel Tom Parker were walking around the gardens of Elvis' luxurious Memphis home, Graceland, when they spotted a man filling a suitcase with leaves from the trees on the estate. When asked what he was doing, the man replied, 'The folks in New York will pay $10 for Presley leaves!'

Disc, 20 October

☆ ☆ ☆

ELVIS THE RECORD KING. A recent survey of Elvis Presley's continuing success in the record market indicates that his discs annually account for ten per cent of RCA-Victor's entire business and have grossed $150,000,000 so far.

New York Daily News, 3 December

1963

ELVIS the KING RETURNS

WIN · A WORD
· DATE

EVEALING
S SHOCK'
CRET

appearan
of Elvis

ELVIS PRESL

STAR OF STAGE, SCREEN, RADIO, RECORDS AND T

**ELVIS PRESLEY
MAY VISIT LONDON**

"Evening News" Reporter

AMERICAN rock 'n' roll king, Elvis Presley, may come to London next year. He has been offered about £250,000 a Johannesburg to make 25 per ances in Euro

ELVIS ARMY

ELVIS

kissed me

ELVIS 50th

RESLEY — that's all we had at the ele on ELVIS

ELVIS PRESLEY

CHART ENT

The year began for Elvis with a flood of stories that he was becoming a recluse, rarely seen in public, and totally committed to films and the occasional recording session. Prominent among these reports was one in The New York Times *of 21 January which read: 'Elvis is never seen at public restaurants or night clubs, never attends star-studded premieres, and is completely out of the social whirl.' The newspaper also quoted a Presley 'associate' who said, 'Elvis has become more and more of a recluse. He makes his three movies a year in Hollywood and while there keeps to himself in his Bel-Air mansion. The minute shooting is finished he heads back to Memphis.' Typical of the newspaper and magazine stories which appeared at this time and found their way into the pages of the scrapbooks is the* New Record Mirror *report, 'Is Elvis Becoming A Hermit?' reproduced here. While some of the facts are undoubtedly correct, the reporter's persistence in describing Elvis' home as being in Nashville does throw a question mark over much of the rest of the speculation!*

Fans worried that Elvis might be turning into a Howard Hughes figure, were assured their hero was alive and well and still enjoying life in his actual home town of Memphis by a letter to a rival pop newspaper, the New Musical Express, *from Valerie Escrett, an English girl living in the same town. It appeared in the issue of 19 April and read as follows:*

ELVIS: GETTING AROUND IN STYLE!

Dear NME Readers:

You will be interested to know that Elvis is home and has been seen around on his motor-bike, which he finds much easier to manoeuvre through the traffic. He goes out in a yachting cap, a navy-blue polka dot shirt, slim continental-style black trousers and thick leather boots.

His motor-bike is a powerful one with a headlight, two spotlights and two side-lights on the front of it and has, of course, a windscreen and two wing mirrors.

It also has a very comfortable pillion seat on which Priscilla Baileau, an 18-year-old girl whom he met when he was in the Army in Germany and who is the daughter of a US Army officer, has been a frequent passenger.

Elvis has told us that Priscilla is attending the Immaculate Conception High School in Memphis and is staying at Gracelands as a guest of his father, Vernon Presley, who is a great friend of her father's. Priscilla's family are coming back to the States soon, but until then, she will stay at the Presley mansion.

Naturally the Press is trying to link Priscilla and Elvis romantically, but about this Elvis said last week: 'As soon as they see us together, people say "This is it." But my comment is that I am still undecided about marriage, as it would be unfair to any girl. I am far too busy making movies to think of it.'

Elvis is thinner due to the fact that he lost about a stone in weight while making 'Fun In Acapulco.'

Elvis is happy about this, as he felt he was getting far too plump and admitted that when he made *Kid Galahad* he weighed only one pound under 14 stone!

Elvis has been amusing Memphis friends by revealing that he had a letter recently, suggesting that his film parts were too tame. 'A well-wisher said I should get drunk or do something colourful in my pictures, but the

IS ELVI

NASHVILLE they say is the heart of C & W music. It is also more or less the home of Elvis, who has bought a house large enough to be called a mansion just outside it.

It is surrounded by a wall, and nobody but nobody is let near it. Quite rightly so, of course, for in his earlier days Elvis had more fans on the rampage after him than anyone else. He still gets these fans on the lookout for him, but they don't get much of a chance now.

SECRET

For the truth is that Elvis is virtually becoming a hermit. Apart from visits to the recording studios, and to his other homes in various places, El. seldom ventures outside his two homes, the one in Nashville, and the other in Bel Air.

That is of course apart from the frequent visits to Hollywood for the making of his many motion pictures.

His private life is something kept completely secret—his love life is virtually unknown. Reports that he is secretly married still keep cropping up. They are of course completely unfounded. Elvis and **Tom Parker** know better than that —and also Elvis makes a point not to date the femmes from his own field of entertainment.

He has found in the past to his own cost that they talk too much. Many a young starlet has had the sudden door slammed metaphorically in her face after talking just a little too much to a reporter from one of the more lurid mags that Hollywood thrives on.

Elvis himself, say some of his closest friends, has grown sick of being mobbed everywhere he goes.

So he has built his own private world, surrounded himself with his friends and the things he likes best, and apart from business he keeps very much to himself.

There is no need for El. to go on stage dates or touring, simply because

he doesn't need the money. You [ ] blame him for wanting to keep hi[ ] to himself.

Or can you . . .

Some fans say he is taking it to[ ] In the States teenage girls are posedly sent crying away from his [ ] In Britain the perpetual fruitless about 'why doesn't Elvis come here' still goes on.

And all the time Elvis sits at hom[ ] plays with his pet monkey.

He still earns more money tha[ ] other 'pop' singer—probably even than Sinatra, the only other singer income can match his.

But let's look at the whole from Elvis' point of view.

For six long years he has bee[ ] world's top singing star. For th[ ] those he has gradually been earnin[ ] respect of the older generation unti[ ] he is accepted by them.

His style of singing has mature[ ] his looks have been toned down. [ ] is still pursued by the fans who [ ] be content with his discs and wi[ ] films.

PLEASURE

Elvis gives pleasure to millio[ ] people but many of them want h[ ] give them more.

They don't realise here in Britai[ ] the fans in the States are as distan[ ] him as we are here, and that th[ ] likely to remain that way.

His fans want him to do thing[ ] themselves would not think of Why should the biggest singing s[ ] the world continually make the [ ] of tours like a young up and comi[ ]

The answer is he should not. Al[ ] Elvis is making a hermit of hims[ ] has a right to. For in those seve[ ] years he has been on the scene [ ] worked hard enough to merit a r[ ] long one.

So let him rest, fans. . . .

BECOMING A HERMIT ?

WESLEY
LAINE
takes a
look at the
continued
non-
appearance
of Elvis
... both
in Britain
and in the
States . . . .

ELVIS: A still from "FOLLOW THAT DREAM". Is he in real life forced to live in a dream world to ensure some rest?

type I am making now are doing so well it would be silly to change the formula,' he said.

Elvis has been relaxing in Memphis and one of the best ways to do it is to watch films. Two that he has recently been most enthusiastic about are *Lawrence of Arabia* and *To Kill A Mockingbird* (for which Gregory Peck won the 'Best Actor' Academy Award).

Elvis arrived in Memphis in his mobile bus that can sleep eight, which means that he can bring his entire retinue with him and can avoid flying – which he fears.

Valerie Escrett
Memphis

While Elvis was making the first of his 1963 films, Fun In Acapulco, *a production assistant named John del Valle who had worked on all the pictures he had made for Paramount, published a fascinating account of what a typical week in the star's life was like. The article was reprinted in both America and Britain and provided an interesting insight into Elvis the actor.*

A WEEK FILMING WITH ELVIS

Elvis Presley pulled the small calendar bearing his picture out of his pocket.

'Looks like another busy week ahead.' He smiled, crossing off another day on the calendar, a replica of those sent to all members of the Presley fan clubs.

Elvis was too modest to say all his weeks are busy, especially when he's at work in Hollywood.

Here's a typical week, taken during his recent filming of the colourful and tune-filled *Fun In Acapulco.*

Monday

7 a.m. finds Elvis turning off the alarm and burying his head under the covers for a few minutes' more sleep.

'I just hate to get up on Mondays,' he admits. 'But once I'm on my feet I feel fine.'

By 8 a.m., Elvis has showered and dressed, gulped down toast and coffee, and is ready to be driven to the studio.

A shiny, black 1962 Rolls-Royce is standing in the circular drive of the Bel Air mansion Elvis rents while he's in Hollywood. At the wheel is Allan Fortas, one of Elvis's friends from Tennessee, who takes care of all the Presley automobiles. Elvis sits in the rear seat, while five of his friends and employees from home jump in to accompany him to work.

Elvis is quiet on the 35-minute drive to Paramount Studios in Hollywood.

'Usually I like to look out the window and enjoy the scenery,' he explains, 'but most Mondays I feel I should be concentrating on the script.'

At 8.35, the beautiful car pulls into the De Mille Gate of the studio. Elvis waves to the guard and the car slows down to the pre-scribed seven miles per hour to drive Elvis to his dressing-room. There, a make-up man is already waiting to put on the necessary tan make-up which Elvis needs for his role as a singing sailor who gets fired off a private yacht in Acapulco.

Director Richard Thorpe holds out his hand as Elvis walks on to Stage 14 and says, 'I hope you're feeling good, boy. You'll be working hard today.'

Elvis grins, and says, 'Oh, yes, sir I'm ready.'

On the day's agenda is a fight sequence. Elvis and a stuntman standing in for one of the other actors in the film are due to slug it out in a brawl.

From 9.15 until noon, Elvis and the stuntman work carefully, punching each other as tourists scream and the furniture collapses.

Elvis and the boys drive back to the dressing-room for lunch and another change of clothes.

One hour later, Elvis is back, ready to

resume fighting – they finish up their fight scenes exactly at 5.30, half an hour earlier than scheduled. Elvis, the stuntman and their director all shake hands and leave.

As the car passes the gate on the way home, it pauses momentarily for the Presley fans waiting outside to get a glimpse of their hero. Box cameras go clicking madly, and Elvis waves as the car speeds off.

Elvis arrives back at the mansion at 6.45. He and the boys have dinner on trays in the living-room, where they all watch TV. At 10 p.m., Elvis excuses himself to go to his

A revealing behind-the-camera photograph of director Richard Thorpe filming a scene for Fun in Acapulco

bedroom. There, he plays records, mostly spirituals, while he goes over his lines for the next day's filming. At 12.15, the lights in his bedroom go out, Elvis' least favourite day, Monday, is over.

Tuesday

Elvis wakes up promptly at 7 a.m., showers, dresses, has a leisurely breakfast, and once again arrives at Stage 14 on time.

The morning and afternoon have love scenes on the schedule. Elvis joins beautiful Mexican actress Elsa Cardenas in a small sports car parked on the set in front of a panorama of the Acapulco Bay.

In the film, the gentle Elsa plays an aggressive lady bullfighter. Her part in the day's filming calls for her to romance Elvis. But Elvis plays hard to get (in the film, at least), and finally poor Elsa is forced to kiss him. 'I'll bet there are a million girls who wish they were here right now,' she tells Elvis with a laugh.

The scenes go on all day, and because camera trouble causes numerous delays, Elvis doesn't arrive home until almost 7 p.m. Elvis and the boys eat dinner and then go into the spacious billiard room, where they play pool until 11.30.

Wednesday

Elvis oversleeps. 'I don't know what happened,' he declares. 'I guess I turned off the alarm in my sleep!' At 8.15, the boys begin pounding on his bedroom door, and a worried Elvis dresses 'faster than I ever did before' and rushes to the studio.

He's on the set at 9.10 apologising for any delay he caused. 'Actually, it doesn't matter today, Elvis,' Director Thorpe says kindly. 'If you'll look at your shooting schedule more closely, you'll see we aren't going to begin work until 9.30!'

Elvis quickly takes his place on the set and at 9.30, when the cameras start turning, he's ready to sing 'Margarita,' in the setting of a beautiful nightclub.

All day Wednesday, Elvis sings and flirts with Ursula at her table.

At 6 p.m. that night, Elvis leaves the studio, pausing a moment, as usual, to wave to his fans. Again, pool is the entertainment of the evening.

Thursday

When Elvis arrives for work, he finds himself in a new setting. He, Ursula and her film father, Paul Lukas, are gathered in the kitchen of the Acapulco Hilton Hotel. As chef of the hotel, Lukas is testing vichysoisse. Elvis? He has a rendezvous with Ursula. Elvis, Ursula and Lukas trade lines all that morning.

That afternoon, as Elvis relaxes between scenes, one of the middle-aged extras approaches him. Elvis looks up politely and smiles.

'Did you get that picture for me yet, Elvis?' the man asks.

'Yes, sir,' Elvis says graciously.

Like hundreds of others with whom Elvis has worked, the man wants a specially-autographed picture of 'The King' for one of his children.

'Don't these interruptions bother you?' someone asks with an amused smile. 'No, they certainly don't,' Elvis answered quietly, but firmly. 'It's when they don't ask, I'll be bothered!'

That evening, Elvis stays in his bedroom after dinner, making telephone calls to several of the girls he dates when he's in Hollywood. Then he plays records, studies his script, and falls asleep just after midnight.

Friday

Elvis is in good spirits as he's driven along Sunset Boulevard to the studio, this time in a white Chrysler station waggon. Elvis is smiling and happy as he looks out at the beautiful homes along the wide street in Beverly Hills.

That morning, he works for three hours in another nightclub scene in which both Ursula and Elsa are seated in the audience. Elvis sings a new song, 'Which Way Do I Turn?' as he ponders how to get out of what might prove to be an embarrassing situation. Finally, he manages to send word to Ursula to meet him outside, and he escapes through a window to get away from his ever-present lady bullfighter.

For a time Elvis wanted to be a professional American footballer and here he demonstrates his skill at the game!

That night, Elvis throws a party, inviting some of the girls he and his friends like to date. The group listen to records, watch a movie and talk. The party doesn't break up until 2 a.m., and Elvis doesn't fall asleep until almost 4 a.m.

Saturday

Elvis sleeps until 2 p.m. and then eats a huge breakfast. He and a group of ten friends go out on the huge lawn in front of the mansion to play touch football.

'I could play football for ever,' Elvis says, his eyes lighting up. 'I'll never be the world's greatest player, but sometimes I like to pretend I am.' The group play until dusk, making numerous trips to the coke cooler on the side of the lawn.

Elvis doesn't go to sleep until 3 a.m., after the last guest has left. The boys are still down in the living-room, but Elvis wants to write a letter to his father in Memphis.

'We usually talk on the telephone,' Elvis explains, 'but sometimes there's things that you can say only in a letter.'

Sunday

Elvis and company drive to a park not far from home for another afternoon of touch football. This time, a group of young actors from another studio are the opposition. A small crowd gathers to watch the fleet Elvis.

Ken Ferguson reports on...

● The strange story behind the romance of Elvis Presley and Ann-Margret began on the set of M.G.M.'s *Love in Las Vegas*. Hardly ever has Elvis finished a picture without his name being romantically linked with his beautiful co-stars unless, of course, they happened to be married!

Elvis and Ann soon became constant companions when the film went into rehearsals. On location in Las Vegas they went everywhere together. They danced cheek to cheek, went boating and shared intimate dinner dates. Back in the Hollywood studios the romance got warmer. Every day the couple dined alone in Elvis's dressing-room.

Finally Ann said, " Elvis is the warmest, nicest, most attractive man I've met in ages—he has everything a girl finds desirable in a man."

She was quick to spread the word that she and Elvis were very close. In London on a visit to attend the premiere of *Bye Bye Birdie* she was happy to talk of her warm interest in the Tennessee charmer. She even wore a diamond ring on the third finger of her left hand. When asked if Elvis had given her the ring, the smiling bundle of high explosive shook her head.

" The ring," she said, " is a present from my managers for being a good girl in accepting their advice."

Elvis did not say much about their romance apart from such quotes as " I think Ann is a very, very attractive girl. I like her. We see each other, but we're not going steady."

But things reached a boiling point when Ann showed a photographer a king-sized, round, pink bed in her new hillside home and explained that it was a present from Elvis.

When *Love in Las Vegas* was completed, Elvis went straight into *Kissin' Cousins* also for Metro.

On the set of this picture he was asked why he gave Ann a round, pink bed despite the fact that he had announced they were not going steady.

Elvis looked astounded. " A what? " he shouted. " Did you say a bed—that I gave Ann-Margret a bed ?

They danced cheek to cheek, they dined alone, and their romance hit the headlines, but how long will it last now that Elvis is again dating an old flame...?

THE ELVIS ANN-MARGRET

AFFAIR

never heard of that before. A bed—that sure would be an unusual gift, wouldn't it."

Meanwhile Ann still talked about her interest in Elvis. But Elvis continued to make it clear that Ann-Margret wasn't the only girl in his life at the time. He was publicly seeing Priscilla Beaulieu, the young teenager he had met in Germany while he was serving in the Army.

His close friends knew that Priscilla had come back into Elvis's life. Their relationship made every gossip column in Hollywood when it was discovered that she was staying in Graceland, his Memphis home. There were even reports that Elvis had secretly married Priscilla! When she was asked about this rumour she replied, " You ought to ask Elvis. He'll tell you what he wants you to know."

Even before Elvis met Ann, Priscilla was constantly seen in his company. Then when Ann came on the scene the general public almost forgot that he knew Priscilla at all.

The Sunday before Ann left for Europe on the *Bye Bye Birdie* exploitation trip she went along to cheer Elvis who spent his free day playing football with a team from the Metro studios. On the following Saturday night, Elvis called at Ann's home to help her pack for her trip. But when she left the next day he was not at the airport to wave goodbye.

While Ann was in England, Priscilla replaced her as Elvis's constant companion. She was his guest at the big studio party held at the end of the *Kissin' Cousins* shooting. After that Priscilla vanished. It was assumed she had gone home to her parents. Then it was discovered that she had in fact gone to Graceland.

Her mother was asked if she had heard any news that Elvis and Priscilla had secretly married. She said she had not, but added that she would be charmed to be Elvis's mother-in-law.

" We like Elvis very much," she said, " very much. You know, we met him in Germany and became very fond of him. I think he is a very fine young man."

As far as we know, Priscilla is the first girl to visit Graceland as a houseguest since Elvis's pre-army days.

Priscilla's mother went on to say she didn't think Elvis and her daughter were married. " Elvis is too honest, I don't think he'd keep it a secret from us, if he and Priscilla were married."

Where does all this leave Ann-Margret?

Does she fit in to Elvis's future at all? Or did their romance begin and end with *Love In Las Vegas*.

One thing is certain, Elvis is no two-timer. He has never encouraged any girl to think his intentions were serious when they weren't, nor has he ever dealt dishonourably with any girl in his life.

If and when he marries it will be done openly by telling the girl's family and inviting all their friends. And in Hollywood they're saying there's a strong chance that little Priscilla may well become Mrs. Elvis Presley. Who knows?

But, as usual, he keeps his mind on the game and ignores the sighs from the female spectators. At 6 p.m., after the last point has been scored, he politely signs autographs and chats with his fans on the way to the car.

Elvis and the boys have a special treat for dinner that night – Elvis' favourite dinner of pork chops, mashed potatoes with gravy and lots of Coca-Cola.

'During the week, I watch my weight,' he declares, 'but on the week-ends I generally allow myself something real special – and it's always something fattening.'

The boys all gather around the television set, but Elvis goes over his script. He tries to memorise the lines for each day of filming. At 11 p.m., he puts on a record of soft mood music and thumbs through a book of poems. It's after midnight when Elvis goes to sleep.

And soon another busy week will begin.

Elvis' second picture of 1963 resulted in the strongest rumours for some time of a romance – as well as an extraordinary report that he had been given the brush-off when trying to contact his former German girlfriend, Margrit Buergin, now living in America and working as a model. This story broke in May; and was followed soon afterwards in August by reports that Elvis and another Margaret, the Swedish-born actress Ann-Margret, had fallen in love while filming Viva Las Vegas. *The couple were described as 'the sexiest partnership for the screen since Gilbert and Garbo', and were reported frequently to be seen together off-screen dining and going to the cinema. Ann-Margret herself told inquisitive reporters, 'Elvis and I are going steady. You can take it from there. We are both great ton-up motor-cycle fans. When I am not out on my own machine, I am often riding pillion to Elvis. But I'm not ready for marriage yet.' Of the many accounts of this romance, Ken Ferguson's report for* Photoplay *was perhaps the most objective – and, in the light of hindsight, the most accurate. Elvis and Ann-Margret in fact remained good*

..and Elvis gets the brush-off from Margrit

By LEO GUILD

IS Elvis Presley, the teenagers' heart-throb, trying to revive an old romance?

That is the question intriguing Hollywood today. And it is causing a few laughs, too.

Because Elvis got a very quick brush-off when he phoned lovely German-born Margrit Buergin, his former girl friend, the other day.

He wanted her to accompany him to a film première. But Margrit gave him a very curt brush-off. She said simply: "No." And slammed down the phone.

Sweet sixteen

Now Elvis, one of the world's most eligible bachelors, is not used to receiving such cavalier treatment from the girls.

But this Margrit is quite a girl. Elvis met her in Frankfurt, Germany, when he was doing his army service in 1959.

Margrit was just a sweet-sixteen then. She fell for the richest soldier in any man's army. And Elvis certainly went overboard for Margrit.

She told me: "I once said to him:

"'Am I just another girl to you?' He swore that I was different. I was, too.

"First, I was very young. I was German. And I really cared. Sometimes when he sang to me, I melted into a hot, little ball. His singing really reached me."

But, as the affair progressed, there was one thing that Elvis was extremely shy about. He never talked of marriage.

Eventually Margrit put her foot down and told him: "Darling, either we get married or we are through."

But Elvis had to consider his image as the teenagers' heart-throb. His millions of girl fans might not like it if he gave his heart to just one.

So he said he belonged to his public . . . he could not desert them.

"I'm a corporation, not a man," he said. "Sure I want to get married and have kids. But for me it's impossible."

Margrit then did something that few other girls would have considered—she walked out on the heart-throb of millions. Just like that. Leaving Elvis with only his guitar to fill his empty arms.

Now Margrit is in America carving out a career as a model. She is also hoping for a career in films.

And Elvis has no part at all in her plans.

---

friends for the rest of the singer's life and she was among the mourners at Presley's funeral.

The year ended with Elvis playing a dual role as an Air Force officer and a hillbilly in Kissin' Cousins, *the story of a dispute over the siting of a missile base in the Smoky Mountains. Some of the picture was shot on a closed site location high in the mountains of California and reports of the work were given to the press by Tom Diskin, Colonel Tom Parker's assistant, who was by this time increasingly becoming the spokesman for all Elvis' plans.*

ELVIS AND DOUBLE GET BOTH GIRLS!

By Tom Diskin

Elvis and the Colonel are on location in California for *Kissin' Cousins*. This picture is going to have everything – authentic scenery, lots of laughs, great music.

They've gone into the mountains for the scenery because in one of his dual roles Elvis plays a rough mountain boy. Most of the comedy emanates from Arthur O'Connell who played Elvis' father in *Follow That Dream* and has the same role in *Kissin' Cousins*.

For the music, Elvis went back to Nashville, where you will remember he made all those early big hits, and waxed the whole soundtrack before shooting the film began.

Though he isn't getting double salary for his dual role, there is one thing that's pleasing Elvis tremendously – he wins two leading ladies! Each of the brothers he plays gets his woman in the end – that really pleases our boy!

We keep getting asked if Elvis will perform in concert again. The answer is we hope so, but at the moment his entire schedule has been from one picture to the next.

The Colonel always says that in films Elvis can reach his fans in the remotest corners of

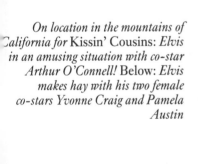

On location in the mountains of California for Kissin' Cousins: *Elvis in an amusing situation with co-star Arthur O'Connell! Below: Elvis makes hay with his two female co-stars Yvonne Craig and Pamela Austin*

the world – something it would take the best part of his life to do on personal appearances.

We don't fit concerts in between his films because they require a great deal of preparation on Elvis' part. He would never just pick up a guitar and walk out on a stage after all this time of playing to nothing but movie cameras. He is a dedicated performer – one who gives himself completely.

Billboard,
3 November

PRESLEYMANIA – 1963

HIGHWAY PATROL PROBLEMS. Elvis Presley's popularity is causing problems for the Tennessee State Highway Patrol. The stream of visitors to the Presley home have worn holes in the road. Gravel doesn't work because girls carry away the pebbles for souvenirs. Asphalt turned out to be the solution.

New York Post, 9 January

ELVIS PRESLEY SENSATION. 'Tentative plans for the invasion of this country by Elvis Presley, the biggest phenomenon show business has ever known, have already been outlined, and it is virtually certain that his visit will include a date at Wembley Stadium.'
Sheffield Star, 25 February

☆ ☆ ☆

THE UNIQUE ACTOR. 'I've never seen anything like it,' Ben, the white-haired major domo of the big silver gates at Paramount Studios in Hollywood declared. 'I've been at this gate for thirty years, and I've seen 'em come and go … Dietrich, Chevalier, Barrymore, Jimmy Dean, all the rest. But I've never, in all my born days, seen a star like Elvis Presley. I've never seen so many people of all ages waiting so long outside the gates for just one glimpse of Elvis …'
Photoplay, March

ELVIS, HIS LORDSHIP AND THE BEATLES

HOUSE OF LORDS,
Westminster,
London, S.W.1.

10th December, 1963

Dear Sir,

I cannot understand this Beatle mania.

I appreciate they have attractive personalities but when it comes to a question of rhythm, Elvis Presley has it all the way.

Yours faithfully,
Massereene and Ferrard.

RICHEST MAN IN SHOW BIZ. Elvis Presley at 28 is just about the richest man in show business. He earns $600,000 a picture plus a percentage of the profits; an estimated $200,000 a year from the sale of records; plus royalties from the sale of Presley T-shirts, rings and other trinkets. His gross income is estimated at $2,000,000 a year, and it is safe to guess that his take so far has totalled more than $10,000,000.

Cashbox, 13 April

☆ ☆ ☆

ELVIS SUED! Rock 'n' Roll star Elvis Presley is being sued for $500,000 by a women who alleges that one of the singer's cars knocked down and killed her husband. The woman, Mrs Leona Henslin, in the action filed in Santa Monica yesterday, named Richard Davis, driver of the car, as a co-defendant. Presley was not in the car at the time of the accident last March.

Evening News, 11 May

☆ ☆ ☆

MARRIAGE WARNING! Says Colonel Tom Parker, 'I'm glad a British clairvoyant has warned us that Elvis is getting married this autumn. It's little enough time to start considering his added financial responsibilities and possible tax reduction.'

New Musical Express, 5 June

☆ ☆ ☆

ELVIS NEEDS PUBLICITY. 'Elvis Presley should announce his engagement!' That's what Bob Marcucci, manager of Frankie Avalon, Gary Clarke and others says. 'You see, I've noticed that Elvis' publicity has gone down considerably in the past few months. The fans aren't quite as interested in him as they once were. That's why I believe Elvis should announce he's getting married. You can just bet that thousands of fans will sit up and take notice of Elvis. They don't want their hero to marry and they'll say so!'

Mirabelle, 29 July

☆ ☆ ☆

ELVIS TO WED? Colonel Tom Parker, Elvis Presley's manager, told us, 'Our boy had one hobby last year. He has the same hobby this year – pretty girls. I've met Ann-Margret, of course, and she's real pretty. But there'll be others to follow.'

Hollywood Reporter, 19 September

☆ ☆ ☆

NATURAL GIRLS FOR ME. Elvis Presley says: 'Doesn't matter to me whether she's blonde, brunette or redhead – so long as she's out-and-out feminine. Also, she must be real down to earth – I don't dig a chick who tries to put on a sophisticated act, or make herself out to be something she's not. I go for someone who looks up to me as a man, and who makes me feel a little superior just for that one reason. I like a girl who's happy just doing the ordinary things on an evening out. Like movies, followed by hamburgers, cokes and listening to the juke box. I shan't marry till the right girl comes along – whether I happen to be thirty, forty or even fifty.'

Film Stars, October

☆ ☆ ☆

DOUBLE THE FEE? On hearing that MGM wanted his star, Elvis Presley, to play two roles in a new movie, *Kissin' Cousins*, manager Colonel Tom Parker retorted, 'That's just fine. But does he get double the salary?'

Cashbox, 30 November

1964

ELVIS the KING RETURNS

WIN · A WO
· DATE

EVEALING
S SHOCK
CRET

appearan
of Elvis

ELVIS PRESL

TAR OF STAGE, SCREEN, RADIO, RECORDS AND T

ELVIS PRESLEY
MAY VISIT LONDON

"Evening News" Reporter

AMERICAN rock 'n' roll
king, Elvis Presley, may
come to London next year. He
has been offered about
£250,000 a Johannesburg
to make 25 per
nces in Euro

ELVIS kissed me

ELVIS 50th

PRESLEY—that's all we had b
at the ele
on ELVIS

ELVIS PRESLEY

HART

Unlike Elvis who was never to cross the Atlantic, the Beatles had no sooner conquered Britain than they flew to America in February 1964 and were given a hysterical reception when they appeared on the Ed Sullivan Show. *Elvis himself watched this show and undoubtedly felt a sense of* déjà vu *as the four young men were besieged by press and public alike. The Colonel and Elvis sent a congratulatory telegram to the Beatles and their manager, Brian Epstein, and by so doing learned that the biggest ambition of the four Merseysiders was to meet the man they called 'The King'. Unfortunately, on neither the brief visit in February, or during the Beatles' 32-day tour of the major cities of the USA in September–October, was it possible for them to get together – though Paul McCartney did speak to Elvis on the telephone. The Beatles experienced the same teenage mass-hysteria that Elvis had done and when, finally, the 'summit meeting of the super stars' took place at Elvis' home in Hollywood in August 1965, this was one of their major topics of conversation. Both Elvis and the Beatles recorded their impressions of each other which are quoted hereunder.*

WELCOME TO THE USA

A Telegram from Colonel Tom Parker to Brian Epstein

DEAR MR EPSTEIN – ON BEHALF OF ELVIS AND MYSELF WELCOME TO THE USA. STOP. SINCERE GOOD WISHES FOR A SUCCESSFUL TOUR AND A WONDERFUL TRIP AND TO ALL YOUR ENGAGEMENTS. STOP. IF THERE IS ANY WAY I CAN BE OF SERVICE TO YOU AS A FRIEND DO NOT HESITATE TO CALL ON ME. STOP. ALTHOUGH THERE IS NOT MUCH I CAN DO AS I HAVE BEEN LAID UP WITH A BACK AILMENT BUT MY EFFORTS MAY BE OF SOME HELP IF NEED BE. STOP. IF YOU HAVE TIME GIVE ME A CALL WHEN YOU COME TO TOWN. STOP. SINCERELY THE COLONEL.

THE BEATLES

By Elvis Presley

I'll say that the Beatles have got what it takes, and in great abundance, and they have been given a heck of a vote of confidence. They have appeared on three Ed Sullivan shows in this country and I have watched them all.

I have been asked if their success bothers me? Of course not. They are entertainers like myself and I guess they are as dedicated as the rest of us. In the long run, this is all that matters.

As to their music I don't think I should tell you what I really feel about them. I don't think it would be fair to fellow entertainers.

Remember I have been a lucky guy myself. I've never forgotten that. It's too vivid in my memory. But let me add I sure wish them luck.

Weekend, 10 June

ELVIS PRESLEY

By The Beatles

JOHN LENNON: 'There was only one person in the United States that we wanted to meet and that was Elvis. We can't tell you how we felt. We just idolised him so much. When we first came to town, these guys like Frank

Sinatra and Dean Martin and all these people wanted to come over and hang around with us simply because we had all the women, all the chicks. We didn't want to meet those people. They didn't really like us. We didn't really like them or admire them. The only person we wanted to meet was Elvis Presley. We can't tell you how much we wanted that.'

GEORGE HARRISON: 'We admire him very much, but we preferred his earlier discs, especially his first LP, to the ones he's being releasing lately. There's no getting away from it though – he's still the greatest.'

PAUL McCARTNEY: 'I like Elvis' voice, it reminds me of Blackpool on a sunny day.'

RINGO STARR: 'The last two years his records have been going down the nick, but Elvis is great.'

In April, Elvis confounded those critics who felt his days were numbered as a result of the emergence of the Beatles and other beat groups, when his latest release, 'Crying in the Chapel' leapt into the British top ten. The achievement made front-page news in England – especially as the number had been recorded some five years earlier! It also produced an article apparently written by Elvis – though more probably ghosted by a member of Colonel Parker's staff – in which the singer talked about himself and his career. 'The Record Scene and Me' appeared in Hit Parade *magazine, was carefully pasted into the scrapbooks, and is reprinted here as another rare piece of Presley memorabilia ...*

ELVIS PRESLEY WRITES:
'THE RECORD SCENE AND ME'

Hi, this is Elvis Presley. I guess the first thing most of you want to know is how it feels to be

Elvis Pops Back Into The Top Ten

"Evening News" Reporter

ELVIS PRESLEY swings the surprise of the week in both the *New Musical Express* and *Melody Maker* charts. For the first time in nearly a year the Pelvis is back to-day in Britain's Top Ten.

He's had a lean time over here ever since the British beat groups began their domination of the pop world.

Now Elvis. 30 years old and a multi-millionaire, makes a flourishing come-back with a record he put "in the can" five years ago.

back in the British top ten again. I'll answer that right away – it feels great.

I really mean that. You know, when I was making the top of the charts regularly a few years back now, I was the happiest guy alive. My fans were always kind to me and, no matter what type of song I did, they liked it.

But when things kinda cooled off a little for me, I began worrying. After all, I wasn't used to that kind of thing. I spoke to my manager, Colonel Tom Parker, and he admitted to being a little puzzled as well.

Honest, we got to thinking about things and we couldn't come up with an answer. We called a conference with songwriters and music publishers and people like that, but at the end we didn't have a reason for the dropping off period in Britain.

Here in America, my records were still selling as well as ever. But in Britain, they wouldn't get too high before they started dropping. As usual in these cases, there were always plenty of people around to tell me what was wrong and what I should do to improve my overseas position. But I always place the greatest trust in what Col. Parker says. He is the man who has done most for me and I am convinced that if he says for me to do something, that it is the best thing in my interests.

In the meantime, I had a heavy schedule of film-making. When I started out to be an actor, there were some people who said I'd never make it. I hope now I've proved them wrong.

My films do well at the box office and the albums of the sound track sell in large numbers. It is also very important that we have a lot of fun on the sets. The cast always gets together and messes around swimming, having barbecues and driving. If you get a happy cast, you're well on the way to getting a good picture. I always remember that and so far it's worked out just fine.

If you asked me to name one film I'd enjoyed more than any other, I couldn't tell you. There are so many good things I remember about several of my motion pictures. I could tell you something, and that is the way in which my films have changed along with my image.

Do you remember *Jailhouse Rock* and *King Creole*? If you do, you'll visualise me as a hard-talking, fighting kind of person who was more or less a loafer. At the time, that was all fine. I used to wear long sideburns, flashy sports jackets or denims and very tight trousers.

When my Army stint came, Col. Parker decided it was time for a change, and he began the gradual process. The old mean Elvis gave way to a new cleaned-up version that I admit I have grown fond of over the years. *GI Blues* first showed the public what to expect from then on in. Luckily, they took to the film and the new image.

If they hadn't, I don't know what we would have done. I don't think we could have gone back to the old style after all the work that went into the new bit, things would just have taken a little longer, I guess.

I get puzzled when people give the opinion that my films are responsible for my records not being as successful as they used to be. That doesn't figure to me at all. It's still the same person singing, and we all decide on the songs before we record them. If a song isn't suited to my style, we forget it. I wouldn't record a song just because it fitted a film if it didn't fit me.

That's what a whole lot of people think happens, but they're wrong all along the line. With my film commitments, I don't have all that time to go into a recording studio and do additional songs. So when we get a film to do, we study the songs and if one of them seems a likely prospect for the charts, we issue that as a single.

The success of 'Kissin' Cousins' has finally proved that we were right. Now let's hope we can follow up with some more hit songs from my movies.

In April, Elvis filmed Roustabout, *the story of a travelling carnival show, at Thousand Oaks in California. His co-star was the talented Barbara Stanwyck. The film afforded Elvis another chance to get back on his bike.*

Elvis' second picture of 1964 was Girl Happy *in which he played a night club entertainer hired to keep an eye on a rich man's daughter only to fall in love with her! Filmed at Ford Lauderdale, the picture was the first of three he made with pretty Shelley Fabares (the others being* Spinout, *1966, and* Clambake, *1967.) Elvis and Shelley subsequently became close friends, though there was never a suggestion of a romance despite a well-remembered moment during the filming of* Spinout *when they held a kiss for almost three minutes after director Norman Taurog had called 'Cut!' Perhaps not surprisingly, it was widely believed that Shelley was Elvis' favourite co-star! Following the making of* Girl Happy *she gave the interview here to* Disc *magazine.*

MAKING LOVE WITH ELVIS

Shelley Fabares talks about Filming with Presley

What's it like to play romantic lead opposite Elvis Presley? Millions of girls would like to know the answer to this question, but the only girls who CAN speak with any knowledge on the subject are those who have actually filmed with El.

Latest in the line of romantic screen leads to play opposite Elvis is glamorous, hazel-eyed blonde Shelley Fabares, who stars with him in *Girl Happy*, the MGM movie.

To find out just what it is like to film with Elvis, and to give fans a personal view of the sort of person he really is, I put in a call to Shelley's Beverly Hills home.

Legends have grown up around the fact that Elvis is basically a rather shy person when he is not performing for the fans. And Shelley was able to confirm this.

'This is the first film I had made with him,' she told me.

'Actually the first time we met was the very first day of rehearsals for the picture – the day before we started filming.

'But I found him very nice indeed. He put me at my ease right away.

'Of course, as a singer myself, I was always interested in his style of singing.

'He's fun to work with, but he is very quiet and shy. Even with a lot of people around on the set, he doesn't mix with them much.

Dances

Practically nobody on the set ever sees him between filming, because he goes off with his own circle of friends. Socially, I didn't meet him at all.

'But when it comes to filming, he will talk about all the choreography and stuff – the different songs and dances we had to do together.'

Two such scenes with Shelley are the 'Meanest Girl In Town' night-club speciality and the beach-party number 'Do The Clam' – the title of Elvis's latest charts-rider.

The 'Meanest Girl' song is a speciality sequence featuring Shelley with Elvis's group – and it is really a scene-stealer.

In the 'Do The Clam' scene Shelley and El wind up their lively dance sequence rolling down a sand dune together.

Right top: *Another behind-the-scenes shot of Elvis on location with co-star Barbara Stanwyk filming* Roustabout; *and* right bottom *let loose on a motor-bike once again*

And just what is it like to go into a romantic clinch with Elvis?

'Just like any actor doing a scene – that's all there is to it,' says Shelley – maybe destroying a few romantic illusions in the eyes of the fans!

There was no faking in the dancing Elvis and Shelley did together. Adds Shelley: 'Naturally, Elvis did all the dancing in the picture himself. He is a very good dancer, you know.'

A dramatic highspot in *Girl Happy* is the scene where Shelley gets tipsy and goes into a 'striptease' – much to the horror of El, who has been commissioned to keep an eye on her by her father – who wants to keep the Fort Lauderdale wolves at bay.

Blushes

Elvis saves the day – and Shelley's blushes – by starting a scene that winds up with a tremendous fight by all present.

'This was fun – and it all worked without anyone getting hurt,' says Shelley. 'Every punch was planned, of course. Elvis rehearses scenes like this a lot – and he makes them look very convincing.'

And Shelley's favourite number in *Girl Happy*? 'I enjoyed doing "The Meanest Girl In Town."'

For my money, 'The Meanest Girl In Town' and 'Do The Clam' – plus the fight scene – were the high-lights of *Girl Happy*.

But you can bet Elvis admirers won't find much to grumble about during the rest of the film either. Especially the male members of the audience when they see the swinging Shelley Fabares!

The third of Elvis' 1964 pictures, Tickle Me, *in which he played a down-on-his-luck rodeo rider in search of hidden treasure produced strong rumours of a romance with his co-star, the voluptuous Jackie Lane. There was particular interest in this possibility in Britain, for Jackie was an English-born starlet who had moved to Hollywood to further her career. Despite reports such as the one here from the* Daily Sketch *of 14 November, the story proved to be just one more of Elvis' 'relationships' made in headlines rather than in real life.*

JACKIE 'JUST FRIENDS' WITH ELVIS

It was a lift she accepted in Elvis Presley's Rolls-Royce that started the rumours.

Then off-the-set meetings between Britain's Jackie Lane and Elvis, her co-star in the new Hollywood musical *Tickle Me*, really set the tongues wagging.

In the film, Jackie and Elvis marry. But 25-year-old Jackie denies any real romance with the pop star.

Amateur astrologer Jackie explained: 'Elvis is a Capricorn and I'm a Taurus, so we get along well together.'

She added, predictably: 'We are just good friends.'

Red-haired Jackie does, however, find American men 'more interesting than men anywhere else in the world.' And the man interesting her most at the moment is her constant companion, bachelor Glenn Ford.

Also interesting her are her career – which is coming along very nicely, thank you – and her latest investment, a villa she and her sister Mara are having built in Spain.

Wedding plans? 'The stars say I'm supposed to marry next year,' said Jackie. 'But I can't think who I might be marrying.'

PRESLEYMANIA – 1964

ELVIS GIVES AWAY YACHT: Singer Elvis Presley is giving away a luxury yacht he bought for £19,640 at an auction at Long Beach, California. The yacht belonged to the

Shelley Fabares, the beautiful brunette with whom Elvis made three movies and who was said to be his favourite co-star. Seen here in Girl Happy

late President Franklin D. Roosevelt, and Presley said as he did not have time to use the vessel he was handing it over to a children's charity in Los Angeles. The charity is a fund started by Mr Roosevelt to aid polio victims.

Evening News, 31 January

☆   ☆   ☆

LIPSTICKED: Ed Sullivan recently recalled Elvis Presley's answer when a newspaper-woman asked, 'Don't you resent it when bobby-soxers deface your brand new white limousine with lipstick?' Presley answered, 'I can't very well resent it because if it weren't for those kids, I wouldn't have a limousine.'

New York Post, 9 February

☆   ☆   ☆

ALMOST KISSED TO DEATH! Police in New Rochelle, NY got an unusual complaint. A young boy reported that a teenage girl grabbed him and kissed him. He said she broke his sun glasses and almost suffocated him. When questioned, the girl broke down and confessed that the boy looked so much like Elvis Presley she had an uncontrollable compulsion to grab him!

National Enquirer, 21 February

Jackie Lane with Elvis in Tickle Me

ELVIS STREET? A Presley fan asks: 'I've heard that there's a road called Elvis Street somewhere in England – is this true?' Our resident expert replies: 'Well, it's not true, but there is a street called Presley Drive in Yorkshire and it was given that name in Elvis' honour.'

Mirabelle, 4 April

☆ ☆ ☆

SAVE OUR PIN-UPS! Fifty teenage girls on the top of a blazing seven-storey college yesterday were told, 'Get out quick!' They started to make a dash for it – then remembered their 'valuables': Pin up photographs of singer Elvis Presley.

Daily Mirror, 16 May

☆ ☆ ☆

THE BEATLES AND ELVIS. Talking on the set of Elvis Presley's new movie, *Roustabout*, producer Hal Wallis said: 'Why haven't I gone after the Beatles the way I went after Elvis? My answer is that I have no use for them. I doubt that they can last more than a couple of pictures. I don't want to be unkind and call them a flash-in-the-pan, but they are no match for Elvis, the unknown Elvis of 1956. Not that I haven't had a good look at them. I have. And I found them wanting. They have no sound, no rhythm. I wouldn't touch them. It's as simple as that.'

Weekend, 16 June

☆ ☆ ☆

CASH REGISTER GROUP. Asked what he thought of the Beatles, Colonel Tom Parker, manager of Elvis Presley, who sent a greeting telegram to the British group on their US debut, said: 'They're the greatest – they sure play the finest tune on the cash register that I've ever heard.'

Photoplay, March

☆ ☆ ☆

ELVIS THE BEATLE: A Los Angeles theatre showing Elvis Presley's *Kissin' Cousins* has billed the star as 'the original Beatle'. Hollywood columnist Mike Connolly noted that the occasion reminded him of the time Johnnie Ray told him, 'I'm last year's Elvis Presley.'

New Musical Express, 15 March

☆ ☆ ☆

DOUBLE ROOMS: Elvis Presley is regarded as so important a star at MGM that while he is there making *Girl Happy* he has been given two dressing room suites. They were once occupied by Spencer Tracy and Clark Gable.

Billboard, 20 July

MANSION OF SECRETS. The garden walls of Elvis Presley's Bel-Air home in Hollywood are seven feet high. Anyone getting a chance to peek over can see Elvis' house through the trees. The most closely guarded secret in the palatial mansion is the star's personal telephone number. Only nine people, including Colonel Tom Parker, have the number and it is changed every six months.

Daily Express, 9 August

☆　☆　☆

ELVIS AND LIZ. Words of economic wisdom from Colonel Tom Parker, Elvis Presley's manager: 'The difference between Elvis getting a million dollars and Elizabeth Taylor getting a million dollars per movie is that Elvis never takes longer than five weeks to shoot. So the good folks at the studios make a nice profit on us.'

Disc, 25 October

PETER PAN ELVIS. Veteran motion picture director, Norman Taurog, who has just completed *Tickle Me*, starring Elvis Presley, says: 'Being young today is an attitude – it's like belonging to a secret society. Elvis is its symbol: he's the leader. And now he's got a whole new crop of teenagers running after him, proving what I've always said – he's Peter Pan.' And of his progress as an actor, Taurog added, 'If we gave him serious roles to play, he would be recognised as one of the best actors. And you know something? I'd like to direct him as a cold-blooded killer!'

New Musical Express, 23 November

☆　☆　☆

GOLD SUIT TOUR? Asked why Elvis Presley no longer tours, manager Colonel Tom Parker said, 'Elvis is unavailable for personal appearances because of his filming commitments. I've just sent his gold Cadillac on a tour of America. Matter of fact, it's so successful I'm thinking of putting his gold suit on tour, too!'

Cashbox, 16 December

1965

ELVIS the KING RETURNS

WIN · A WO...
· DATE

EVEALING
S SHOCK'
CRET

appearan...

of Elvis

ELVIS PRESL...

STAR OF STAGE, SCREEN, RADIO, RECORDS AND T...

ELVIS PRESLEY MAY VISIT LONDON

"Evening News" Reporter

AMERICAN rock 'n' roll
king, Elvis Presley, may
come to London next year. He
has been offered about
£250,000 a Johannesburg
... to make 25 per
...nces in Euro...

ELVIS ARMY

ELVIS

kissed me

...PROVOCATIV'
CAREEP

...RESLEY – that's all we had h...
...at the ele... on. ELVIS P

ELVIS 50th ELVIS PRESLEY

...HART...

8 January 1965 marked a major milestone in Elvis' life – his thirtieth birthday and the tenth anniversary of his rise to fame. It is also the moment in Presley history where the scrapbooks found in the fan club attic end. The fabulous decade in which Elvis had risen from being an unknown Memphis truck-driver to undeniably the most famous singer in the world, was over and the fans who had collected and filed the newspaper accounts of these phenomenal times now apparently began new books for the years to come. The final items are a reflection of what had passed and the hope of greater things to come. That Elvis never surpassed this first decade was perhaps inevitable, though his few attempts to match it are perhaps more regrettable still.

As the Beatles were the only artists to seriously challenge Elvis' unparalleled popularity, it seems appropriate that the tribute to 'The King' on the occasion of his birthday should be from the pages of the Liverpool paper, Mersey Beat. Equally appropriate, the survey of Elvis' achievements was written by Albert Hand, then the President of the British Elvis Presley Fan Club who had met Elvis and even stayed at Graceland for a week. The British fans, too, marked this special moment in their hero's life by voting him yet again the top male vocalist with almost twice as many votes as his nearest rival, Cliff Richard.

The early days of 1965 also produced what was to be the last of the notorious 'Elvis To Appear In UK' stories, though this time those involved had the good grace to apologise for once again vainly raising the hopes of British fans. The many rumours about Elvis marrying ceased, too, when news was given that he was actually going to wed Priscilla Beaulieu, who had been quietly living in Memphis all the while since her return from Germany.

Finally, Elvis and Colonel Tom Parker also celebrated ten years together: the Colonel proudly telling the press that his client had grossed over $150 million dollars in record sales for RCA Victor, and $125 million for the various companies who had released his pictures. The prestigious American weekly magazine Time devoted several pages of its show business section to Elvis' achievements, entitled with a great sense of presentiment, 'Forever Elvis' – an extract from which concludes this book.

ELVIS IS THIRTY!

By Jeff Rigby

Today Elvis Presley reaches another milestone in his phenomenally successful life for he has arrived at the ripe old (!) age of 30. Yes, girls, Elvis Presley is 30 years old.

Will this make any difference to his mammoth female following? Who knows, perhaps he'll increase in popularity with the mums and dads as he is 'getting on'.

During El's years as top 'pop' idol he has been awarded over THIRTY gold discs.

But now, what does the future hold for the American idol? Will his popularity increase or fade? Will he make more, or less, records? Will we be honoured by that long awaited and much needed visit from the 'daddy' of it all?

These are questions only time and patience will answer! But, rest assured, they will be answered and Elvis Presley will either rise, fall, or trot along as he is doing now.

Mersey Beat, 9 January

World's outstanding male singer

ELVIS PRESLEY

World's outstanding musical personality

ELVIS PRESLEY

ELVIS STAYS AS TOP MALE SINGER

1	Elvis Presley	4,808
2	Gene Pitney	2,035
3	Cliff Richard	1,884
4	Bob Dylan	1,454
5	Roy Orbison	705
6	Mick Jagger	542
7	Buddy Holly	439
8	John Lennon	438
9	P.J. Proby	428
10	Del Shannon	282
11	Marvin Gaye	146
12	Jim Reeves	145
13	Chuck Berry	99
14	Donovan	89
15	Billy Fury	81
16	Roger Miller	72
	Ben E. King	72
18	Paul McCartney	62
19	Frank Sinatra	61
20	Eric Burdon	54

ELVIS THE GREAT!

The Presley Saga Wags Showbiz By the Tail
By Albert Hand

Ten years of the immortal Elvis, ten years of being a Presley fan, ten years of listening to the greatest artist in the pop music business – that's been a decade of pure pleasure to this particular Presley fan. But it's also been ten years of close in-fighting against the stupidity of the people who persist in saying that Elvis is finished – a point of view they have been constantly plugging for the same ten years!

Yet the legions of Elvis Presley fans themselves go on their triumphant way, happy in the knowledge that their idol is in precisely the same position – even chartwise – as he was when his very first disc erupted into Britain's entertainment world back in 1956.

Did I hear somebody snigger? Do I detect a murmur of disbelief?

Brush the hair out of your eyes and read on …

In 1956 and 1957, Presley made 15 records altogether, starting with 'Heartbreak Hotel.' They made these positions in our charts: 2, 9, 12, 2, 9, 11, 25, 6, 1, 3, 9, 2, 27, 15 and 7 – or an average placing of between ninth and tenth position.

That was a fantastic achievement, you'll agree, I'm sure! But consider the story in the years 1963 and 1964: despite what most of the Press would have us believe, Elvis did even better!

In this second period, he made a total of nine discs – counting 'Ain't That Loving You, Baby' which, as I write, I estimate will probably reach a maximum placing of seventh position – and these achieved the following British chart positions: 1, 8, 2, 10, 10, 16, 9, 13 and (my guessed position) 7 or 8.

The average placing here is eighth to ninth, even higher than before!

And this in the teeth of the gale of popularity today for groups, which have (quite admirably, I think) turned the music business upside down all over the world.

During this eight-year production period, in which Elvis cut for the British market no less than 47 singles, 19 EPs and 23 LPs, he didn't exactly play around with his film output either. After his first movie, *Love Me Tender* (remember it – that film the critics said would finish him off for ever as a potential movie star?), he followed up with no

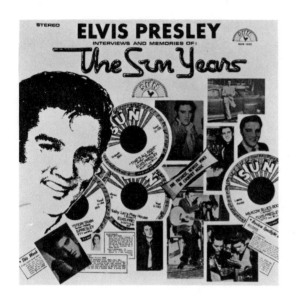

less than 15 more screenies up to *Roustabout*, and added to this, he's already got one more in the can, and is half-way through yet another!

Brother, that's what I call production!

Sixteen movies! All box-office hits! All 100 per cent, vintage Presley – and this despite an enforced, two-year stretch in the U.S. Army, where he submerged himself in the identity of G.I. No. 53310761, one bleak morning in March, 1958.

Of course, this turned out to be a blessing in disguise, for it was the Army that really turned the tide for him, as regards universal adult *and* teenage acceptance. Until then, the wider world outside his teen legions had brushed him off as a hiccoughing, gyrating, guitar-twanging, surly, slack-mouthed, side-burned great fool, who couldn't even sing! And they thought also, one gathered, that in addition he boasted the morals of a moron, the manners of a pig and the general attitude to life of a spoiled movie star!

Actually, of course, Elvis wasn't – and never had been – anything of the sort. It's just that the Army, with its usual disciplinary

attitude and enforced tidiness – plus some very hard-working public relations officers! – simply accentuated and revealed to the world an Elvis who was a human being. Like I say, he had been 'human' all the time, but his stage and screen image had simply hidden the fact from the public! And, naturally, the Press did what it always does to a rebel – the papers didn't help one little bit!

Today, however, the demobilised Elvis, almost five years later, still stands right on top of his pinnacle ... and gazes affectionately down on the 50,000,000 fans who have loved – and helped – him over the past ten, tumultuous years.

Why is it, then, that non-Elvis fans so firmly believe Elvis is on the wane?

There are three very good reasons:

(1) The publishers and newsagents

Now early on in Elvis's career, the big publishers churned out enough written and pictorial stuff on Elvis to kill a normally talented artist stone dead. So much stuff, in fact, that the kids were 'out-pocketed': they just couldn't afford to keep up with it and the stuff wouldn't sell any more. The publishers saw the red light – but instead of cutting down to a sensible output, they stopped publishing altogether! The newsagents acted similarly. Finding Presley books gathering dust on their shelves, instead of cutting down their stocks, they just ceased to stock Elvis books any more!

As a result, the shops were suddenly emptied of Elvis. At the same time, the magazines stopped using him on their covers and Elvis's smiling face no longer gazed down on the shoppers who passed by the newsagents. Not unnaturally, the public began to think that Elvis was on the way out, too, and this same belief could easily have become stark, straight fact, if it had not been for one thing: a publication called *Elvis*

ELVIS TOPS THEM ALL

LIFE begins at 30! That's what Elvis Presley is thinking these days. He's riding high on all fronts.

"Crying In The Chapel" is in the Top Ten both sides of the Atlantic. His films continue to be world-wide best sellers. He's a contented and prized citizen of Hollywood and Memphis. And he's happy, so happy.

The other day he broke his usual silence to say: "I'm a lucky guy—and a grateful one, too."

He talked about his films and the fact that the plots are simple and samey.

"I realise that I must never bite off more than I can chew. I know I can repeat the kind of picture I make now without much worry. But if I made an art picture and it clicked, I'd be scared I couldn't repeat it."

Sound, logical judgment. Elvis is very honest with himself. Another important asset Elvis has is his assessment of people.

Keep away

"I've learned about folk fast and keep away from those who can land me in trouble.

"Girls specially. I find it difficult to meet up with a girl who has a good sense of humour, simplicity and loyalty."

The time has passed when Elvis couldn't marry without hurting his career. But he still remains single, explaining it with: "As I get older I get more choosey. A girl who would have attracted me a few years back isn't so appealing now. But I have no ambition to end up a bachelor."

Elvis likes reading books on politics (he backed Johnson for President) and medical books.

"But don't get the idea I'm a hypochondriac," he chuckled. "I read medical books because I find them interesting—wanted to be a doctor once—but I never connect the disease described with myself.

"Fact is," he said, "I never seem to get sick."

Elvis still has his six bodyguard buddies on the payroll. One of their chief functions is to play touch football with Elvis when he feels in the mood. A wag said:

ELVIS as he appears in his forthcoming "Harem Holiday" (renamed from "Harem Scarem").

"They're probably the highest paid footballers in the business."

Not so, however, Elvis doesn't pay them colossal salaries.

Mention of money brings in his manager, the famous Colonel Tom Parker. There's a lot of humour in the way he handles the fabulous deals for Elvis.

Take the case of the producer who said: "Your boy will win an Oscar if he takes this rôle. It's worth dropping 50,000 dollars of his fee for such a part."

Colonel Parker didn't bat an eyelid. "Tell you what. You pay our fee—350,000 dollars—and if Elvis wins an Oscar I'll refund you 50,000 dollars."

No wonder Elvis thinks the world of the Colonel!

Monthly. Now this booklet, too, is obtainable from newsagents. *So, as sure as sure, if the rumours had, in fact, been true, its sales should also have dropped.*

But they didn't. In fact, the reverse was the case. During the past six months, its sales have leapt by over eight per cent, despite the fact that it already boasted a quarter-of-a-million readership over the past three years. As I write, it has again grown in sales this month! It is easy to reason further that if it wasn't for the newsagents who are scared that the copies wouldn't go if they ordered extras 'on chance,' the sales might have increased even more. Which brings me to:

(2) The Spate of Films

Elvis made only four films in his first four years at the top – one each year. Naturally, on this small output and with his huge following, everywhere the films were shown the houses were absolutely packed. But how times change! Nowadays with his output up to no less than three films per year, plus the fact that his old films are still constantly re-doing the rounds, the obvious has happened: the houses are half empty!

But if the box-office takings for *the whole year* for 1964 were placed alongside his takings for 1960, I'll wager that very little revenue loss would appear on Elvis's balance sheet. Three half-full houses equal one and a half houses, by my reckoning – which is a 50 per cent increase on 1957–60!

Nevertheless, as I say, to the casual film-goer, those empty seats do very little to destroy the fallacy that Elvis has lost his popularity. Then there's:

(3) The Record Shops

Here again, just like the newsagent, the shopkeeper suddenly discovered that Elvis's new releases were not selling at the same rate as did his past hits – quite natural, really, because nowadays there are more LP's knocking around. But instead of just cutting down on single supplies, they've clamped down on his whole range of past singles, EPs, LPs, the lot! Out they came from the windows; in went the group LPs. And, once again, the passer-by saw the change and came to the conclusion: he's finished. Once again though, I can personally prove otherwise.

I own a very large record shop, and I can tell you this: after a single leaves the charts, no matter how good it is, you may as well chuck the surplus copies in the dustbin. They just stop selling.

Unless they are by Elvis Presley. With Elvis it's a very different matter. You dare not chuck them away. Would you care to know my last month's best-sellers of Elvis, for instance? You'll be surprised – and note the year of release!

1 'Ain't That Loving You Baby' (of course!);
2 'Such A Night' (a 1964 release);
3 'Kissin' Cousins' (once again, 1964);
4 'Wooden Heart' (1961);
5 'All Shook Up' (1957);
6 'Are You Lonesome Tonight?' (1961);
7 'It's Now Or Never' (1961);
8 'Rock-a-Hula Baby' (1962);
9 'A Fool Such As I' (1959);
10 'Surrender' (1961).

Only one of these numbers, you will note, was released in 1962, supposedly his best year.

These are my own store's top sellers only, of course. You must bear in mind, too, that never a week goes by without I sell at least three copies of every disc Elvis has made, which is more than I can do for any other artist you care to mention, including the groups. And would *you* dare to wager that 75 per cent of the past year's Number Ones will even be *in existence* on a single, let alone still selling, in five years time?

Albert Hand, President of the British Elvis Presley Fan Club, meeting Elvis

I'll bet you wouldn't. You'd lose your money, for sure!

These three reasons, then, are why I and most of the other Elvis fans I know firmly believe that the public is being blissfully hoodwinked into thinking that Elvis is finished. They also make the main reason why the mere thought of the non-Elvis fan thinking that Elvis is finished, makes the real fan smile. Dwellers in Elvisville just shrug the whole thing off!

They've become bored by the whole thing. And, in any case, their minds are, at present, on a greater thing. The greatest thing, in fact, since P-Day, March 4th, 1960, when the U.S. Army returned their hero, unscathed and handsome as ever, to their tender care once more!

JANUARY 8th, 1965, will be the day: Elvis will once again make show business history, so make a note of the date in your diary.

It all began here in Britain, where the fans felt that, as Elvis's thirtieth birthday coincided with his celebration of a decade in show business, he should have something a cut above his ordinary fan clubs. And so The Elvis Presley International Appreciation Society was formed.

This is a fan club with a difference: only those who have proved their faithfulness over the years can join – though, of course, anyone can apply.

All rules governing the Society are voted by an elected Committee, comprising leading figures from fan clubs all over the world. The Society intends to hold an Annual International Convention at which two representatives from every fan club in every country will attend.

The Society is dedicated first and foremost to the cause of furthering Elvis's popularity, and to uniting his existing fans throughout the world. But another major job is high on the list: the raising of money for charity, on a large scale. The Society is completely non-profit making.

The biggest problem for the fan is to be allowed to join in the first place! For membership of the Society is strictly limited to those who have been fans for a long time. However, the Committee's view is quite reasonable. They point out that there is an Elvis Fan Club in almost every country already and that, for a small fee, a fan can join any one of them – even if he or she has only been an Elvis fan for a day or a week! Therefore, if the Society applied the same system itself, not only would it interfere with the affairs of many fan clubs and be unfair to their hard-working presidents; it would also be pointless to have such a Society, for there would be nothing special about it.

The system of choosing inaugural members is simple. There are nomination secretaries all over the world, each of which knows most of the Elvis stalwarts in his (or her) country, and these fans' names are passed through immediately. But those not so chosen need not despair! The Committee reasons that, should a person apply to join again and again over the months, this fact alone reveals the truly keen fan – so in the end, such persistent tryers will inevitably be

A contingent of fans from Elvisville – a.k.a. Heanor – make their mark at Land's End which Elvis passed just once by sea on his way to Germany

allowed to join. And then, automatically, it's for life!

The inauguration of the Society in London on January 8th, 1965, Elvis's thirtieth birthday, was to be under the guidance of that famous Luxembourg disc-jockey, Peter Aldersley (a great Elvis fan himself) and the whole proceedings were being recorded, edited and broadcast later on Luxembourg.

Independent Television, planning their own Elvis celebrations (possibly an hour show on Elvis's life) were hoping to join this cream of Elvis fanship, by taking their cameras along, too. So there's not exactly a lack of interest on the air!

Make no mistake, per 100 of the population, this country is the greatest Elvis country in the world; its Elvis-organisation is unequalled; its Fan Club has more members than the rest of the world's fan club members put together.

On the Continent, too, every Elvis poll that crops up is conducted like a military campaign and the Elvis fans literally 'slaughter' the groups in poll 'battles,' on almost every occasion.

This is, admittedly, due mostly to the solidarity and enthusiasm of the Presley clubs – for it is estimated that, although the Elvis fans have a 'wagon' with, worldwide, around 50,000,000 fans aboard, fans of the Beatles and other beat groups have a 'wagon' with probably *three times* that number on it!

But how many of them have just jumped on for the ride, because they see all the others there? How many of them will last? How many are *genuine* fans of the artists – and, when the inevitable happens and the groups lose ground, how many will jump off, and how quickly?

Elvis's 50,000,000, we think, are there to stay.

Big ones, little ones, young ones, old ones, he-males, she-males – all still Elvis fans, all still singing Elvis songs, all still claiming he's the greatest!

But now, with the formation of the new Society, it's for life!

ELVIS HERE!

He's virtually certain to appear on the Palladium Show in April
By Richard Green

Elvis Presley is 70 per cent certain to star in a charity show at the London Palladium on April 29, *Record Mirror* was exclusively told this week.

Agent Malcolm Feld is flying to America on February 18 hoping to clinch what would be the deal of the century.

He told me: 'I wrote and asked the possibility of Elvis appearing in a charity show at the Palladium on April 29. Colonel Tom Parker has indicated that there is a 70 per cent chance of Elvis accepting.

The Colonel

Malcolm will spend three weeks in America. He will meet Colonel Parker and Elvis for negotiations early during his stay.

'I think he would come to show people he is not scared of coming to England,' said Malcolm. 'If he comes, it will be for public relations, but I would love to put him on elsewhere.'

The show promises to be one of the show business events of the year. Top British and American stars have been asked to appear, and several have already accepted.

Buddy Greco, Tony Bennett, Jack Benny, Julie Grant and Eddie Calvert are set, and Al Burnett will compere.

Sinatra

Frank Sinatra, Dean Martin, Sammy Davis, Jnr., Barbra Streisand, Jerry Lewis, Connie Francis, Frankie Laine, Johnny Mathis, Louis Armstrong and Perry Como have all been asked to appear and replies are expected shortly.

The three-hour show is in aid of the Greater London Fund for the Blind and it is hoped that the Queen Mother will attend.

Malcolm Feld is a nephew of the late Isidore Green, former editor of *Record and Show Mirror*.

ELVIS PRESLEY – AN ANNOUNCEMENT!

Our recent announcement that Elvis Presley was seventy per cent certain to appear at the London Palladium on April 29, created an immense amount of interest. As a service to *RM* readers we printed the story based on statements made to us by Mr Malcolm Feld and checked their authenticity as far as possible.

In the light of certain events which have occurred since the story appeared, we again spoke to Mr Feld. We put to him certain questions and print below his verbatim replies.

Is Elvis Presley coming here for you next month?

No.

Why isn't he now coming?

He is in the middle of making a film at Paramount, then he goes over to do another film.

Is there any possibility of Elvis Presley visiting this country for you?

It is not true to say that Elvis Presley will never appear in England. It is just a question of when he has time.

Record Mirror, 20 March

I would like to apologize to anyone who was inconvenienced by the article on Elvis Presley in the February 13th edition of the Record Mirror. *As you may appreciate, trying to put on a show of this size takes a great deal of preparation and things do not always work out as planned.*

Malcolm Feld

James Craig writes: We've received a great many letters about that controversial theorising on whether Elvis Presley would be visiting Britain. Many have complimented Mr Malcolm Feld for his efforts to bring over Elvis, even though they failed. Fair enough! But some have attacked the *Record Mirror* for printing the original story and then for printing, accurately and concisely, the story of the breakdown in negotiations. The *Record Mirror* position is simply this: The original story was checked as fully as possible – though, clearly, only a phone call to Elvis himself would have settled it. And that is not practicable, alas! And when the trip was definitely 'off,' we put matters as fairly and squarely and concisely as possible. Incidentally, the London Palladium management have asked us to say that all letters sent direct there have been forwarded

BM037 MGA199 MEMPHIS TENN 76 13 1215P

ALBERT HAND

41 DERBY RD HEANOR DERBYSHIRE

ALBERT PHYLIS AND SON DEAR FOLKS ALLOW ME TO EXPRESS MY DEEP

AND SINCERE APPRECIATION FOR YOUR CELEBRATING MY BIRTHDAY IN

ENGLAND WOULD APPRECIATE IF YOU WOULD PASS ON THE GRATITUDE

TO ALL THE FANS IN ENGLAND WHO PARTICIPATE IN THIS CELEBRATION

MANY MANY THANKS ANXIOUSLY LOOKING FORWARD TO THE TIME WHEN

I CAN VISIT ALL OF YOU OVER THERE SINCERELY YOUR FRIEND I

BEG TO REMAIN

ELVIS PRESLEY

A typical telegram from Elvis to his British fans; and (below) Elvis with one of the messages of tribute from his fans on this side of the Atlantic

for attention to Mr Feld – except those which enclosed money (they were dealt with direct to the senders). We believe in keeping our readers fully in the picture – and the original story was said to be '70 per cent certain,' only.

Record Mirror, 20 March

FOREVER ELVIS

It was just ten years ago that Elvis Presley signed a contract with RCA-Victor, made a few records like 'Heartbreak Hotel' and 'Hound Dog', and overnight became the rage and outrage of the US. A year later, everything from lipsticks to T-shirts bore the Presley imprimatur. He made his first movie, and his take from all and sundry was estimated at $1,800,000. Then came two years in the Army to put a damper on Elvis. As an ex-G.I., he was given an ecstatic welcome home by his fans. And at the end of a decade of strutting and strumming he is bigger than ever – moneywise. This year he personally figures to make at least £5,000,000.

At 30, Elvis is the grand-daddy of big-time rock 'n' roll. His second-skin jeans have been replaced by somewhat wider slacks. His sideburns have been shortened 1½ inches. And his gyrations have calmed down to a dull twitch. He no longer appears on television; he has not even made a personal appearance in four years. All he does is make a few records and three movies a year. Not one of his pictures has ever lost money; he is the No.6 box office attraction in the US, and No.4 in Britain.

The remarkable thing is that Elvis the private human being has not been terribly touched by it all. He still calls elders of a year or more by their surnames, keeps in top physical shape with touch-football games, holds a black belt in karate, and can split a brick or a stacked pair of two-by-four boards with his right hand (which, as a result, is slightly deformed.) He does, however, indulge a few personal whims. He likes peanut-butter-and-banana sandwiches with Pepsi or Nesbitt's orange soda to drink. He owns half-a-dozen cars, including a gold-trimmed Cadillac that has been spray-painted with 40 coats of crushed diamonds. But since that is a bit showy for everyday and is being used by RCA on promotion tours, a black Rolls-Royce does the journeyman work.

Still a bachelor, he has surrounded himself with eight Tennessee buddies. They earn their pay by keeping everyone else away, and Elvis leads a totally encapsulated life. His managers and agents, headed by the ever-canny Colonel Tom Parker, would like to present the image of a monk in sideburns but, admits Elvis, 'I have looked for years. I don't plan to become a Hollywood creation who has several marriages. I pray I will find the right girl and raise a little Elvis Jnr.'

Between pictures, Elvis does just about what he wants, usually takes off cross-country with his cronies to Memphis and his 18-room, $1,000,000 hideaway, Graceland. 'I withdraw not from my fans but from myself,' he drawls. 'After work, I just give out.' He gives out into a place with jukebox at poolside, a den for his 31 gold single records. There is a private suite for him and another for his grandmother, Mrs Minnie Presley, 74. He doesn't like to think about Elvis the idol when he's not working. 'I don't regard money or position as important. But I can never forget this longing to be someone. I guess if you are poor, you always think and want more than those who have everything when they are born.'

Time, 7 May

Elvis Reported Marrying The Girl He Met in Service

Palm Springs, Calif., April 30 (Special)—Elvis Presley, one of the most eligible bachelors in show business, was reported giving up that role today for marriage to a girl he met while in the Army in Germany.

Persistent reports circulated that he was being married at the home here of his agent, Col. Tom Parker, to Priscilla Beaulieu, daughter of an Air Force officer. Elvis is 32, Priscilla 22.

She Saw Him Off in '60

When Elvis returned to the United States in 1960, after 17 months in Germany, the girl who saw him off tearfully at Frankfurt was Priscilla, then a high

Elvis Presley
His bachelor days over?

Priscilla Beaulieu—a baby doll from Texas.

school student whose father was a captain at Wiesbaden. She and Elvis had been going steady in Germany, but parted with no promises.

For the past year, back in this country, they have been going steady again. Priscilla, whose home town is Austin, Tex., is described by friends as a baby doll with reddish hair, and a beautiful dresser.

Elvis had romanced many leading ladies, among them Jocelyn Lane, Ann-Margret and Juliet Prowse, but it was the non-acting girl who was reported to have won his heart.

No Confirmation

The reports of the marriage, while current for several days, were not confirmed immediately and it was not possible to reach the home of Parker, the man who promoted Elvis to a place as the highest-paid star in show business.

Born in Tupelo, Miss., Jan. 8, 1935, Elvis made his first record in 1955 as a surprise for his mother—he paid $4 to have it cut —and a year later he set teen-age girls swooning with his "Heartbreak Hotel."

Since then, he has made more than 40 "gold" records for RCA.

He made it even bigger in the movies, with more than 20 feature films, among the latest being "Frankie and Johnny," "Spinout" and "Easy Come, Easy Go." All of them, beginning with "Love Me Tender" in 1956, were big at the box office.

THE MANIA CONTINUES – 1965

BIRTHDAY TRIBUTE: Columnist Peter Bart writes of Elvis Presley at 30: 'The loud, leering figure of a decade ago has turned into a mellow, diffident, rather thoughtful young man who is steadfastly courteous and holds the acting craft in high esteem. "Ah wants to be a better actor," he drawls. "Ah want to act in serious pictures. It will come some day. Ah don't want to rush it." '

The New York Times, 8 January

☆ ☆ ☆

BIRTHDAY GIFT. Elvis Presley's 30th birthday present from his Hollywood studio, MGM, is a new contract to make three new films for them. It's the kind of generosity that pays, of course. Since 1956, Presley's 16 feature films have grossed over £53,000,000.

Daily Mirror, 9 January

That unforgettable face …

☆ ☆ ☆

GOOD TRIBUTE. Elvis Presley spent the evening of his 10th showbiz anniversary at home watching on television a 'Tribute to Elvis' edition of British producer Jack Good's *Shindig* show. All ten artists on the bill sang numbers Presley made famous. Elvis always watches *Shindig* and has struck up a friendship with Good.

Photoplay, February

☆ ☆ ☆

LAST WORD. Boffo days ahead for rocker-turned-legit Elvis Presley and his manager, former carny hustler, Colonel Tom Parker, celebrating ten years of togetherness. Says the ole Colonel, 'Why, boy, you add up the annual gross from his movies, from his records, from all the Elvis merchandise and you get a total gross of up to $35 million a year. And every year more money rolls in. …'

Variety, 4 April